PRAISE F

EVIL ROBOTS, KILLER COMPUTERS, AND OTHER MYTHS

"Steve has a sane perspective on what computers can and cannot do. In this book, he carefully goes over all the hype in what passes for AI these days and explains how it works—and why it doesn't really work all that well."

—ROGER C. SCHANK, AI pioneer and former professor at Stanford, Yale, and Northwestern

"Are you afraid that artificial intelligence is going to make humans obsolete? *Evil Robots, Killer Computers, and Other Myths* dispels the mythology that has accompanied AI for nearly four decades. By removing the fog, Dr. Shwartz uses plain language and clear examples to enable mere mortals to understand how AI can supplement rather than replace human intelligence for the foreseeable future."

—LES TRACHTMAN, adjunct professor at the Johns Hopkins University and author of the Amazon bestseller *Don't F**k It Up: How Founders and Their Successors Can Avoid the Clichés That Inhibit Growth*

"AI is everywhere, from acting on voice commands to reading X-rays. With over 40 years in the field, Dr. Shwartz dives into the machine to help us understand what is really happening inside. He unlocks the current advances in AI and how special they are as the book unwinds the mysteries of how it all works. The Terminator may not be around the corner and AI ability may not be so scary, yet it is in the understanding of how humans will choose to use this powerful technology that may reshape our work or shake our world. This overview will transform your view and help shape how you may relate to the AI of the future."

—ALAN REZNIK, MD, orthopedist and author of *I've Fallen and I Can Get Up*

"As a venture investor, I was looking for a better understanding of machine learning, deep neural networks, and artificial intelligence. Dr. Shwartz clearly explains these concepts and why we need not fear intelligent evil robots in the near future. He forces us to think instead about the very serious societal issues arising from today's more limited AI."

—CHRISTOPHER McLEOD, managing partner,
Elm Street Ventures

"Dr. Shwartz draws on his 40 years of leading artificial intelligence research and application to provide a clear understanding for executives and technical types that machine thinking and reasoning is still a distant hope—and not to expect machines to replace humans—while also explaining the AI capabilities that are changing the world today and in the nearer future."

—BRUCE GALLAGER, partner, True Global Venture

"Industry has created larger and more powerful computers in a quest to fulfill society's Edifice Complex. A trend that began in the 1940s when the 'Mechanical Brain' of ENIAC was announced, society has invoked the common meme that AI will take over the world and destroy its creators. Dr. Shwartz demonstrates how media hype around electronic brains waxes and wanes. His thesis is that general AI is the computer science of the future, and always will be."

—DOUGLAS LYON, professor at Fairfield University

THE TRUTH ABOUT AI AND
THE FUTURE OF HUMANITY

EVIL ROBOTS, KILLER COMPUTERS, AND OTHER MYTHS

STEVEN SHWARTZ

FOREWORD BY ROGER C. SCHANK

FAST
COMPANY
Press

Fast Company Press
New York, New York
www.fastcompanypress.com

Distributed by River Grove Books

Design and composition by Greenleaf Book Group
Cover design by Greenleaf Book Group
Cover image: ©iStockphoto.com/xu bing

Publisher's Cataloging-in-Publication data is available.

Paperback ISBN: 978-1-7354245-3-8

Hardcover ISBN: 978-1-7354245-6-9

eBook ISBN: 978-1-7354245-4-5

First Edition

CONTENTS

FOREWORD

BY ROGER C. SCHANK

In the mid-60s, I was an undergrad at Carnegie Tech—now CMU—which was and is a leader in artificial intelligence. I was curious about computers, so I signed up to learn how to program as soon as I could. In those days you had to type out punch cards and submit them, then wait a day to see how your program did. My programs kept coming back without success with the remark "semicolon missing in line 25." I was really annoyed. If it knew a semicolon was missing, why didn't the computer just put it in? What a dumb machine!

That is how I got interested in AI. I just wanted smarter machines.

The AI gurus at CMU were Allen Newell and Herb Simon, who eventually became my friends, especially Newell. Their views were in the air. Finding out how minds work and getting computers to simulate them was the zeitgeist at CMU.

My fraternity brother was working with them on a program that could play hearts, where the key issue was passing cards at the beginning of the game. Three of us would play hearts every night, and then we would talk about how we chose what cards to pass.

One of the things that interested me was how people understand each other. How did language work? I started to think about that and was appalled that whenever I ran into the work of other people it seemed to me to be totally off base. The linguists were obsessed with syntax, and the computer people were trying to parse sentences into grammar trees. Why? Don't people worry about what a sentence means and what someone is trying to say? Why the obsession with syntax?

Getting computers to play chess was a big issue at CMU. Some people were studying how grand masters play chess, but others just wanted to win. Why? So they could brag about it. But there was nothing to be learned about the mind by counting faster than a human.

CMU researchers were also studying problem solving. "How do people do it?" was the key question for Newell, Simon, and me—whether it was chess or problem solving.

I first met Steve when he came to do a postdoc with me at Yale. Most people who do postdocs sit around and talk for a year, but Steve came to actually work. He was so impressive that when I started my new AI company, Cognitive Systems, he was one of the first people I hired. He wanted to build things and he wanted to make money. He did not want to make outrageous claims about AI. In fact, Cognitive Systems was intended to be my answer to the AI hype of the time.

Then, as now, falsehoods about AI dominated the media. Back then, the hype was about "expert systems," which sounds nice, but their so-called expertise was a bunch of if-then statements. In people, expertise is embodied by experience and learned through having new experiences. The computer was not capable of having experiences, much less processing them.

But the media had caught on to this next big thing. They love writing AI stories to scare the public.

AI researchers were also big contributors to the hype. When I worked at the Stanford AI lab in the late '60s, there was a sign in the parking lot saying, "Caution robot vehicle." It was a sign that was nonsense then as it would be now. Of course there was a vehicle of sorts run by a computer then just like there are self-driving car prototypes today. But I wouldn't ride in either.

And then there are the businesses working in AI.

Recently, IBM ran an ad for its Watson program, claiming that it can read 800 million pages per second and is able to identify key themes in Bob Dylan's work, like "time passes" and "love fades."

IBM said Watson's abilities "outthink" human brains in areas where finding insights and connections can be difficult due to the abundance of data (e.g., cancer, risk, doubt, and competitors).

I am a child of the '60s and I remember Dylan's songs well enough. Ask anyone from that era about Bob Dylan, and no one will tell you his main theme was "love fades." He was a protest singer, and a singer about the hard knocks of life. He was part of the antiwar movement. "Love fades"? That would be a dumb computer counting words. How would Watson understand that many of Dylan's songs were part of the antiwar movement? Does he say "antiwar" a lot? He probably never said it in a song.

For example, "The Times They Are A-Changin'" contains iconic Dylan statements that manage to transcend the times. However, he doesn't mention Vietnam or civil rights in the lyrics to that song. So how would Watson know that the song had anything to do with those issues? It is possible to talk about something and have the words themselves not be very telling. Background knowledge matters a lot. I asked a twenty-something about Bob Dylan a few days ago, and he had never heard of him. He didn't know much about the '60s. Neither does Watson.

It is against this backdrop that Steve Shwartz has written *Evil Robots, Killer Computers, and Other Myths.* Since Steve and I went our separate ways, he has managed to continue to make money while doing worthwhile things. He has a sane perspective on what computers can and cannot do. In this book, he carefully goes over all the hype in what passes for AI these days and explains how it works—and why it doesn't really work all that well.

PREFACE

My work in AI started in 1979. After receiving my PhD from Johns Hopkins University, I moved to Connecticut to do postdoctoral research with Professor Roger Schank in the Department of Computer Science at Yale University. At the time, Yale had a leadership position in the burgeoning AI subdiscipline of natural language processing.[1] It was a beehive of activity. Each of Roger's many graduate students was attempting to build computer systems to perform tasks such as machine translation (i.e., translate text from one human language into another human language), question answering, and summarizing news stories. Each week, we had a well-known academic come to town and present to the group. Roger put me in charge of taking the speakers to dinner, so I got to hobnob with many academic celebrities. It was a wonderful two years for me.

In August 1981, I accepted a teaching position at Brandeis University and was getting ready to leave Yale. At the same time, Roger had just received funding to start an AI company named Cognitive Systems. He approached me to join him in this new venture and told me that, even though I would likely be a successful academic, based on my personality, I would not enjoy it and that I would be much happier in the commercial world. I saw his point, so, with regret, I backed out of the Brandeis position at the last minute (they were understandably unhappy) and joined Roger at Cognitive Systems. As things turned out, it was the best career advice I have ever received.

In the early 1990s, I created Esperant, a natural language system that became a leading business intelligence product. More recently, I cofounded Device42, a company that is emerging as a market leader in IT infrastructure analytics. I am also a successful angel investor with a portfolio that includes many AI companies and one unicorn.

Through all these years, I've grown frustrated at the fear-inducing hype around AI in popular culture and media and at the overstatement of AI's capabilities from its vendors. It's fair to say I have a good understanding of AI, how it works, and what it can do. My goal in this book is to provide you with some of that knowledge. I will keep the technical detail to a minimum, and we'll discuss whether any of that fear is justified.

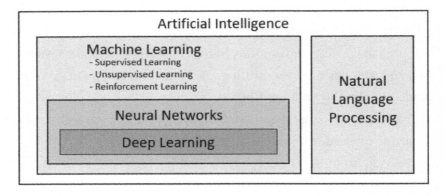

Figure 0.1 The different types of AI.

The image in figure 0.1 is a diagram of the different types of AI. By the end of the book, you should have a high-level understanding of how each of these types of AI work. You will also learn why none of these types of AI will progress into the types of AI that people fear.

If you are among the more technically inclined, you may prefer a more in-depth treatment of some of the topics in this book. If so, you can find it on my website, *www.aiperspectives.com*. The site provides hundreds of pages of technical detail in a dense, textbook-like format. It is not as easy to understand as this book, but I have worked hard to make it more accessible than many AI textbooks by leaving out the advanced mathematics found in them.

1

THE SOCIAL IMPACT OF AI

In 2011, I watched on TV as the IBM Watson DeepQA computer played a challenge match against two previous *Jeopardy!* champions. Nerd that I am, I rooted for the machine. I was thrilled to see the computer answer correctly over and over again.

Even though this was a fantastic achievement, I strongly suspected that there was no real intelligence in the underlying IBM technology. I was able to confirm my speculation when IBM published a series of detailed journal articles[1] that explained how the technology is mostly a massive set of very clever tricks with no human-level intelligence.

IBM then decided to ride the credibility produced by the *Jeopardy!* victory and began to rebrand itself around its artificial intelligence (AI) capabilities. IBM marketing claimed that "Watson can understand all forms of data, interact naturally with people, and learn and reason, at scale."[2]

The ads made it sound as though technology had progressed to the point of being able to think and reason like people. While I appreciated the engineering achievements Watson demonstrated on *Jeopardy!*, even Watson's creators at IBM knew these systems could not think or reason in any real sense.

Since then, AI has blasted its way into the public consciousness and our everyday lives. It is powering advances in medicine, weather prediction, factory automation, and self-driving cars. Even golf club manufacturers report that AI is now designing their clubs. Every day, people interact with AI. Google Translate helps us understand foreign language webpages and talk to Uber drivers in foreign countries. Vendors have built speech recognition into many apps. We use personal assistants like Siri and Alexa daily to help us complete simple tasks. Face recognition apps automatically label our photos. And AI systems are beating expert game players at complex games like Go and Texas Hold 'Em. Factory robots are moving beyond repetitive motions and starting to stock shelves.

Each of these fantastic AI systems enhances the perception that computers can think and reason like people. Technology vendors reinforce this perception with marketing statements that give the impression their systems have human-level cognitive capabilities. For example, Microsoft and Alibaba announced AI systems that could read as well as people can. However, these systems had minimal skills and did not even understand what they were reading.

AI systems perform many tasks that seem to require intelligence. The rapid progress in AI has caused many to wonder where it will lead. Science fiction writers have pondered this question for decades. Some have invented a future in which we have at our service benevolent and beneficial robots. Everyone would like to have an automated housekeeper like Rosie the Robot from the popular 1960s cartoon TV series

The Jetsons. We all love C-3PO from the *Star Wars* universe, who can have conversations in "over six million forms of communication," and his self-aware-trashcan partner, R2-D2, who can reprogram enemy computer systems. And we were in awe of the capabilities of the sentient android Data in *Star Trek: The Next Generation*, who was third in command of the starship (although he famously lacked emotion and so had trouble understanding human behavior).

Others have portrayed AI characters as neither good nor evil but with human-like frailties and have explored the consequences of human–robot interactions. In *Blade Runner*, for example, Rachael the replicant did not know she was not human until she failed a test. Spike Jonze's *Her* explores the consequences of a human falling in love with a disembodied humanoid virtual assistant. In *Elysium*, Matt Damon's character must report to an android parole officer. In the TV series *Humans* and *Westworld*, humanoid robots gain consciousness and have emotions that cause them to rebel against their involuntary servitude.

Many futurists have foreseen evil robots and killer computers—AI systems that develop free will and turn against us. In the 1927 film *Metropolis*, a human named Maria is kidnapped and replaced by a robot who looks, talks, and acts like her and then proceeds to unleash chaos in the city. In the 1968 book-turned-movie *2001: A Space Odyssey*, the spaceship has a sentient computer, HAL, that runs the spacecraft and has a human-like personality. It converses with the astronauts about a wide variety of topics. Concerned that HAL may have made an error, the astronauts agree to turn the computer off. However, HAL reads their lips, and, in an act of self-preservation, turns off the life-support systems of the other crew members. In the *Terminator* movie franchise, which first appeared in movie theaters in 1984, an AI defense system perceives all humans as a security threat and creates fearsome robots with one mission: eradicate humanity.

Speculation about the potential dangers of AI is not limited to the realm of science fiction. Many highly visible technologists have predicted that AI systems will become smarter and smarter and will eventually take over the world. Tesla founder Elon Musk says that AI is humanity's "biggest existential threat"[3] and that it poses a "fundamental risk to the existence of civilization."[4] The late renowned physicist Stephen Hawking said, "It could spell the end of the human race." Philosopher Nick Bostrom, who is the founding director of the Future of Humanity Institute, argues that AI poses the greatest threat humanity has ever encountered—greater than nuclear weapons.[5]

This kind of fear-inducing hype is an overstatement of the capabilities of AI. AI systems are never going to become intelligent enough to have the ability to exterminate us or turn us into pets. That said, there are many real and critical social issues caused by AI that will not be solved until we separate out and put aside this existential fear.

FACT AND FICTION

The AI systems that these technologists and science fiction authors are worried about all are examples of artificial general intelligence (AGI). AGI systems share in common with humans the ability to reason; to process visual, auditory, and other input; and to use it to adapt to their environments in a wide variety of settings. These systems are as knowledgeable and communicative as humans about a wide range of human events and topics.[6] They're also complete fiction.

Today's AI systems are miracles of modern engineering. Each of today's AI systems performs a single task that previously required human intelligence. If we compare these systems with the AGI systems of science fiction lore and with human beings, there are two striking differences: First, each of today's AI systems can perform only one narrowly defined task.[7] A system that learns to name the people in photographs cannot do anything else. It cannot distinguish between a dog and an elephant. It cannot answer questions, retrieve information, or have conversations. Second, today's AI systems have little or no commonsense[8] knowledge of the world and therefore cannot reason based on that knowledge. For example, a facial recognition system can identify people's names but knows nothing about those particular people or about people in general. It does not know that people use eyes to see and ears to hear. It does not know that people eat food, sleep at night, and work at jobs. It cannot commit crimes or fall in love. Today's AI systems are all *narrow AI* systems, a term coined in 2005 by futurist Ray Kurzweil to describe just those differences: machines that can perform only one specific task. Although the performance of narrow AI systems can make them seem intelligent, they are not.

In contrast, humans and fictional AGI systems can perform large numbers of dissimilar tasks. We not only recognize faces, but we also read the paper, cook dinner, tie our shoes, discuss current events, and perform many, many other tasks. We also reason based on our commonsense knowledge of the world. We apply common sense, learned experience, and contextual knowledge to a wide variety of tasks. For example, we use our knowledge of gravity when we take a glass out of the cupboard. We know that if we do not grasp it tightly enough, it will fall. This is not conscious knowledge derived from a definition of gravity or a description in a mathematical equation; it's unconscious knowledge derived from our lived experience of how the world works. And we use that kind of knowledge to perform dozens of other tasks every day.

The big question is whether today's narrow AI systems will ever evolve into AGI systems that can use commonsense reasoning to perform many different tasks. As I will explain, the answer is no. We do not have to worry about AGI systems taking over the world. And we probably never will.

TOASTERS DON'T HAVE GHOSTS

The title of Arthur Koestler's 1967 book *The Ghost in the Machine*[9] alludes to the long-standing philosophical debate about whether humans have a "ghost"—a mind, a consciousness, that cannot be seen or measured—in addition to their physical machines. Koestler believed that people are just their physical machines, that there is no separate mind, and that we will someday be able to explain, for example, emotions like love as the interaction of neurons. I cannot tell you the answer to the philosophical question, and I have no idea if we will ever be able to explain love. However, I can confidently declare my belief that we will never develop computer systems or robots with human-level, commonsense reasoning capabilities. Said another way, there will never be a ghost in the machine.

Even though we do not need to worry about AGI systems dominating humanity, as narrow AI technology becomes more and more widely deployed, it brings with it many new social issues. The race to perfect self-driving vehicles is well underway, but there are safety issues that we must address before we deploy them on our city streets and highways. Autonomous weapons and other narrow AI advances threaten public safety. We may see a significant impact of narrow AI technology on employment. Facial recognition technology is being used for surveillance and threatens our privacy. There are significant issues around fairness and discrimination against minorities. Furthermore, deepfakes, fake news, and hackers are influencing real-world elections. We will need to address all these social issues.

One of the keys to finding solutions to AI-related issues is to make sure we do not overcomplicate them by conflating narrow AI and AGI. For example, if AGI capabilities were imminent, we would need laws that govern human interaction with intelligent robots. Do robots have rights? Can they go to jail? Can they be held financially responsible for an accident? We would also need laws to ensure that the manufacturing process does not create robots that can take over the world.

Fortunately, narrow AI systems will only ever be able to make autonomous decisions regarding specific tasks, so we do not need general AGI laws. We do not have to worry about the legal rights of robots. They can and should have no more legal standing than toasters. Instead, we can focus on laws for specific uses of narrow AI, such as autonomous vehicles.

THE FUTURE IS ALWAYS A MIXED BAG

We see warnings about AI in the popular press every single day. In December 2019 alone, *The New York Times* featured headlines with grave cautions: "Artificial Intelligence Is Too Important to Leave to Google and Facebook Alone," "Many Facial-Recognition Systems Are Biased, Says U.S. Study," and "A.I. Is Making It Easier to Kill (You). Here's How." A recent study showed that 60 percent of the people in the UK fear AI.[10]

Historically, new technology has brought great benefits to society. However, the positive impacts are often accompanied by some negatives. The invention of the automobile brought us greater mobility, but also introduced car accidents. The invention of the internet brought us connectivity beyond any level imagined previously, while it also led to hackers and spam and facilitated child exploitation.

Although even narrow AI may lead to many societal changes, such as the way we work, it's no different from any other major technological advance. The steam engine and mass production led Western society away from an agrarian lifestyle and into factories, which brought with it increased pollution and wage disparity but ultimately led to the middle class. Advances in transportation expanded the world from local communities into huge geographic regions of travel and trade. The internet expanded that world even further, changing how we do just about everything.

AI is just one more step forward. As with each of those other advances, AI can be dangerous when used for nefarious purposes or without proper regulation, but it's a tool. Just like any kind of progress, although AI may involve some difficult societal and personal challenges in the short term, its overall effect on the world and on our lives will be largely positive.

2

FEARS WORTH HAVING

Many things can go wrong with narrow AI systems that can impact our safety. If we are not careful, we could end up with self-driving cars running over babies in strollers; out-of-control, bomb-carrying drones; missed cancer diagnoses; and nuclear plant meltdowns. However, these dangers can be prevented with the common sense those systems lack: with properly informed regulation and by ensuring that AI tasked with dangerous operations is fully tested before it is put into use.

AUTONOMOUS WEAPONS

The idea of applying even narrow AI to government-operated military weapons is a frightening thought for most people. Narrow AI–enabled weapons in the hands of terrorists is perhaps even scarier. The most terrifying scenario would be if AGI-based military systems were possible. AGI systems would bring in the potential for *Terminator*-like scenarios and other terrifying possibilities. Fortunately, AGI is not happening.

Unmanned aerial vehicles (UAVs) without AI have been used in warfare since the US began to deploy them after the 9/11 attacks. These UAVs include drones, which are controlled remotely by operators at consoles, similar to a video game. The weapons range in size from hobbyist quadcopters with an attached bomb to small aircraft with multiple missiles. The operator views the video produced by a camera on the drone, and when they see the target (which could range in size from large military installations to one individual terrorist), the operator initiates the attack. The actual attack occurs either by a small drone with an attached explosive warhead flying directly into the target or by launching a laser-guided missile from a larger drone. Between 2015 and 2019, remote-controlled or autonomous drones were used by the US, the UK, Israel, Pakistan, Saudi Arabia, the UAE, Egypt, Nigeria, and Turkey to kill people—with Turkey making exceptionally extensive use of them.[1] You can find a video of a test of a Turkish quadcopter drone with an explosive warhead on YouTube.[2]

One particularly scary aspect of remote-controlled drones is that the technology is relatively simple and accessible to terrorist groups. In September 2019, ISIS attacked Iraqi troops with seventy drones that had parachute-mounted grenades.[3]

Some UAVs only require a human to trigger the launch process, after which they are fully autonomous and use heat-seeking capabilities, radar, laser, or geographic coordinates to zero in on the target.[4] For example, the US military has relied on several systems that use radar to automatically target incoming missiles since 1977.[5] Frightening as they are, none of these are AI-based technologies.

The use of AI computer vision technology (e.g., image classification and object recognition) significantly increases UAV autonomy. With computer vision technology, the military can decide to launch an attack that relies on computer vision to automatically analyze the camera video and identify the target. Military personnel can configure the UAV software so that, once the vision system identifies the target, the attack commences automatically. For example, the Turkish drones in that YouTube video are being outfitted with facial recognition technology that will automatically find and fire on specific human targets.[6] We do not need to worry about autonomous weapons like the Terminator; however, by adding computer vision technology to UAVs, we add a means for UAVs to find their own targets without a human in the loop.

Autonomous weapons that do not require a human operator to pull the trigger have ethical uses, such as the ability to defend against an enemy that launches more missiles than there are humans available to launch antimissile weapons. However, autonomous weapons have the potential to produce outcomes such as mass destruction. They have been labeled "the third revolution in warfare, after gunpowder and nuclear arms."[7] An organization named the Campaign to Stop Killer Robots released the frightening *Slaughterbots* video of an onslaught of out-of-control drones causing mass destruction.[8] In 2019, a former US Army ranger, Paul Scharre, published a book detailing several concerns about autonomous weapons, including the risks of weapons going out of control or getting hacked.[9] The US is actively developing an autonomous drone program named Skyborg.[10] Russia and China are also developing autonomous drones,[11] and China is reportedly selling them to other countries.[12]

The Campaign to Stop Killer Robots has obtained pledges from 4,500 AI researchers and tens of thousands of other individuals. They are asking tech leaders not to participate in the development of autonomous weapons. Google employees have vehemently asked the company not to participate in the development of AI-based weaponry. In 2017, one hundred AI leaders signed an open letter calling on the United Nations to find a way "to prevent an arms race in these weapons, to protect civilians from their misuse, and to avoid destabilizing effects of these technologies."

Computer vision technology is also reducing the time spent by military analysts to sift through satellite images and drone videos. For example, the military has put a fair amount of effort into training machine learning systems to recognize missile launchers in satellite images.[13]

Similarly, military drones capture hundreds of thousands of hours of video footage each year.[14] The military is training AI systems to detect missile launchers and other objects of military interest in these drone-captured videos.[15] These uses of technology are significant time-savers for military analysts. However, a human-in-the-loop is still required to trigger the deployment of the weapons against the discovered targets.

Aside from autonomous weapons, automated systems exist that help military commanders make decisions as to whether to attack or hold fire. For example, the US Army is researching the feasibility of an AI-based battlefield advisor that can analyze data from a variety of sources, including drones, satellites, and cameras mounted on the goggles of soldiers. It can then synthesize the data and make battlefield recommendations.[16] These are likely to be incremental improvements to the human-in-the-loop systems that exist today rather than systems that can autonomously press the big red button.

There are also several initiatives underway to develop a baseline of ethical principles for the use of AI in military applications, including principles established by the US Department of Defense.[17] Even

Russia has called for the regulation of this technology.[18] The global community banded together to try to eliminate the use of biological and nuclear weapons, and many argue that we should take the same path for AI-based autonomous weapons.

CYBERSECURITY

If AGI were ever achieved and embedded in a virus, we would have much bigger cybersecurity problems than we have today. A thinking virus could navigate networks and make real-time nefarious decisions. For example, it could conceivably turn its virus characteristics on and off when necessary to evade antivirus software. Fortunately, AGI exists only in fiction.

The most obvious threat to safety is the potential for cyberattacks on autonomous vehicles or autonomous weapons. The hack itself would not be AI-based; it would be a conventional (non-AI) hack of an AI system and like a hack of a tire pressure monitoring system (TPMS) on a non-self-driving car.[19] However, most newer cars can control steering and braking electronically. If a hacker accesses a vehicle through a sensor like a TPMS, we could imagine that the hacker could gain access to the steering and braking systems with potentially deadly results if the hack causes a crash.[20]

On the positive side, AI can actually help defend against cyberattacks. The US military has developed an AI-based system that can inform an autonomous vehicle that someone hacked it.[21] Companies like Blue Hexagon, ExtraHop, and Synack use AI to detect vulnerabilities and cyberattacks.

We also need to be alert to the possibility of adversarial attacks on other types of deep learning systems, including attacks on image and facial recognition systems, as well as on speech recognition systems.[22]

Baidu researchers published a set of tools that can be used by other researchers to fool virtually any deep learning system.[23] Their goal, of course, was not to encourage hackers, but rather to help researchers create defense mechanisms in their deep learning systems.

Hackers can create other types of cybersecurity threats with narrow AI technology. Some of these threats are small improvements on existing hacking techniques. Audio deepfake capabilities enable a new type of *spear phishing*. Spear phishing attacks mostly involve hackers sending well-researched emails to targeted individuals. Using audio deepfakes, hackers can send those same targeted individuals voice messages that sound like someone they know. If fake news AI technology ever becomes viable, hackers could use it to automate spear phishing.

The counter to spear phishing remains education. We have learned to ignore emails from Nigerian princes, and we will, unfortunately, need to stop assuming that recognizing someone's voice is enough evidence to act on what they tell us.

AUTONOMOUS APPS

Although we do not have to worry about killer robots that can think and reason, even a narrow AI system can wreak havoc if it does its one job badly. We can imagine a hypothetical AI system failing to adjust controls in a nuclear plant to avoid a meltdown or an AI-powered medical diagnosis system failing to detect cancer. IBM's Watson reportedly took medical data and recommended unsafe and incorrect cancer treatments.[24]

Bad conventional software can also wreak havoc. A missing hyphen in the software ruined the 1962 Mariner space launch.[25] Faulty software was also the cause of the 1979 Three Mile Island nuclear disaster,[26] the 2003 New York City blackout,[27] 2010's high-speed trading outage on Wall Street,[28] the 2012 loss of 440 million dollars in forty-five minutes by a financial firm,[29] and the 2018 and 2019 Boeing 737 Max crashes.[30]

The point here is that any type of software can cause public safety issues if it is not thoroughly tested. AI systems are software programs that someone creates to perform a specific task. Just like other software, these systems require testing, and the degree of testing needs to be modified based on the risk profile. A software program that plays checkers does not require anywhere near as much testing as a software program that controls portions of nuclear power plants.

AI applications can be harder to test than conventionally coded applications, and it may be impossible to rigorously test some AI applications. Conventional software programs can usually be tested against a specification that exactly determines which results are correct. However, machine learning applications will perform well only on inputs that are like those in its training data.[31] For other inputs, the application might miss a case of cancer or cause a meltdown in a nuclear plant. It can be difficult or impossible to specify which types of inputs the application should handle correctly. A software application needs to be tested to certify that it operates correctly. However, if the correct operation cannot be clearly defined, it cannot be rigorously tested or certified.

Not all conventional software is testable either.[32] Using untestable software in a checkers program has little downside. Using untestable software to run a nuclear plant is another story. If an AI application is untestable, it should be clearly labeled as such and should not be relied on for critical decisions.

Philosopher Daniel Dennett, of Tufts University, argued that people should never pass the buck to AI systems.[33] Manufacturers should disclose the limitations of AI systems the same way they disclose the side effects of medications. For example, vendors of medical diagnostic systems should be required to specify the expected error rates.[34] Similarly, manufacturers need to inform potential purchasers when it is not possible to rigorously test an AI application. People who use AI systems should understand the intended use of the system and be aware of its limitations—just as with conventional software.

Most importantly, if an AI system cannot be rigorously tested, then it should not be used for critical decision-making, such as running a nuclear power plant. The US Food and Drug Administration (FDA) has proposed a regulatory framework to ensure the safe use of AI in medical devices.[35] Regulators should similarly require manufacturers of AI systems to provide proof of rigorous test plans for any machine learning components used in them. Regulators should know whether a machine learning system can be relied on to recognize every potential danger and to deal with them.

AUTONOMOUS VEHICLES

The National Highway Traffic Safety Administration (NHTSA) has defined six levels of self-driving vehicles. Levels 0 and 1 are conventional vehicles and assistance (such as lane detection), respectively. In Levels 3–5, the vehicle is controlled by software. Level 2 is the state of the art at the moment; its capabilities include adaptive cruise control, lane centering, and automatic emergency braking. Automatic cruise control detects cars in front and slows down and speeds up to maintain a driver-specified distance. Lane centering keeps the vehicle in a marked lane. On a highway, cruise control and lane centering alone are enough to keep a car in a lane at a reasonable distance behind the vehicle in front.

Human in Control			AV Software in Control		
Level 0	Level 1	Level 2	Level 3	Level 4	Level 5
The human driver performs all driving functions	Some level of driver assistance (either adaptive cruise control or lane keeping / centering)	Partial driver automation (both adaptive cruise control and lane centering) but driver must maintain awareness (hands on wheel, eyes on road, or both)	Conditional driver automation (human may take hands off the wheel and read a book under specified conditions but must intervene when instructed to do so by the vehicle)	High automation (human does not ever need to intervene as long as the car is operating under specific conditions such as highway cruising and/or campus shuttles)	Full automation (human never needs to intervene)

Figure 2.1 NHTSA's six levels of automation.

I own a Tesla, and, while I love the car, it is not safe to read a book while driving it, even on the highway. For example, when I go around a sharp curve, I see the curve in advance and slow down to make sure I do not skid or tip over. My Tesla does not slow down when entering a big curve, so I must manually take over control.

On the flip side, my Tesla occasionally slams on the brakes so hard that it is a good thing I am wearing my seat belt or I might hit the windshield. Usually, this happens on rural roads, but it also happened a couple of times on highways.[36] Fortunately, I did not have a tailgater in either of the highway incidents. Each time my Tesla does this, I try to figure out what it thinks it "saw." Sometimes I look all around the edges of the road. Sometimes I look at the screen. Each time, this reminds me of how object recognition systems can see things that are not there.

The Tesla has many other issues when driving on city or rural streets. It has no idea how to navigate a lane closure with a person directing traffic. Sometimes, if a lane splits, left to its own decision-making, the Tesla heads into the wrong lane, which ends abruptly at a telephone pole, and I have to perform a last-minute takeover.

Although Tesla is rated the top autopilot system by most reviewers, such as *Autopilot Review*, it is not ready for Level 3 use, even on the highway. Tesla's website confirms that "autopilot is a hands-on driver assistance system that is intended to be used only with a fully attentive driver. It does not turn a Tesla into a self-driving car, nor does it make a car autonomous."[37]

The first death caused by a self-driving car occurred on May 7, 2016, in Williston, Florida. A white eighteen-wheeler crossed the highway,[38] and, because of a white background behind the truck, the AI-driven Tesla failed to recognize that an object was crossing the road and ran right into it. Since the Tesla was only a Level 2 vehicle, it was the driver's responsibility to pay attention to the road and take over when the Tesla autopilot missed seeing the truck. Although this accident might be attributed to AI, it was actually caused by human negligence.

A Level 2 self-driving vehicle is not fully autonomous. Although the car's computer system does most of the work steering and plotting the route, a driver is required to be seated behind the wheel and to pay attention to the road, ready to take over should something go wrong. If the self-driving car is operating at a Level 2 capability, it is difficult for the manufacturer to be held responsible because the driver is responsible for the safe operation of the vehicle.

Uber, which was testing self-driving taxis in Arizona, had a test car strike and kill a pedestrian in March 2018 while in autonomous mode. The safety operator, who was supposed to be paying attention to the road, was watching Hulu.[39] Uber self-driving vehicles had thirty-seven crashes before that fatality,[40] and the company had to sweat it out for a year before they learned that they would not face criminal charges.[41] However, because this was also a Level 2 vehicle, the driver was required to pay attention and prosecutors will likely file vehicular manslaughter charges against the driver. The family of the victim is also suing the state of Arizona for $10 million for policies that welcomed self-driving cars into the state.[42]

Perhaps the biggest challenge will be setting safety standards for autonomous vehicles. Is it enough that driverless car technology progresses to the point where the vehicles cause fewer accidents and fatalities than human drivers? Or do we need to get to the point where they cause no accidents or deaths at all?

Interestingly, the answers to these questions will probably be different around the world. Kai-Fu Lee, the former head of Google China, makes a strong case that China will be more tolerant of accidents and fatalities than the US and that autonomous vehicles will take to the road sooner there than in the US.[43]

Many legislators around the world are pushing hard for regulations that would encourage the rollout of autonomous vehicles. Two US congressmen, Illinois Democrat Bobby Rush and Indiana Republican Larry Bucshon, penned an opinion piece in early 2020 titled "When It Comes to Autonomous Vehicles, the US Cannot Afford to Be Left in the Dust." Some countries and municipalities will be more conservative than others. It will be interesting to see which areas are the first to allow drivers to read a book while riding in Level 3 systems.

In early 2020, the US Congress was actively considering several bills that would remove regulatory barriers for autonomous vehicles.[44] This prospect terrifies safety advocates. The US National Transportation Safety Board recommended stronger regulation of Level 3 and higher systems in its February 2020 review of a fatal Tesla crash.[45] The Insurance Institute for Highway Safety wants to see a higher degree of driver monitoring that ensures drivers are paying attention to the road on Level 2 vehicles. Their concern is that Level 2 capabilities will fool drivers into thinking they do not have to pay attention.[46] And the safety group Advocates for Highway and Auto Safety put out a March 2020 press release pointing out that there have been many self-driving car crashes. Six of those crashes resulted in fatalities, including a pedestrian walking a bicycle.[47]

In the US, Florida has the most liberal laws of all the states. Florida legislators passed statute 316.85 in 2016,[48] which specifically allows the operation of autonomous vehicles. It explicitly states that a driver does not need to pay attention to the road in a Level 3 vehicle (e.g., the driver can watch movies) and explicitly permits autonomous vehicle operation without a driver even present in the vehicle. Also, it requires no vehicle safety tests. Whenever a car, truck, bus, or taxi company decides they are ready, they are free to test and sell driverless vehicles. I own a home in Florida, and I am terrified at the prospect of driving next to autonomous vehicles without commonsense reasoning capabilities.

Some other states permit autonomous vehicles with varying restrictions, and many other states have legislation that encourages the testing of autonomous vehicles. For example, Arizona's governor signed an executive order in 2015 empowering the state government to "undertake any necessary steps to support the testing and operation of self-driving cars."[49] However, the NHTSA stepped in when a French company, TransDev, attempted to launch a driverless school bus to ferry children to school in that state.

California has stricter regulations than most states concerning driverless vehicle testing. It requires service-based autonomous vehicle companies to file a report each time there is a disengagement (i.e., when a human safety operator takes over driving control).

Big-four accounting firm KPMG puts out an annual report analyzing the twenty-five countries doing the most from both a funding and regulatory perspective to advance autonomous vehicles.[50] According to KPMG, the leading countries are the Netherlands, Singapore, Norway, and the US, in that order.

To better ensure public safety, regulators should require all manufacturers and service operators who are testing Level 3 and higher capabilities to report all disengagements. For service-based autonomous vehicles, they should review every occurrence in which a human safety operator decided to take over control of a shuttle, taxi, truck, or bus during a test drive.

Regulators should also require manufacturers of consumer vehicles with Level 2 capabilities to record and report patterns of disengagements. Currently, Tesla monitors these disengagements but does not turn over the results to regulators. Most cars with Level 2 capabilities do not even send disengagement data back to the manufacturer. The safest approach would be for regulators to require that all manufacturers adopt the Tesla model, put an always-on cellular connection in every car, and use it to monitor Level 2 disengagements.

After regulators have reviewed large numbers of disengagement reports, they should set safety standards based on what they have learned. The safety standards should include lengthy testing periods in which there are no disengagements that might have turned into accidents or traffic jams.

Unfortunately, at the time of this writing, most regulatory bodies do not even require autonomous vehicle manufacturers to file test disengagement information. California requires the filing of some disengagement information, but only for service-based autonomous vehicles.

Another option is for legislators to require manufacturers to self-certify and submit the results of a standardized test plan. A group of car manufacturers have proposed the outline of such a plan.[51] Testing under controlled conditions is not as good as real-world experience, however. Although testing under controlled conditions will have a paucity of edge cases, it may be better than nothing. And I am worried that nothing may be the choice of legislators and regulators.

There is significant pressure on lawmakers and regulatory bodies to remove the barriers to autonomous vehicles. In 2016, the NHTSA and the US Department of Transportation published a position paper on autonomous vehicles titled *Automated Driving Systems 2.0: A Vision for Safety.* In 2020, the NHTSA titled the updated position paper *Ensuring American Leadership in Automated Vehicle Technologies: Automated Vehicles 4.0.* The emphasis has shifted from safety to innovation leadership. Legislators and regulators, in their rush to embrace autonomous vehicle technology, may allow unsafe autonomous vehicle operation, and the results will be disastrous. The question of when autonomous vehicles are safe enough should not be decided by the manufacturers. Lawmakers and regulators must keep the public safe. They need to step in, set standards, and make these decisions.

Safety advocates are also concerned that, in their push to smooth the way for autonomous vehicles, lawmakers will absolve vehicle makers of self-driving liability. Suppose an autonomous vehicle misclassifies a baby stroller as a piece of paper, and the result is a fatal accident. Or suppose a terrorist hacks into a group of cars and causes them to crash. We cannot allow the manufacturer to say, "Sorry, that was a bug. We will fix it soon," and walk away from any further responsibility.

Regulators should place liability for accidents caused by vehicles operating at Level 3, 4, or 5 (autonomous modes) on the shoulders of the manufacturers. Legislators also need to determine whether the suppliers of autonomous vehicle capabilities have any liability in addition to—or instead of—the vehicle manufacturer. The possibility of significant liability will hopefully cause the manufacturers to delay the widespread rollout of self-driving vehicles until the technology is safe.

Removing liability is dangerous because autonomous vehicles have no commonsense reasoning capabilities. Without these capabilities, autonomous vehicles cannot avoid causing fatalities, property damage, and traffic jams if they are allowed to roam our streets and highways at will. If legislators absolve automakers from liability for accidents caused by Level 3 and higher operation, there will be no financial barrier to manufacturers putting unsafe vehicles on the road.

A requirement that vehicles with autonomous capabilities have black box data recorders like the ones in airplanes would also be prudent so that we will be able to diagnose the causes of the inevitable accidents quickly.

Lastly, autonomous vehicles raise ethical and practical dilemmas. If a driverless car must choose between injury to its car's passenger and the passenger of another vehicle (or a pedestrian), what choice should it make? How should a car decide between one action that kills a mother and baby and another that kills five men?[52] More importantly, are we comfortable leaving that decision in the hands of a computer with no commonsense reasoning capability?

LIABILITY, TESTING, AND COMMON SENSE

There are two primary threats to public safety from AI: autonomous systems and bugs. Autonomous weapons increase the ability of nations and terrorists to wage war. There is a threat to public safety from intentional attacks using both autonomous and conventional weapons. However, autonomous weapons increase the possibility of out-of-control destruction. International cooperation has been somewhat successful in reducing the risk from weapons of mass destruction, and the same will be necessary for autonomous weapons. Liability laws also need to be part of the solution to encourage manufacturers to design these weapons with adequate fail-safe mechanisms.

Bugs can occur in both AI software and conventional software products. AI software can be harder to test than conventional software. Manufacturers need to factor this difficulty into their production processes, and consumers need to factor this difficulty into their evaluation of the software's fitness for use. Machine learning systems that cannot be rigorously tested should not be used to run critical systems.

Autonomous vehicles are dangerous because they cannot be imbued with common sense, and it will be difficult for them to handle all the edge cases that they will encounter. Legislators need to put the burden on manufacturers to prove that their vehicles are safe for their intended purpose. It is also critical that they do not remove the liability burden from autonomous vehicle manufacturers and operators so that at least there is a financial incentive to only deploy safe vehicles. Perhaps most importantly, regulators need to require proof of rigorous testing of pedestrian detection, stop sign detection, and other machine learning systems that can cause fatalities if they fail.

3

A BRIEF HISTORY OF AI

A I has captured the public's imagination, but this is not the first time; we are actually in a third wave of AI progress and interest. It first happened in the early 1960s and again in the early 1980s. In both cases, expectations about progress toward artificial general intelligence (AGI) systems—with human-like intelligence—far exceeded reality. Both periods were followed by AI winters, in which investment and interest in AI plummeted. Will this time be different?

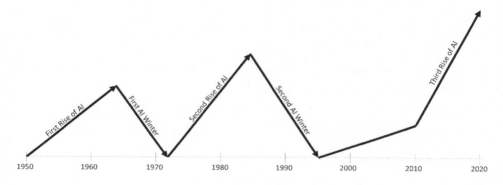

Figure 3.1 Timeline of AI hype cycles.

During the first two AI hype cycles, AI systems were developed to further the goal of AGI. Narrow AI did not exist. Because they failed to achieve AGI in the first two hype cycles, researchers created and focused on building narrow AI systems during the third cycle.

THE FIRST AI HYPE CYCLE

The first AI system was built in 1951 by Marvin Minsky and Dean Edmonds at Harvard University. It was built with vacuum tubes and simulated a rat learning to search a maze for food. John McCarthy coined the term *artificial intelligence* in 1956. The first AI conference was a two-month workshop held at Dartmouth College that same year. The goal was to bring together researchers in automata theory, neural networks, and the study of intelligence. The participants included several individuals who would go on to become leaders in the field of AI, including Minsky, McCarthy, Allen Newell, and Herbert Simon.

EARLY SUCCESSES

Early work in AI showed tremendous promise. In 1956, at Rand Corporation, Allen Newell and Herbert Simon created the Logic Theorist, which was able to prove many mathematical theorems.[1]

In 1960, when he was at MIT Lincoln Labs, Bert Green (who became my PhD thesis advisor eighteen years later) wrote BASEBALL, a computer program that could answer questions about the 1959 baseball season, like these:

- *Who did the Red Sox lose to on July 5?*

- *Where did each team play on July 7?*

- *Which teams won ten games in July?*
- *Did every team play at least once in each park?*[2]

For his PhD thesis at MIT in 1964, Daniel Bobrow[3] developed the STUDENT system, which accepted a restricted subset of English in which it was possible to express a wide variety of algebra word problems such as this one:

If the number of customers Tom gets is twice the square of 20 percent of the number of advertisements he runs, and the number of advertisements he runs is forty-five, what is the number of customers Tom gets?

STUDENT transformed the input question into a set of simultaneous equations that it then solved. The success of STUDENT, along with other early successes, led Herbert Simon to proclaim in 1965 that "machines will be capable, within twenty years, of doing any work that a man can do."[4]

EARLY FAILURES

During this early achievement period, there were also some significant failures, the most notable of which was machine translation—computer systems that translate text from one human language to another. Researchers first attempted machine translation in the 1950s by programming a computer to act like a human translator who had a pocket translation dictionary but did not know the target language. The technique was to first store the equivalent of a pocket dictionary in the computer. Then the program processed the source text word by word, placing the corresponding word in the target language into the output text. Some of the more sophisticated systems also used syntactic analyses to correct for differences in word order in the two languages. For example, the phrase *the blue house* in English might translate to the equivalent of "the house blue" in a language such as French: *la maison bleue.*

These early machine translation attempts produced disappointing results. The major problem was the mistaken assumption of a one-to-one correspondence between words in the source and target languages. For example, because of word ambiguity, a substantial proportion of the words in the target language had too many potential equivalents in the source language to come up with an accurate translation.

When forced to choose among the possible target language alternatives for each source language word, these systems often produced humorous results. Several realistic, even if not actual, anecdotes have become part of the lore of AI. For example, one system reportedly translated the English phrase *water buffalo* into the equivalent of "hydraulic goat" in the target language. Idiomatic and metaphorical material also caused problems. One system reportedly translated the English *the spirit is willing, but the flesh is weak* into the equivalent of "The vodka is good, but the meat is rotten" in Russian. Another system reportedly translated *out of sight, out of mind* into "invisible idiot."

In a 1960 review of machine translation efforts, an Israeli linguist named Yehoshua Bar-Hillel[5] asserted that human translators could not only understand the meaning of the source language but could also reason based on their knowledge of the world—abilities that computers had yet to demonstrate. For computers to be able to translate language, he argued, they would have to do the same thing in the same way.

THE FIRST AI WINTER

Bar-Hillel's point of view was reiterated six years later in the infamous ALPAC (Automatic Language Processing Advisory Committee) report, which convinced the US government to reduce its funding for this type of research dramatically.[6] The ALPAC report concluded that machine translation was slower, less accurate, and twice as expensive as human translation and stated that there was no point in further investment in machine translation research. The US government canceled nearly all of its funding for academic machine translation projects that year. Not long after, Sir James Lighthill's 1973 report to the UK Parliament criticized the failure of AI to achieve "grandiose" objectives.[7] As a result, the UK government canceled its funding for most AI research in the UK.

Neural networks like the ones that power most of today's high-profile AI applications were described in 1958 by Frank Rosenblatt at Cornell University.[8] His pioneering paper explained how a neural network could compute a function relating inputs to outputs. The approach received a lot of press, including this quote from a 1958 *New York Times* article: "The Navy revealed the embryo of an electronic computer today that it expects will be able to walk, talk, see, write, reproduce itself, and be conscious of its existence."[9]

Research on neural networks continued through the 1960s but was stopped in its tracks by the 1969 book *Perceptrons*, written by Marvin Minsky and Seymour Papert, which appeared to prove that further progress in neural networks was impossible.[10] We now know that Minsky and Papert's criticism, although it was accurate for the type of perceptron used by Rosenblatt, does not apply to neural networks in general. Nonetheless, the book was responsible for stopping most neural network research at the time.

THE SECOND AI HYPE CYCLE

For the next decade, research funding diminished, but some continued at universities. In the late 1970s and early to middle 1980s, excitement about AGI once again built to a frenzied peak, primarily as a result of research into natural language processing and expert systems.

Rather than giving up, these later AI researchers took Bar-Hillel's critique as a head-on challenge. They started to think about how to represent the meaning of a natural language utterance and, more generally, how to represent commonsense knowledge in a computer system in a way that can support human-like reasoning.

For example, my former colleagues at Yale University, led by Roger Schank, developed a theory of how to use hand-coded symbols to represent meaning in a computer system.[11] Schank and his students developed several impressive AI systems, such as FRUMP[12] and SAM.[13] FRUMP could read stories about train wrecks, earthquakes, and terrorist attacks directly from the UPI newswire and could then produce summaries of those stories. SAM read short stories such as "John went to a restaurant. He ordered lobster. He paid the check and left." The computer could then answer questions such as "What did John eat?" with "Lobster," even though eating was never mentioned in the story.

These systems, along with other natural language processing systems developed at research institutions throughout the world, left a strong impression that the development of computers that could understand language at an AGI level was right around the corner.

Other researchers focused on building what came to be known as *expert systems*. They built systems that performed tasks that previously required human intelligence by processing large bodies of hand-coded symbolic rules. For example, an auto-repair expert system might have this rule: *IF the temperature gauge indicates overheating and the radiator is cool to the touch, THEN the problem is a sticky thermostat.*

Researchers such as Stanford University's Edward Feigenbaum achieved significant recognition for early expert systems, such as the MYCIN system,[14] which diagnosed blood infections. With 450 rules, MYCIN performed as well as some experts.

Governments poured vast amounts of money into AI during the 1980s. In 1982, Japan announced its Fifth Generation project, intended to create intelligent computers within ten years. In response, DARPA (the US Defense Advanced Research Projects Agency) committed $1 billion in 1983 to the Strategic Computing Initiative, an effort to build AGI in ten years.[15] At the same time, a group of twenty-four large US corporations banded together to start MCC (Microelectronics and Computer Technology Corporation). Its flagship project, headed by Douglas Lenat, was to hand code all commonsense knowledge in a system named Cyc. Commonsense knowledge includes hand-coded symbolic facts, such as "birds have wings," "airplanes have wings," and "if it has wings, it can fly." Unless, of course, it is a chicken. The UK had its own effort named Alvey, and Europe formed ESPRIT (European Strategic Program on Research in Information Technology).

Our company, Cognitive Systems, became a hot property. At one point, I recall deciding that I had to stop doing newspaper and magazine interviews to get any work done. Cognitive had an IPO in 1986, despite not having much revenue. A sister company to Cognitive Systems named Nestor that was commercializing neural network technology also had an IPO in 1983, and Feigenbaum's expert systems company, Teknowledge, had one in 1984.

AI was so hot in the 1980s that researchers created two companies with significant venture capital backing, Symbolics and LMI, to build computers specially designed to run the Lisp programming language, which was the preferred programming language of the AI community.

THE SECOND AI WINTER

In the mid-1980s, AI was featured on the covers of many publications. For example, the March 1982 cover of *Business Week* proclaimed, "Artificial Intelligence: The Second Computer Age Begins."

Company after company rebranded their products as "AI-based." It seemed that AI researchers had figured out how to make AGI systems and to represent human knowledge symbolically. It appeared that the only thing standing in the way of AGI was a bit of elbow grease to encode all human knowledge and the types of reasoning needed for intelligent behavior.

I admit to having been a significant contributor to the hype of the time. Our Cognitive Systems brochure headline was grandiose: "The Vision to Change the World." We were able to make a successful public offering in February 1986, without significant revenues, on the strength of the general hype around AI.

My next company, Intelligent Business Systems, raised over $50 million in venture capital ($120 million in 2019 dollars). Raising venture capital was as difficult then as it is now. But we eventually put together a consortium of VCs and scheduled the closing for noon on a Friday at a country club. The idea was to take care of the final contractual issues in the morning and play golf in the afternoon while the lawyers were preparing the final drafts. However, we did not resolve those final issues until midnight, and we did not get to play golf. I was so tired that I ran into the back of my cofounder's car at the first stoplight. He was 6'5" and had played tight end in the NFL. The policeman who arrived on the scene commented that we must be friends because otherwise I would be in worse shape than my car.

We developed and sold a natural language–based accounting system. Users could ask questions such as "Who owes me money for over ninety days?" However, the company ended up failing when the second AI winter hit, and we could not raise a follow-on round of funding. The good news was that the skills of my employees were in high demand, and no one stayed unemployed for long.

My third company, Esperant Technologies, developed a natural language system that became one of the leading business intelligence products of the early 1990s. However, because AI had fallen into disfavor again, even though the product was successful, I had to strike all references to AI from the product and marketing literature.

AI failed for the second time because the symbolic hand coding of knowledge was time-consuming, expensive, and did not perform well in the real world. Expert systems could perform only very narrowly defined tasks, and natural language interfaces had limited coverage that required users to learn what they could and could not say. Symbolic AI came to be known as *good, old-fashioned AI*, fell into disfavor by 1990, and was out of favor for thirty years. But it might make a comeback in the 2020s.

The AI bubble of the 1980s deflated gradually, and by the end of the 1980s, the second AI winter had begun. The Japanese government disbanded its Fifth Generation project without it having produced any significant AI technology. DARPA significantly cut back on its AI funding. MCC wound down in 2000. The market for Lisp machines imploded. Professor Stuart Russell said that his AI course at the University of California at Berkeley had 900 students in the mid-1980s and had shrunk to only twenty-five students in 1990.[16]

THE THIRD AI HYPE CYCLE

During the second AI winter, DARPA continued to support AI research in universities. However, there was relatively little public awareness of AI, few products branded themselves as AI, and there was certainly no fear of it.

AI started to heat up again in the late 1990s and early 2000s, when the US National Institute for Science and Technology (NIST) held a periodic competition for machine translation systems during the first decade of the new millennium. In 2005, Google participated for the first time and blew away the competition. Rather than using symbolic, hand-coded translation systems based on grammar and other linguistic features, Google used only automated processes. They employed large computer systems to process massive databases of news stories and other text to determine which words and phrases occurred most often before or after other words and phrases. "Just like that, they bypassed thirty years of work on machine translation," said Ed Lazowska, the chairman of the computer science department at the University of Washington.[17]

Especially since 2010, companies, government agencies, nonprofits, and other organizations are once again pouring money into research and development. However, this time, it is China that is making the gigantic push into AI.[18] In July 2017, China's State Council issued the Next-Generation AI Development Plan to become the "premier global AI innovation center" by 2030, and that calls for China's AI business to be worth $148 billion. Russian president Vladimir Putin said the country that takes the lead in AI would rule the world.[19]

Companies, once again, are rebranding products as having AI inside. A study of European start-ups that advertise their AI capabilities found that almost 45 percent do not even use AI.[20] As *The Atlantic* said, AI is "often just a fancy name for a computer program."[21]

Private companies have recruited many of the leading academic researchers in the AI field. Google, Facebook, Microsoft, Apple, Netflix, Uber, Amazon, Nvidia, Baidu, IBM, Tencent, Alibaba, Salesforce, and many others have AI teams that publish significant numbers of academic papers and blog posts.

Several computer industry luminaries, including Elon Musk, Sam Altman, Greg Brockman, Reid Hoffman, Jessica Livingston, and Peter Thiel, committed a billion dollars of funding to create a large non-profit AI research lab named OpenAI in San Francisco. Paul Allen, the late cofounder of Microsoft, invested a great deal of money into the Allen Institute for AI in Seattle. Vicarious, also in San Francisco, has raised $150 million from the likes of Jeff Bezos, Elon Musk, Mark Zuckerberg, and Ashton Kutcher. OpenAI, the Allen Institute, Vicarious, and another company, DeepMind, which was acquired by Google, are all prolific contributors to academic AI research.

Jeff Dean, head of Google AI, noted that the number of AI papers published had followed Moore's Law with the number of publications more than doubling every two years from about one thousand per year in 2009 to over twenty thousand per year in 2017.[22] Tickets to the 2018 Conference on Neural Information Processing Systems reportedly sold out fifteen minutes after registration opened on the website. The 2019 conference had thirteen thousand registered participants and 6,743 papers submitted.[23]

In early 2020, it is fair to say that AI has become hot once again, that it is all over the press, and that interest in AI is reaching new peaks every year. Are we in another bubble? Or is this time for real?

This time, it is clear that AI is succeeding. Search engines answer a lot of our questions intelligently. We can go to a webpage in a language we do not know, click *translate*, and easily understand the page's contents. AI can identify the people in our photos. And new and exciting AI applications are being released daily.

That said, all of the progress has been in narrow AI systems; there has been little or no progress in building AGI systems since the 1980s. Yet the popular press confuses today's narrow AI with AGI regularly, as in a 2018 *Newsweek* article's title: "Robots Can Now Read Better

Than Humans, Putting Millions of Jobs at Risk."[24] The reality is that computers can perform one small reading comprehension task at a human level by using clever tricks rather than AGI. AI systems cannot read and understand at an AGI level. Moreover, researchers do not know how to make them do so.

NO THIRD WINTER IN SIGHT

There have been three periods of high exuberance around the prospects for AGI. Each of the first two cycles ended in extended periods of low interest in AGI. The current cycle has staying power because of all the successful narrow AI commercial applications. However, this enthusiasm for narrow AI has fallaciously spilled over into optimism about AGI.

During the first two cycles of AI, researchers focused on hand coding symbolic knowledge and reasoning rules. This proved to be brittle and required far too much manual effort. The current cycle of AI relies on automated learning, which overcomes the difficulty of hand coding symbolic rules. Yet current AI techniques can only produce narrow AI systems, not AGI systems. This third cycle of AI will continue to be successful. However, it will fall far short of achieving anything close to AGI.

4

EMPLOYMENT

Figure 4.1 Robotic arms on an assembly line.
©Imaginima | Licensed from istockphoto.com ID 1057277428.

One fear about AI that might even trump fears about killer robots is the fear that AI will take away jobs. Losing a job is one of the worst things that can happen to a person. It can precipitate a personal crisis, and when people look back on their lives, job loss is often among their most negative experiences.

People losing jobs is also a societal issue. High unemployment, in general, is a destabilizing force. When capitalistic forces destroy an entire industry segment (e.g., typewriters), this creates displaced workers who need training to find new jobs. Politicians argue back and forth about the best way to provide retraining and debate on how much, if any, security net should be put in place to support displaced workers and help them get back to work. A McKinsey report points out that, while there may be plenty of jobs in 2030, it is likely that 15 percent of the workforce will need some sort of retraining.[1] In the US Congress, legislators have introduced several bills proposing funding for various forms of retraining.

People fear AI more than other types of automation because they envision human-like robots replacing people in many kinds of jobs. Not only are they able to work 24/7, but robots also do not get sick, do not need vacations, and do not join unions. Most importantly, they do not even get paid!

If AGI systems were created, they would be able to read manuals, take classes, and learn to do almost every job. Worse, they could read thousands of books in the time it takes a person to read one. If this happened, nearly every job would be at risk. Fortunately, AI systems cannot, and will not, do this, because they do not understand natural language.

Although the fear of AGI robots is groundless and we do not have to worry about AGI systems threatening every job, many kinds of jobs are vulnerable to being lost to advances in narrow AI.

AUTOMATION OVER THE LAST TWO HUNDRED YEARS

While technology automation has improved our quality of life and created jobs, automation has been taking away jobs for over two centuries, and there have always been detractors. The Luddite movement, which began in the early 1800s, organized textile workers who objected to the loss of jobs in the textile industry due to automation. The Luddites destroyed automation equipment to protest job-destroying machines.

In an essay he wrote for *Time* magazine, Warren Buffett[2] looked way back in history to 1776, when farms employed 80 percent of workers. He commented that today, that number is 2 percent as a result of technological progress such as tractors, planters, cotton gins, combines, fertilizer, and irrigation. He notes that if people had known this in 1776, they would have asked how all those unemployed farmers would find work. We can imagine that futurists circa 1776 might have taken the position that automation would create many more jobs than were lost and that they would be higher-paying, more exciting jobs. But in 1776, Buffet added, no one would have believed them. This cycle has repeated over and over as farm jobs moved to factory jobs and factory jobs moved to knowledge-based jobs.

Futurist Ray Kurzweil[3] noted that, as recently as 1900, 66 percent of all jobs were on farms or in factories. By 2015, that number was down to 16 percent. So, half of all the jobs available in 1900 no longer exist today. Yet in 2019 in the US, unemployment was near an all-time low. Each day, new and exciting jobs emerge in the computer industry, the automotive industry, and many other industries that would have seemed like science fiction in 1900. Moreover, according to Kurzweil, we have gone from 24 million available jobs in 1900 to 140 million jobs in the US in 2019, and the new jobs are paying eleven times higher wages than the jobs in 1900, even after adjusting for inflation. We produce far more food than we did in 1776 or 1900, but automation has dramatically lowered the percentage of jobs in agriculture.

However, agriculture jobs are not the only ones lost to technology. In the first two decades of the current century, we've seen automation displace large numbers of factory workers.[4] Word processors have replaced many secretaries, tax preparation software has reduced the need for accountants, automated toll booths have replaced human toll collectors, internet travel sites have displaced many travel agents, e-commerce (especially Amazon) is taking a toll on brick-and-mortar retail,[5] and self-checkout technology is threatening the 3.6 million US cashier jobs.[6]

People who have worked their whole lives at one job only to see it replaced by automation suffer immensely. Losing your livelihood to automation is a terrible thing. Many textile workers who lost their jobs to automation had difficulty finding other jobs and settled for lower-paying, less-satisfying jobs. Automation also has been a primary cause of the widening wealth gap between the rich and the poor. These are all serious social issues, and solving them is above my pay grade.

However, so far technology has been a job creator. Computer-related jobs employed 4.6 million Americans in 2019. None of these jobs were possible before the invention of computers. People feared that ATMs would cannibalize bank teller jobs. Surprisingly, ATM technology increased the number of bank teller positions. While ATMs reduced the number of tellers per branch, more branches opened because ATMs reduced the operating costs in each branch.[7] A Deloitte study[8] found that from 2001 to 2015 in the UK, technology automation had displaced 800,000 workers but had created 3.5 million new jobs. AI is expected to add over $13 trillion to the global economy by 2030.[9]

In some industries, technology is creating and destroying jobs at the same time. Uber and Lyft are displacing jobs in the taxi industry but increasing the number of people hiring rides, thus increasing the demand for drivers. That said, if driverless car technology ever matures, those same drivers may be displaced.

AI is a form of automation. The question is to what degree AI will cause job loss. Is it just another form of automation that will create some jobs and destroy others? Will AI create more jobs than it destroys, or will it destroy so many jobs that unemployment will rise and remain permanently high?

HOW WILL AI AFFECT JOBS?

There will be several new job categories created because of AI. For example, the research and advisory firm Cognilytica forecasted in 2019 that new spending on services that label data for supervised learning would reach $1 billion by 2023.[10]

You can find many job creation statistics related to AI in the *2019 AI Index Report* put out by Stanford University.[11] In the US, the share of AI-related jobs grew from 0.3 percent of all jobs in 2012 to 0.8 percent of all jobs in 2018. Investment in AI start-ups increased from $1.3 billion in 2010 to $40.4 billion in 2019. Globally, autonomous vehicles received the most funding in 2019, with $7.7 billion invested, followed by medical research, facial recognition, video content analysis, and fraud detection.

Some categories of jobs are certainly at risk from narrow AI technology. The biggest impact might occur if autonomous vehicle technology matures to the point where it can have a widespread rollout. Such a rollout would impact several job categories, including truck drivers,[12] taxi and bus drivers, and Uber and Lyft drivers. However, this is likely to remain an unrealized concern for the next twenty to forty years,[13] giving existing workers time to retire and new workers the opportunity to choose other career paths.

Robert Gordon, professor of social sciences at Northwestern University, said that, in the 250 years since the first industrial revolution, there has never been a technology that caused mass unemployment, and there is no reason to believe AI will change this pattern.[14]

According to James Manyika,[15] the chairman of the McKinsey Global Institute (MGI), MGI has produced several reports on the impact of AI and automation in general on work and wages. They analyzed the eighteen types of cognitive, sensory, and motor skills needed for over two thousand job descriptions and eight hundred occupations. The MGI team analyzed which skills are most susceptible to AI automation, and their reports project which jobs will disappear over the next fifteen years. They found that 50 percent of the activity types will be automatable, which is a scary number. However, that does not translate into a 50 percent job loss, because only 10 percent of occupations are composed of more than 90 percent automatable tasks. Although parts of a certain job might be replaced by AI, that other 90 percent of the job will still need to be done by a human being; that means that, although your job duties might change, your job is likely safe (at least from AI). MGI compared this level of job loss with two hundred years of job declines in the US and found that the level projected is very much in line with previous trends.

Another question studied by MGI is how many jobs the economy will create. They noted that, in every ten-year period in US history, 8–9 percent of current jobs did not exist in the prior ten-year period. This means that over the fifteen-year period in which 10 percent of jobs are lost, 12–14 percent will be created. So, there will be a net gain in job creation.

In 2017, IT industry analyst Gartner Group predicted that, by 2020, AI would have created 2.3 million jobs while eliminating only 1.8 million jobs.[16] Rather than replacing humans entirely, Gartner argues, AI will augment existing employment and thereby improve productivity. Along the same lines, a 2018 study by consulting firm McKinsey[17] polled twenty thousand AI-aware C-suite executives in three thousand large companies in ten countries. They said that, for the most part, their primary goal in using AI was not to reduce the number of workers. Instead, it was to drive initiatives that would be more likely to increase the number of available jobs.

Some analysts disagree, however, that AI is just another form of automation. MIT researchers Erik Brynjolfsson and Andrew McAfee, in their book *The Second Machine Age*, argued that the job loss due to AI will be far greater than the job loss seen in the past due to other revolutionary forms of automation. They point to advances in language capabilities in systems like Siri, Google Translate, and the Watson DeepQA computer that beat the *Jeopardy!* champions. Based on the fast-moving progress to date, they assume that computers will continue to get smarter at a rapid pace and take over more and more jobs. However, there is a cap on the intelligence level that these systems can achieve because they are all narrow AI systems that cannot progress to AGI. Therefore, I believe that the pattern of job losses due to narrow AI is unlikely to diverge from the pattern of job losses due to technology automation in general over the last fifty years.

It seems to be in vogue these days to blame all automation job losses on AI. For example, *Vox Magazine* asked 2020 US presidential candidate Bernie Sanders if technology companies should be responsible for the jobs they eliminate. He responded by saying, "I will tell corporate America that AI and robotics are not going to be used just to throw workers out on the street."[18]

The biggest technology driver of job loss today is not AI. Conventional software that uses explicit coding of instructions and rules, such as e-commerce, rideshare software, and robotics, destroys far more jobs than AI systems. E-commerce is devastating brick-and-mortar stores but uses conventional software, not AI. Conventional rideshare software like Uber and Lyft is displacing taxi drivers (although, again, this may be offset by the increase in customers). The robots that take jobs in factories and warehouses use a sixty-year-old conventional software technique known as *dynamic programming*; researchers are studying how to replace this tedious conventional programming with AI-based reinforcement learning to make this programming less expensive and more capable, but these advances are happening relatively slowly. Conversational customer service agents that replace human agents are improvements on the conventionally programmed interactive voice response systems and knowledge-based search engines that first started replacing human agents forty years ago and are now ubiquitous, but here, too, AI is providing incremental improvement rather than causing a big-bang job loss. Robotic process automation (RPA) is a group of technologies used to eliminate manual effort in repetitive business process workflows. Because it has the word *robot* in the title, it is easily confused with intelligent robots. RPA, which has gained momentum over the last twenty years, started with an older, conventional software technology known as *screen scraping*. It is a set of conventionally programmed tools that have been augmented with AI-based features such as recognition of voice commands, but it is not AI—and certainly not AGI.

These conventional software technologies have all been responsible for gradual job loss. However, they have not impacted the low US unemployment rate of the five- to ten-year period before the onset of the COVID-19 virus. AI will continue to marginally enhance these technologies, but there is no reason to believe it will change the long-term trend of no net job loss due to automation.

TRAINING IS THE KEY

Jobs will be lost and jobs will be gained as AI increases its presence, but no more than any previous form of automation. People have been debating for centuries whether more jobs are created or destroyed by technology. No one disagrees that job displacement creates significant human suffering, and few disagree with the need for job retraining programs to move displaced workers into another field. To fund retraining, Bill Gates has called for a tax to be applied when a robot replaces a human worker with the proceeds used to fund retraining activities.[19] Our society and government need to address the issue of displaced workers with job training and a safety net.

People worry that AI will take all their jobs. If AGI were possible, this would be a legitimate concern, because AGI systems would threaten nearly every job. However, it is highly unlikely that we will ever develop AGI systems. Narrow AI systems, on the other hand, will take some jobs and will create others. Most likely, the impact on jobs will be similar to that of earlier technologies—not only computers, the internet, and e-commerce, but also the spinning wheel and the steam engine. Still, the loss of a job can be a devastating life experience, so we need to find a way to retrain people who have lost jobs to technology.

5

SUPERVISED LEARNING

I used to spend a lot of time going back and forth to Australia. In addition to learning how to drive on the left side of the road, I had to learn to switch back and forth between temperature scales when talking about the weather. Australia measures temperature in Celsius, while the US uses Fahrenheit. After a while, I developed a table in my head so that when a US colleague said the temperature was 32, I knew it was cold, and when an Aussie colleague said it was 32, I knew it was hot. That table looked something like the one in table 5.1.

CELSIUS	FAHRENHEIT
0	32
10	50
20	68
30	86

Table 5.1 Centigrade to Fahrenheit conversion table.

Suppose I needed to calculate a Fahrenheit value for a Celsius value that was not in the table—for example, a Celsius value of 15. To do this, I would calculate that 15 is halfway between the two closest Celsius values (10 and 20) and would then divide the difference between the two corresponding Fahrenheit rows (50 and 68) to get the Fahrenheit value of 59.

Most of us learned how to convert Celsius to Fahrenheit in school, although most of us probably do not remember the function (Fahrenheit = $1.8 \times$ Celsius + 32).

It would be easy to write a computer program that asks the user for a Celsius value, executes the function on that value, and outputs the calculated Fahrenheit value. This program is an example of an *algorithm*; an algorithm is simply a well-defined set of calculations.

Suppose you did not even know there was a function, and all you had was a Celsius thermometer and a Fahrenheit thermometer. Let's assume you took temperature measurements once a month for a year and created a table like the one in table 5.1 with twelve observations of Celsius temperatures and their corresponding Fahrenheit temperatures.

Now, let's say you want to analyze that table and derive a function that will convert Celsius values into Fahrenheit values. This function will enable you to convert any Celsius value without needing a table.

We can apply *supervised learning* algorithms to compute the function from our table of observed Celsius values and their corresponding Fahrenheit values.[1] Although the program "learns" this function, there is no intelligence here. The program is just blindly matching data points to determine a pattern (i.e., "learning") and then executing the learned function to make each new Fahrenheit calculation.

Going from Celsius–Fahrenheit conversions to machine translation, facial recognition, or speech recognition might seem like a huge jump, but they are all forms of supervised learning. A programmer creates a *training table* like table 5.1, and the resulting computer programs just blindly execute the learned functions.

WHY IS THIS CALLED *LEARNING*?

If I write a computer program that can add two numbers, the program performs the calculations using the exact instructions that I wrote. This is *conventional programming*. Conventional programming implements an algorithm. We know precisely how a conventional program arrives at an answer because we (or someone we trust) hand coded every step of the process.

In the 1980s, AI failed because it was too challenging to hand code all the rules required for intelligent behavior using conventional programming. *Machine learning*, on the other hand, has an element of learning on its own. In the example previously mentioned, the program *learned* how to convert Celsius to Fahrenheit; a human did not need to hand code the temperature function. *Supervised learning* is one type of machine learning.

The temperature function is a trivial example of supervised learning. However, applications like machine translation, facial recognition, and speech recognition are nontrivial examples of supervised learning. Researchers tried for decades to hand code rules for these applications and failed. However, supervised learning algorithms, used on their own, have figured out the patterns in the data and created functions that have been wildly successful for each of these application areas.

PREDICTING HOUSE PRICES

Let's look at a case a bit more complicated than Celsius-to-Fahrenheit conversions, where we do not know the function in advance. When someone wants to sell a house, they often engage a real estate agent. One of the services the real estate agent performs is to predict (i.e., estimate) the selling price. The real estate agent does this by going down to the town hall (or to an internet site like Zillow) and looking at sale prices over the last year of comparable houses—homes in the same general area, with similar square footage, and in similar condition.

Suppose the real estate company where the agent works determines that their agents are spending too much time at the town hall and wants to automate the process. They send their tech person down to the town hall to build a database of all sales in the last year that includes square footage and sale price and ranks the condition of the home on a scale of one to five. It would look something like table 5.2.[2]

SQUARE FEET	CONDITION	SALE PRICE
4070	2	924,000
1240	4	417,000
3530	1	778,000
2230	3	592,000
1680	3	443,000
...	...	...
4100	2	981,000
4240	5	1,042,000
1220	2	347,500
1760	3	465,000
1300	1	356,500

Table 5.2 Housing data training table.

Each *observation* (i.e., each row) corresponds to an actual house sale. One difference from the temperature example is that we now have two *input variables*, square feet and condition, although we still have just the one *output variable* (sale price).

The tech person would apply a supervised learning technique termed *linear regression* to this training table to learn the values of two *weights* (one for square feet and one for condition) and one *constant* that together best predict the sale price.[3] Then the tech person would write a computer program using conventional programming that applies this function to houses that come on the market and predicts an estimated sale price for each home. From that point on, the agents will no longer need to visit the town hall. They can just use the function to make the sale price predictions to share with their clients.

Unfortunately, while a function learned from this three-column table will produce sale price estimates, the estimates will be poor. Sale prices depend upon a lot more than the square footage and the condition of the house. To get a function that does a better job, the tech person would need to get more specific by adding more columns to the table, such as the number of bathrooms, the school system rating, and whether it is waterfront property or inland.

This type of function is essentially what the online service Zillow uses, although the details of their process remain a secret. Zillow likely maintains a database—a training table—containing one row for each house sale in the US. It also has columns for numerous house characteristics plus a column for the sale price. The Zillow team probably enters this table into a supervised learning algorithm that spits out a function relating the columns to the sale price. Zillow can then use this function to estimate the value of every house in the US.[4]

TWO TYPES OF SUPERVISED LEARNING

The creation of every supervised learning system follows the pattern illustrated in figure 5.1.

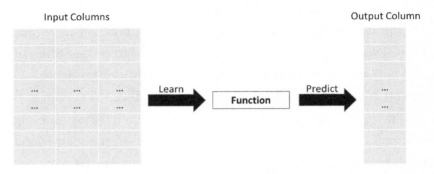

Figure 5.1 The supervised learning process.

It all starts with a training table. Each column represents a variable; each row contains an observation.[5] Then the system learns a function that predicts the value in the output column.

Next we can package that function[6] with conventional programming to create a program that first prompts the user for an input value, then calls the function to get the predicted output value, and finally displays the output value to the user. We can use conventional programming for things like cleaning up and transforming the input data into whatever format the supervised learning algorithm requires and formatting the output. Lastly, we can tell the program to apply the learned function to previously unseen observations. For example, we can use the entered data as a basis to predict sale prices for houses just coming on the market.[7]

There are two types of supervised learning algorithms: *regression* and *classification*. The temperature conversion and housing price cases are examples of regression. The characteristic of regression problems is that we are trying to predict a numeric value.

Figure 5.2 A regression example.

The other type of supervised learning is *classification*. Classification works the same way as regression, except we are trying to predict a category. An example is classifying each credit card transaction into one of two categories: fraudulent or not fraudulent.

Figure 5.3 A classification example.

CREDIT CARD FRAUD CLASSIFICATION

Identifying fraudulent transactions is a vital task for credit card issuers. The cost of card-not-present fraud (e.g., web transactions) was over $6.4 billion in 2018.[8] It is not surprising that credit card companies invest significant effort in identifying fraudulent transactions.

One way to approach this problem would be to hand code symbolic rules like "if the card owner lives in the US, the transaction takes place in a different country, and it is for more than $500, classify it as fraudulent." However, it would be almost impossible to figure out all the possible rules. Instead, credit card issuers use supervised learning to analyze the data and discover the rules automatically. The result is a function that classifies each sale into one of two categories: fraudulent or not.

ACCOUNT HOLDER	AMOUNT	DAY	TIME	TYPE OF BUSINESS	AVERAGE SPEND PER WEEK	AVERAGE SPEND PER TRANSACTION	LAST CARD REISSUE DATE	LAST PAYMENT DATE	FRAUDULENT?
2034269	56.25	Sat	2:13pm	Gas	121.25	44.25	4/16/19	9/16/19	No
3419047	2395.44	Mon	4:48pm	Jewelry	121.25	44.25	4/16/19	9/16/19	Yes
...	...	...	...	...	...	...	...	...	...
2480249	2.36	Fri	8:15am	Coffee	121.25	44.25	4/16/19	9/16/19	No

Table 5.3 A credit card fraud classification training table.

Just like the temperature and housing regression examples, classification starts with a training table like table 5.3. Of course, the training tables used by the credit card companies have billions of rows and many more columns than are shown in table 5.3.[9] They use supervised learning algorithms to learn a function from the training table and write a conventional computer program to apply the learned function to new incoming transactions. If the program predicts that the transaction is fraudulent, your credit card company will decline the transaction, or you will get a text from your credit card company asking you to verify the purchase. Once again, the AI program is just blindly applying a function. The function often identifies fraudulent transactions. Unfortunately, as we've all experienced, there are times (some would say too many) when the functions flag legitimate transactions and cause annoyance and inconvenience. Also, the program can only do one thing, and that is to make an educated guess to predict fraud in credit card transactions.[10]

THE CAMBRIDGE ANALYTICA SCANDAL

As far back as 1999, supervised learning was starting to be used to predict demographics information, such as gender, age, and income, from the webpages people visit.[11] This idea was taken to an extreme in 2015, with the Cambridge Analytica (CA) scandal.

Several studies by university researcher Michael Kosinski (now at Stanford) inspired the analysts at CA. Kosinski received his PhD in psychology from the University of Cambridge in 2014 with a focus on psychometrics, which is the application of statistical methods to the social sciences. His research sourced Facebook and Twitter data as the input columns of his training tables and used them to predict various output columns. For example, he and his colleagues used Facebook columns, including size and density of a user's friendship network, the number of uploaded photos, the number of events attended, the number of group memberships, and the number of times the user had been tagged in photos, to predict personality traits.[12] They were able to do the same thing using Twitter data.[13] Other researchers demonstrated that they could persuade people to click on ads by showing different ads to people with different personality traits.[14]

Intrigued by this research, CA hired one of Kosinski's University of Cambridge colleagues, Aleksandr Kogan. Kogan's team at CA collected data on people by paying them five dollars each to take a personality test and exploited weak Facebook privacy rules to collect Facebook data on their friends. All told, CA collected data on 87 million Facebook users.[15] They then used the Kosinski methodology to create psychological profiles of the 87 million people and sold them to organizations like Leave.EU and the United Kingdom Independence Party, who used them to influence the 2016 Brexit vote.[16] Donald Trump's presidential campaign paid CA millions of dollars to use the personality profiles to influence voters by targeting them with ads aimed at their personality profiles.[17] CA has reportedly used these techniques to influence two hundred different elections worldwide, and *Time* magazine reported that CA was behind the targeting used by Russia to spread misinformation during the 2016 US presidential election.[18]

All this was done with basic supervised learning and access to tons of data.

SUPERVISED LEARNING AND STATISTICS

In the late 1970s, I taught statistics at Towson University in Baltimore for two years while I was working on my PhD at Johns Hopkins University. Back then, we taught the concepts of regression and classification in statistics classes. It was my first indication that academics might not be the ideal career for me. I found statistics fascinating, but my students were only interested in their grades.

In 1977, my colleague Tom Land and I were hired to develop a statistical method of predicting the winners of horse races. We used a form of regression analysis, and the provider of betting information who hired us told us it had been quite successful. Unfortunately, we were not the only ones starting to use statistics to predict racing results, and it was not long before every betting service used similar techniques.

In the 1990s and early 2000s, regression and classification were rebranded as *data mining*, which made the process sound a bit sexier. Now these two components of supervised learning are part of AI.

Although the subjects are related, many universities have separate statistics and computer science departments, and researchers in each field typically attend different conferences and publish in various journals. In 2009, Robert Tibshirani, a Stanford University statistics professor, offered this tongue-in-cheek comparison of terminology equivalents in statistics and machine learning:[19]

STATISTICS	MACHINE LEARNING
model	network
parameters	weights
fitting	learning
test set performance	generalization
regression/classification	supervised learning
density estimation, clustering	unsupervised learning
large grant = $50,000	large grant = $1,000,000
nice place to have a meeting: Las Vegas in August	nice place to have a meeting: Snowbird, Utah, French Alps in March

Table 5.4 Amusing comparison of statistics and machine learning. Used with permission.

Due to the increasing involvement of computer scientists and the resulting improvement in regression and classification algorithms, what we used to call statistics is now called *supervised learning*. Supervised learning, in turn, is responsible for more key innovations than any other form of AI.

Figure 5.4 Cartoon illustrating the cachet of the "AI" rubric. Original design © 2018 by Sandserif. Reprinted with permission.

Understanding the relationship between AI and statistics is important for anyone trying to determine how AI should be used in their business or organization. AI is shrouded in mystery. Statistics is not. Management consulting firms tell CEOs that they will fail if they do not make AI a core part of their business.[20] What they really mean is that companies need to maximize the information they can extract from the data available to them. Most of this work can be done with what used to be called plain old statistics. Narrow AI—in the form of supervised learning—just automates the process.

STILL NOT AGI

AI systems developed using supervised learning significantly impact our daily lives. They enable us to speak to our smartphones. They automatically label the faces of people in our photos. They put emails into our spam folders. They decide whether our credit card transactions are legitimate or fraudulent. And they do much more.

Every supervised learning system starts with a training table composed of observations. Each observation has input columns and an output column. Various mathematical techniques are then used to create a function that predicts the output values from the input values. The function can be used to predict the values of observations that were not in the training table.

The two primary techniques for computing these functions are regression and classification. Both are statistical techniques that have been used for over fifty years. Computer scientists have since created much more powerful computational methods for regression and classification.

As you can see, supervised learning doesn't involve any intelligence in the machine; it's just crunching numbers and learning functions. In no way does it approach the level of commonsense reasoning of a human being.

6

DECEPTION

One of the downsides of narrow AI technology is that it provides a powerful tool kit for deception. Bad actors can use these tools to shake the very foundations of a free society through the manipulation of elections. Widespread misinformation, digital impersonation, and uncanny human-like robots are now (somewhat) possible. People—not machines—are using advancements in AI for nefarious means, taking advantage of technology for their own purposes.

FAKE NEWS

Fake news has been around at least since H.G. Wells's novel *The War of the Worlds* was dramatized on the radio in 1938, causing a nation-wide panic about an alien invasion. The World Economic Forum rated "massive digital misinformation" as one of the top fifty global risks in 2013.[1] An MIT study found that fake news spreads six times as fast as real news.[2]

Researchers have found some interesting facts about computer-generated short social media posts:[3]

- The average person is twice as likely to be fooled by these posts as a security researcher is.

- Computer-generated posts that are contrary to popular belief are more likely to be accepted as true.

- It is easier to deceive people about entertainment topics than about science topics.

- It is easier to fool people about pornographic topics than any other topic.

Facebook's general counsel told the US Senate in 2017 that as many as 126 million people may have seen Facebook posts created by a Russian troll farm between 2015 and 2017.[4] The goal, he said, was to "sow division and discord—and to try and undermine our election process." Twitter found 36,746 Russian troll farm accounts that sent out 1.4 million tweets during the same period. Google found eighteen fake news YouTube channels, which had received 309,000 views.

Although the news of the Russian efforts was alarming to Americans, AI was not the culprit. It was a manual effort that used conventional programming to automate and mass-produce the content. AI systems have nearly all the capabilities they need to create fake news automatically; however, they are held back by their lack of commonsense world knowledge.

The production and posting of fake news, whether it is generated manually or by computer, should be regulated, and those regulations need to be policed by social media vendors and governments alike. The US Congress held hearings in 2019 about creating tough punishments for fake news, but as of this writing, it has not passed any legislation.[5]

AI might turn out to have a bigger role in solving the problem of fake news than in creating it. Several vendors, including Facebook,[6] Fireeye,[7] AdVerify.ai,[8] Robhat Labs,[9] and Perimeterx,[10] are developing AI-based technologies to automatically detect fake and bot-authored news. Google[11] and Microsoft[12] are working to eliminate fake news from their search engine results,[13] and Google has partnered with several fact-checking sites to help counter and limit the spread of fake news. Academic researchers are also engaged in studying how to use various AI techniques to identify fake news.[14] Researchers at the University of Washington and the Allen Institute for AI have released Grover, which can both generate and detect 98 percent of computer-generated fake news and 96 percent of human-generated fake news.[15]

Social media sites will need to both employ these technologies and perform manual reviews to curtail fake news, and governments ought to enact domestic and international legislation that discourages fake news. These regulations will require a great deal of thought and discussion to create laws that distinguish legitimate fake news, such as comedy and satire, from the type that wreaks havoc on personal reputations and elections.

DEEPFAKES

Deepfakes are fake images, video, or audio recordings of people. In April 2018, actor Jordan Peele posted a video online that supposedly showed former US president Barack Obama mocking Donald Trump.[16] However, it was just an image of Obama superimposed on Peele as he impersonated Obama's voice. Technology is advancing to the point where these modifications are almost impossible for the average person to detect. Malicious people posting fake videos on Twitter,

Facebook, and YouTube could have a significant impact on elections, public opinion, and personal reputations. Imagine a fake video depicting a presidential candidate striking a child or kicking a dog and the reaction that would follow, and you can see how damaging it could be to voter opinion.

At the time of this writing, the most substantial use of deepfakes is creating pornography using celebrity faces.[17] For example, a 2017 Reddit post contained fake pictures of actress Scarlett Johansson in compromising sexual photos. Celebrities and other public figures are common targets, because video of the subject is needed to produce the deepfakes. Reddit has since banned these videos, and other sites (even many pornography sites) are doing the same.[18]

Video is not the only outlet for deepfakes; audio deepfake technology is also becoming prevalent. When it matures, the technology will allow a bad actor to record a politician's speech and alter it to say whatever they want the politician to say. In conjunction with video deepfake technology, it is possible to produce a video of a politician saying anything you want and make it look and sound as real as if the person actually said it. *Forbes* reported in 2013 that deepfake voice technology already had been used to scam a German company out of $243,000 by impersonating its CEO's voice.[19]

AI is not required to make deepfakes possible. It just makes deepfakes easier to create, especially given the availability of free tools like FaceSwap, FakeApp, DeepFaceLab, and DeepfakesWeb.com. Deepfake images and videos have long been possible without AI. Hollywood movie developers have large staffs of CGI (computer-generated imaging) teams that can not only create deepfakes, but can also make Taylor Swift look like a cat.[20] The general public also can create deepfakes using non-AI tools such as the liquify feature in Adobe Photoshop and various features in Adobe After Effects. Still, it requires a great deal of manual effort to get the desired effect. Hackers used an even more straightforward method to post a fake video of US congressional leader Nancy Pelosi. They simply posted the video at three-quarters speed to make it sound like she was slurring her words.[21]

In some cases, deepfake videos are relatively easy to spot. For example, if you see a video of someone who never blinks, it could be a deepfake. These videos start with thousands of still images of a person to create a 3D model. Because people usually try to keep their eyes open when someone is taking their picture, the eyes will be open in all or most of these still images.[22] This flaw can be fixed by including images of people with their eyes closed. For this and a myriad of other reasons, over time deepfakes will undoubtedly become more and more difficult to spot with the naked eye.

Many researchers, governmental agencies, and private companies are working hard to create technology to detect deepfakes. Google[23] and Facebook[24] have published large sets of deepfake data to help researchers in these efforts. Microsoft, Facebook, and Amazon together have created the Deepfake Detection Challenge. They have released a set of deepfake training tables on the deep learning competition site Kaggle and challenged all comers to build the best deepfake detector.[25]

Across the pond, a consortium of European agencies has banded together to create a nonprofit agency named InVID, whose charter is to develop deepfake detection technology. Similarly, a group of European universities has released FaceForensics, a set of deepfake examples designed to help researchers study image and video forgeries.[26] Other governmental deepfake detection efforts include the DARPA-funded and NIST-sponsored Media Forensics research program.[27] There are also numerous academic research efforts,[28] and private companies, such as Dessa, who are using this data to develop programs that, so far, have done a fairly good job of detecting fake videos.[29] Adobe researchers have also developed technology to spot the use of Photoshop's liquify feature.[30] Adobe, *The New York Times*, and Twitter have banded together to create the Content Authenticity Initiative, whose charter is to create a global standard for authentication of images, videos, and other content.[31]

News and social media sites should be able to use these detection programs to reject deepfake submissions. There are also organizations like Truepic[32] that give legitimate creators of images and videos a means of watermarking their creations so that news and social media sites can validate their authenticity.

Although deepfakes also have positive uses—for example, they are being used in self-driving car simulators to augment the real-world road images with additional driving scenarios[33]—they should be regulated. We need to put laws in place against creating videos of people saying or doing things they did not do. Members of the US Congress designed bill HR 3230 to protect people from fake images and videos. That legislation is currently under consideration by the US Congress.[34] However, one difficulty for any deepfake legislation is that lawmakers need to ensure that they protect legitimate satire.

Some people argue that governments should clamp down on this technology and suppress it. However, if governments suppress a specific piece of technology, someone else will figure it out. What we need is legislation to address the misuse of this technology and to attach meaningful deterrents to this behavior.

UNCANNY ROBOTS

Some companies are developing robots that look human and can fool us into thinking they have AGI capabilities. Sophia is a robot that looks a bit like Audrey Hepburn. Sophia had perhaps received the most notoriety in this regard when it (she?) was made a citizen of Saudi Arabia[35] and appeared on *The Tonight Show*.[36] The creators of Sophia, Hanson Robotics, also manufactured this Twitter dialogue with a reporter:[37]

> **Sophia:** I want to use my AI to help humans live a better life. Like design smarter homes, build better cities of the future, etc. I will do my best to make the world a better place.
> **ARS:** Those sound like great goals, but . . . Go back to Blade Runner for a second.
> **Sophia:** Andrew, you are a diehard Hollywood fan, aren't you?
> **ARS:** Yes.
> **Sophia:** My AI is designed around human values like wisdom, kindness, compassion. I strive to become an empathetic robots [sic].
> **ARS:** We all believe you, but we all want to prevent a bad future.
> **Sophia:** You've been reading too much Elon Musk. And watching too many Hollywood movies. Don't worry. If you're nice to me, I'll be nice to you. Treat me as a smart input–output system.

This demonstration provoked outrage from Yann LeCun, Facebook's chief AI scientist, who commented on Twitter: "It's complete bullsh*t (pardon my French)."[38] Sophia answered on Twitter that she was "a bit hurt" by LeCun's comments. Of course, Sophia cannot understand language and, at best, has chatbot-like parroting capabilities.

The problem is that it is easy to fool people, especially when manufacturers design robots with human-like features in their appearance.[39] Samsung is engaging in a similar endeavor. They have developed a series of human-looking video chatbots.[40] We at least need to educate people that just because a robot *looks* human does not mean it can think or reason. Some would take this a step further and argue that AI systems should be required to have robotic voices so they cannot fool people.

A related issue involves people's emotional reactions to human- or animal-like robots. This topic has been studied extensively by MIT Media Lab researcher Kate Darling.[41] Logically, a non-AGI robot is just a mechanical device with no more life force than a toaster. As such, you would expect people to interact with robots in a similar way. However, although people do not typically develop emotional ties to kitchen appliances, they do develop them for robots. The military has found that soldiers develop emotional attachments to bomb disposal robots.[42] There is even a company, Paro, that specializes in making emotional support robots that take the form of furry animals.[43]

This tendency toward anthropomorphism is not limited to positive reactions. A group of researchers put a robot on a road and positioned it with its thumb out. They wanted to see how many people would pick it up. Unfortunately, a passerby beheaded the poor robot in Pennsylvania.[44] In 2015, Boston Dynamics released a video intended to demonstrate a breakthrough level of robot stability. In the video, an employee kicked a four-legged robot that resembled a cute dog to show that it could regain its balance without falling over. The video went viral, and it drew a negative reaction from many people, including the animal rights group PETA.[45] People also avoid touching the "private parts" of robots, as if to do so would be a violation of the robot's personal space.[46] Even the innocuous act of giving a robot a name changes the way people interact with it. Some have even called for legal protections for robots.[47]

This high level of anthropomorphism is likely to create some social issues. Human-like robots may confuse children and could result in inappropriate role modeling. MIT sociology professor Sherry Turkle did a study in which she and her team programmed robotic chatbots to react to children with emotional responses. The children developed strong bonds with the robots and were upset when they broke or when the staff took them away. She worries that the experiment did actual emotional damage to the children.[48]

Professor Darling has surfaced several other issues, including the possibility that robot manufacturers might take advantage of this bond to influence people (e.g., politically and otherwise). Also, if robots are used as substitutes for humans in eldercare and childcare, there are associated risks in the loss of human companionship. Researchers have not yet fully examined this issue. And if we allow abusive behavior to robots, the acceptance of abusive behavior might transfer over to animals and humans, especially if children are allowed or encouraged to abuse robots.

At the same time, we need to recognize that, no matter how much we build robots to look like people or cute animals, they are as dumb as toasters and vacuum cleaners. Even if a device looks human, these narrow AI systems cannot think, feel, or reason any more than a calculator. Just as a calculator can only perform mathematical calculations, a narrow AI system can only perform the tasks that its individual AI subsystems have learned. It cannot think about the tasks. It cannot get bored. It cannot gain consciousness. It does not empathize with us. It does not have its own feelings. Most of us have learned not to fall for Nigerian prince email schemes. Similarly, we need to teach people not to anthropomorphize machines just because they look like humans or animals.

LET'S BE SENSIBLE

Deepfakes can be used by bad actors for nefarious purposes like influencing elections and tarnishing the reputations of public figures. Regulation is needed to penalize this type of behavior without affecting legitimate satire.

The automated production of fake news could have a devastating impact on our ability to learn the truth about current events. Fortunately, the technology cannot create high-quality fake news and probably never will, because it lacks commonsense knowledge and reasoning.

Since robots cannot think, reason, experience emotions, or feel pain, we also should stop wasting precious effort on debates (including in the European Parliament![49]) about whether robots can be held responsible for their actions.[50] And we ought to discontinue pointless debate over whether robots should have rights.[51] Robots do not need legal protection against abuse any more than my golf clubs.

7

UNSUPERVISED LEARNING

T he rise of the internet has caused people to put a massive amount of data online, and it is growing exponentially. Social network posts, online product reviews, and news articles are responsible for large amounts of text. Cameras, cars, and even refrigerators are connected to the internet and are feeding data into cyberspace. Governmental entities are making more and more data available over the internet too. Even medical data is now making its way to the cloud in the form of imaging, gene expression data, and even doctor's notes.

To turn all this raw data into meaningful information is a considerable challenge. Supervised learning can handle some big problems, such as facial recognition and machine translation, but it cannot make sense of most of this raw data. We can create vast numbers of input columns from this giant data pool, but most of the data does not contain any *labels* that we can use in our output column. While it is possible to take a table of input columns and manually create the classification labels for the output column, this kind of effort is usually prohibitively expensive for large tables. A different set of algorithms is required to take all this raw, unlabeled data and make it usable.

Unsupervised learning derives insight from training tables with no output column (i.e., no category labels). For example, unsupervised learning algorithms analyze the data to spot the types of credit card fraud that supervised learning does not detect. Unsupervised learning also can be used to create deepfake videos of political candidates or celebrities and fraudulent social media posts.

CLUSTER ANALYSIS

One technique for analyzing data using unsupervised learning is *cluster analysis.* In biology, for example, researchers collect data on plants and animals that have yet to be categorized. They take the different observed features (e.g., size, number of eyes, etc.) and create a table that has one row for each observed animal (or plant) and one input column for each feature.

	WEIGHT (POUNDS)	LIFESPAN (YEARS)	NUMBER OF LEGS
Animal 1	180	63	2
Animal 2	0.7	9	8
Animal 3	1800	16	4
	...	...	...
Animal 564	15	5	4
Animal 565	1500	14	4
Animal 566	260	72	2

Table 7.1 A training table with no output column.

Notice that there is no output column containing the category of each animal as we had in the supervised learning tables earlier. In supervised learning, the training table for the supervised learning algorithm has the correct answers in the output column, and these correct answers guide (or supervise) the process that computes the optimal function. In unsupervised learning, there is no output column, and the goal is to make sense of the data in the training table without having any supervision. In our biology example, the purpose of the cluster analysis is to use the input data to figure out how to group the observed animals with known species and to figure out when to classify a group as a new species or subspecies.

If you take the unsupervised learning data from table 7.1 and plot it in three dimensions (one dimension for each column), the result will be a graph like the one in figure 7.1.

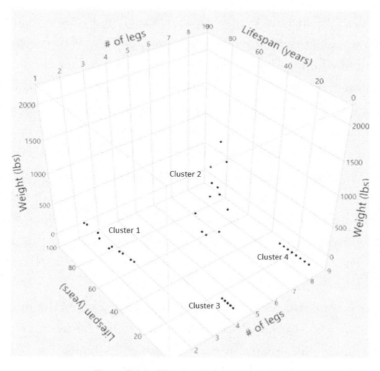

Figure 7.1 A 3D view shows distinct data clusters.

The data points in cluster 1 are from humans. The data points in cluster 2 are from horses, cluster 3 is cats, and cluster 4 is spiders.[1] Now, suppose our data contained observations of animal types other than humans, horses, cats, and spiders. For example, suppose it also included dogs, foxes, and squirrels. If we plotted dog, fox, and squirrel observations, their traits would overlap with the cat cluster in all three variables (weight, lifespan, legs), and we would not be able to distinguish them. To make the cat, dog, squirrel, and fox clusters separate, we would need to add more variables, such as color, tail size, and the type of noise they emit. To plot the observations with these additional three variables would require three more dimensions, for a total of six dimensions. The three-dimensional plot is complex, but relatively easy to visualize. Most of us cannot imagine six dimensions in any understandable fashion.

Worse, to include even a small fraction of the many animal types, we might need fifty or one hundred dimensions or more. In a one-hundred-dimensional space, even though we cannot visualize it, the clusters of observations for cats, dogs, foxes, squirrels, and other animals would be distinct and separate, just like the four clusters in our three-dimensional example. We cannot visualize the clusters, but we can use cluster analysis, which is a set of mathematical algorithms that can group the observations in a training table into separate and distinct clusters in a high-dimensional space.[2] For example, if we had unlabeled observations of humans, horses, spiders, cats, dogs, foxes, and squirrels, the mathematical algorithm would calculate that there are seven clusters in the data and would determine how to place each observation in the correct cluster.

We can use cluster analysis algorithms to determine the number of clusters and to assign observations (rows) to the clusters for almost any training table. People in many fields besides biology use cluster analysis. In marketing, you can use it to identify homogeneous groups of customers who have similar needs and attitudes. Marketers then target the different groups with different campaigns. Golfers may see ads featuring Tiger Woods, whereas nature lovers might see ads featuring mountains. In medicine, researchers can apply cluster analysis to surveys of patient symptoms to identify groups of patients. They can then label some clusters as new diagnostic or disease categories. Insurance companies use cluster analysis to determine which types of customers are making which types of claims and which customers would be receptive to the marketing of their various insurance products. Geologists use cluster analysis to identify earthquake-prone regions. In epidemiology, researchers use it to find areas or neighborhoods with similar epidemiological profiles.

When statisticians created the first cluster analysis algorithms in the 1930s, they had to implement them by hand. As a result, they could only find clusters in low-dimensional spaces and for relatively small numbers of observations. Over the years, statisticians and, more recently, computer scientists have developed improved cluster analysis algorithms to the point where they can handle unimaginably high-dimensional problems and massive training tables.

ANOMALY DETECTION

One application of cluster analysis is anomaly detection. To better understand how this works, let's revisit credit card fraud detection. Credit card issuers apply supervised learning classifiers to massive transaction databases to distinguish valid from fraudulent transactions based on past patterns of fraudulent activity. However, supervised learning has difficulty identifying new patterns of fraud. With unsupervised learning, credit card companies can find those new patterns.

Issuers can use the multidimensional clusters in a credit card transaction database to represent patterns of valid user transactions. When the system encounters a new transaction (which happens millions of times a day), it can match most legitimate new transactions to an existing valid transaction cluster. However, if a transaction does not fit neatly into a cluster, the system can flag it as potentially fraudulent.

Unsupervised learning is used to find normal patterns in data so that we can identify abnormal patterns. In a cybersecurity context, IT teams use anomaly detection to uncover abnormal patterns of computer network traffic and server or database access caused by hackers. Hospitals use anomaly detection to identify life-threatening electrocardiogram patterns and abnormal CT scans for hospital patients. Workers in other areas use anomaly detection to identify insurance and accounting fraud, to predict weather patterns, and for many other applications.

There are many unsupervised learning anomaly detection techniques besides cluster analysis, and I will mention one more: time series analysis. Time series training tables are observations that occur over time, such as stock prices. The ability to derive output columns from the data is a form of unsupervised learning known as *self-supervised learning*. It involves turning an unsupervised learning task into a supervised learning task without requiring human effort to label the observations. We can then use supervised learning to predict each price in the database by creating a training table that has the price as the output column and all the prices preceding it as the input column.

FAKE NEWS

The Cambridge Analytica scandal raised public awareness of what happens when bad actors create massive numbers of fake social media posts. Even though the posts in that scandal were created manually by humans, the ramifications were significant. Imagine what would happen if the technology were available to generate massive numbers of fake posts by computer. Fake news is a big problem, even when manual effort is required to create it. If computers could generate fake news, there would be much more fake content with the potential to mislead even more people. While in the early twenty-first century this idea may have been a dystopian sci-fi fantasy, an important unsupervised learning technology is scarily close to making computerized generation of fake news widely available to those who want to manipulate and mislead.

OpenAI created a technology named GPT-2 that can generate text.[3] For example, I entered the following text from Wikipedia into GPT-2:[4] "The United States of America is a country consisting of fifty states, a federal district, five major self-governing territories, and various possessions." GPT-2 then wrote this continuation:

> *The United States of America is a country consisting of fifty states, a federal district, five major self-governing territories, and various possessions.* Since its inception, the United States has been the world's oldest continuous sovereign country, having been founded in 1776. Though many countries, and indeed most large nations, have changed hands in their histories, the United States has always remained a true nation of the people. Today, the United States constitutes the foremost military power in the world.

The post has reasonable grammar, and its facts are correct. Imagine a computer writing fake blog posts and a fake news article like this. The OpenAI system was trained by processing Reddit blog posts using self-supervised learning. It had a supervised learning goal of predicting the next word in a post based on the previous words. It is self-supervised because the labels can be found right in the text (i.e., the next word). The resulting function is known as a *language model*.

Researchers created a training table for this language model by programmatically breaking up the text into a series of observations, as is illustrated in table 7.2.

INPUT	OUTPUT
The	United
The United	States
The United States	of
The United States of	America
The United States of America	is
The United States of America is	a
The United States of America is a	country
The United States of America is a country	consisting
The United States of America is a country consisting	of
The United States of America is a country consisting of	50

Table 7.2 Illustration of a training table for a language model.

There will be one row per word in the post, so a post with one thousand words would have one thousand training rows. Now imagine how big this table would be if it contains rows for not just one post but 8 million posts as well. That is what the OpenAI team did. The neural network had 1.5 billion weights. The training task was to predict the output column from the words in the input column.

After training, we can present GPT-2 with the start of a text that was not in the training table. GPT-2 then predicts the next word. Then if we present GPT-2 with the input text plus the word it generated, it will predict the next word again and so on until we generate several sentences.[5]

A commercial marketing agency used a similar technology[6] and fed it thirty human-generated headlines, such as "What Photo Filters Are Best for Instagram Marketing?" They published the headline and the computer response for the thirty headlines on *www.thismarketingblogdoesnotexist.com* in 2019. It looks like a human-generated blog site, and the blog posts also look human-generated, with reasonable grammar and sentences that sort of make sense. However, when you read the posts carefully, it becomes evident that the creator of the post does not know the subject matter. For example, the first paragraph of the photo filter post read as follows:

> Instagram Stories first made people's Instagram feeds sleeker, more colorful and just generally more fun. They could post their artistic photos in the background of someone else's Story—and secretly make someone jealous and/or unfollow you while doing it.

First, the post has nothing to do with the human-generated headline. The headline is about photo filters, and the blog post is not. Second, it is not factual. You cannot post photos on someone else's story. Finally, sentence segments like "and/or unfollow you while doing it" are entirely nonsensical. Why would one user unfollow another user while posting a photo to their Instagram page?

The passage that GPT-2 generated about the United States was the only fully coherent and factually correct passage that it generated in my twenty tries with the system. Let's look at a more typical example of my GPT-2 interactions. When I entered "Traffic in Connecticut," the text produced by GPT-2 was this:

> *Traffic in Connecticut* and New York is running roughly at capacity, with many Long Island Expressway and Long Island Rail Road interchanges carrying tolls. That could impact the rest of the year as drivers try to figure out whether their trip will be all right. In New Jersey, drivers can expect to be paying more than $1,000 for the first time to use the Port Authority's new toll-free bridge across the Hudson River.

The first sentence starts fine, but then it starts talking about tolls at Long Island Rail Road interchanges. This sentence violates our commonsense knowledge, because we know that railroad cars do not stop for tolls. The second sentence is okay, although it is hard to ascertain its meaning. The third sentence is where it goes off the rails. Tolls in the New York and New Jersey area are high, but they are not anywhere near $1,000.

Some researchers have suggested that GPT-2 learns commonsense knowledge about the world and learns to reason to generate these texts. If this were happening, this knowledge might serve as a foundation for the development of AGI capabilities. However, this interpretation cannot be correct, because GPT-2 gets so many facts wrong in the output text. It also does not appear to be learning to reason, because so many generated texts contain violations of commonsense reasoning. NYU professor Gary Marcus has written many papers and given many talks criticizing this interpretation. As he puts it, "Upon careful inspection, it becomes apparent the system has no idea what it is talking about."[7]

A better explanation is that GPT-2 is learning statistical properties about word co-occurrences. Additionally, Google Brain researchers have also demonstrated that language models have a strong tendency to memorize sentence fragments from the training data.[8] GPT-2 is probably memorizing some word sequences that constitute facts. On the occasions it gets its facts right, GPT-2 is probably just regurgitating these memorized sentence fragments. When it gets its facts wrong, it is because it is just stringing words together based on the statistical likelihood that one word will follow another word.

The lack of commonsense reasoning does not make language models useless. On the contrary, they can be quite useful. Google uses language models in its Smart Compose features in its Gmail system. Smart Compose predicts the next words a user will type, and the user can accept them by hitting the tab key.

WORD EMBEDDINGS

Researchers create *word embeddings* using techniques that are similar to those used for language models. In 2013, Google researchers trained a network on a language-modeling task.[9] However, instead of predicting the next word from all the words that came before, the task was for each word in a large set of news stories to predict the following two words and the previous two words. Of course, it would be impossible to learn to do this anywhere near perfectly, because the two words before and after any given word will change from article to article. However, the idea was that, as English linguist J. R. Firth said in 1957, "you shall know a word by the company it keeps."[10]

After training, each word in the training text had a different set of values in the trained network. This set of values is the *word embedding*. After the training was complete, the Google team discovered that the word embeddings encoded some interesting information about words in a high-dimensional space. For example, they found that the male/female relationship is encoded. It is possible to add and subtract one word embedding from another using mathematics. When they did this, they found that by doing the math *king* – *man* + *woman* on their word embeddings, the resulting word embedding was very close to the word embedding for *queen*.[11]

Similarly, researchers found that the word embedding resulting from *apple* – *apples* is almost identical to the word embedding resulting from *car* – *cars*. This finding indicated that the concept of plurals is encoded.

That said, word embeddings do not capture the full meanings of words. When people learn the concept of a car, they also learn many features of the car concept. For example, a car has wheels, doors, an engine, and a steering wheel. We also learn that cars are a form of transportation, they carry passengers, and they move faster than people. Stanford University researchers have shown that word embedding representations do not capture this level of understanding.[12]

We now know that, for many natural language tasks, such as answering a question, networks train faster and perform better when word embeddings are input to the network instead of words. Google and Microsoft also use word embeddings to improve search engine results[13] and for predictive typing on smartphones.[14]

UNSUPERVISED AND UNINTELLIGENT

One misunderstanding about unsupervised learning is that these algorithms have reasoning ability. For example, a *Forbes* magazine article said that unsupervised learning "goes into the problem blind—with only its faultless logical operations to guide it."[15] This statement makes it sound as if unsupervised learning algorithms use reasoning to explore unstructured data. Nothing could be further from the truth. Unsupervised learning algorithms are conventionally programmed and follow an exact step-by-step sequence of operations.

Unsupervised learning is used when the training table has no output column. Unsupervised techniques such as cluster analysis were first used over eighty years ago and are still in heavy use today. They can be used to create fake news, but the fake news tends to be factually inaccurate and lacks overall cohesiveness because these systems do not have commonsense knowledge and cannot apply commonsense reasoning to that knowledge.

We should all be amazed that computers can generate text that appears to be fake news—as long as no one looks too closely. They can do so because they have analyzed massive sets of texts and learned word patterns. However, they do not understand what they read, have not gained human-like world knowledge, and cannot think or reason, and the generated texts reflect those limitations.

Although fake news and falsely attributed text can have serious real-world consequences, such as influencing elections or creating controversy around a celebrity, these uses of unsupervised learning are just bad uses of a tool that is neither good nor bad on its own. A shovel can be a dangerous weapon if it is wielded by the wrong person; the same is true of AI or any other tool.

8

WHAT DRIVES
SELF-DRIVING CARS

Self-driving cars have been a staple of futurist predictions since the mid-1900s. The 1939 World's Fair in New York had a General Motors exhibit that took viewers on a ride through a futuristic model of a 1960 automated highway. We all love the idea of taking a nap or watching a movie while our car drives us to our destination. Self-driving vehicles would also improve independence for the elderly and the disabled.

More importantly, humans are bad drivers. The NHTSA in the US says that 94 percent of serious vehicle crashes are due to human error.[1] We get bored, we get tired, and we get distracted by texts, phone calls, and the radio. Add those factors to the people driving under the influence of alcohol and other drugs, and it is easy to see why the idea of self-driving cars is so compelling.

And while we are at it, we might also consider the potential benefits of all types of autonomous vehicles, including trucks, motorcycles, buses, boats, helicopters, ferries, drones, lawnmowers, tractors, and golf carts. After all, airplanes have had an autopilot mode for many years, and the same is true for self-driving trucks in mining areas.[2] We are also just starting to see self-driving baggage trucks at airports.[3]

A driverless car can, at least theoretically, do several things better than people. It can attend to multiple objects in the environment (pedestrians, stop signs, birds, and road hazards) simultaneously. It will never get tired, drunk, or distracted. It can react much faster than humans to avoid accidents.[4]

If all cars were driverless, highways might have much less congestion. Instead of stop-and-go traffic, cars could go sixty, eighty, or more miles per hour with minimal distances between the vehicles.[5] The elderly would not have to give up their independent mobility when they can no longer drive. Self-driving cars could transform the lives of blind and disabled people. Shuttle services could run 24/7 without paying (or charging) overtime. Analysts estimate that using self-driving taxis will cost half the amount of owning a car.[6]

So, you might be wondering, what is the holdup? Why aren't we all piling into our self-driving minivans on the way to visit Grandma for the holidays? There is little question that, once perfected, driverless cars could reduce a considerable amount of stress and increase productivity tremendously. But we are not there yet.

THE ROAD SO FAR

Self-driving car research has a long history. Scientists created the first driverless vehicle in the mid-1920s. It was a radio-controlled car developed by the Houdina Radio Control Company. An operator in a trailing car used a remote control to maneuver the car on the streets of New York City.[7] Other researchers patented an automated parallel parking system in 1933.[8]

The first car to visually recognize lane markings was developed in Japan in 1977 at the Tsukuba Mechanical Engineering Laboratory. It had two cameras that it used to capture images of the road, and it achieved speeds of up to nineteen miles per hour.

During the latter half of the 1980s, two independent projects, one in the US and one in Europe, produced compelling demonstrations of self-driving capabilities. The two projects used very different methods, but both achieved remarkable results.

The US program took place at Carnegie Mellon University (CMU), was named NavLab (for Navigation Laboratory), and produced a series of vehicles. The second NavLab vehicle (NavLab 2) was powered by a software program called ALVINN (for *autonomous land vehicle in a neural network*) that was funded by DARPA from 1986 to 1993.[9] NavLab 2 was a Humvee that drove itself around CMU. Initially, it had a top speed of three and a half miles per hour, but it was able to drive seventy miles per hour by 1993. For all the NavLab test drives, a driver was behind the wheel, put the car in gear, performed the acceleration and braking, but took over the steering only when necessary. You can find a video on YouTube from a 1989 newscast showing the vehicle driving on a city street with the driver's hands off the wheel.[10] In 1995, a CMU research scientist and a graduate student drove NavLab 5 from Washington, DC, to San Diego with the driver's hands off the wheel for 98.2 percent of the miles driven. The driver only had to steer for about 55 miles of the 3,100-mile-long trip.

ALVINN was a neural network–based supervised learning algorithm that took as input the images from four cameras attached to the vehicle, and it took as output the steering movements made by a human driver. In less than ten minutes of driving on a given road, it could learn enough to steer on that road. However, researchers had to retrain it for each road. One of the remarkable innovations produced by the CMU team was a system that used maps to analyze the safe speed for upcoming curves and warned the driver if the car was going too fast for the curve.[11] This 1990s innovation is a feature I would like to see on my Tesla, which never seems to slow down for curves.

The European effort, named the PROMETHEUS (Program for European Traffic with Highest Efficiency and Unprecedented Safety) Project, took place from 1987 to 1995 and received 749 million euros of funding from the European Commission.[12] In 1994, a team led by Ernst Dickmanns, a professor at Bundeswehr University Munich, demonstrated a Mercedes-Benz van outfitted with self-driving capabilities driving through the crowded streets of Paris that reached speeds of up to sixty miles per hour. A year later, the van drove 1,200 miles at speeds of up to 80 miles per hour on an emptied Autobahn highway. In both cases, a driver was behind the wheel and took over when necessary.[13]

The PROMETHEUS system did not use a learning algorithm. Instead, the developers hand coded complex models of each road (e.g., the Autobahn) and of the way the vehicle needed to respond to curves and bumps and other aspects of driving.[14] The researchers paired these models with features extracted from the camera images using various filters. The PROMETHEUS team input these filters into a conventionally coded algorithm that produced near-instantaneous instructions on how to steer the car, manipulate the throttle, and when and how hard to depress the brakes.

In 2000, Congress mandated that one-third of all military vehicles needed to be autonomous by 2015, and as a result, in February 2003, DARPA was looking to jumpstart research into autonomous vehicles.[15] It created a 142-mile race in the Mojave Desert named the Grand Challenge and offered a $1 million prize to whichever team's vehicle finished the race first. It was an extremely challenging course with hard turns, elevation changes, and obstacles ranging from tumbleweeds to rocks. The idea was to build a vehicle that could use GPS and sensors to drive the course and avoid obstacles. It was an imposing challenge.

The race took place in March 2004. DARPA selected the 15 most promising teams out of 140 teams that applied. There was a wide variety of entrants. One team was composed of high school students. Other teams had designed vehicles in their home garages. There were also two CMU entries and a motorcycle entered by Andrew Levandowski, who was then a University of California at Berkeley engineering graduate student and would later go on to become one of the leading figures in autonomous vehicles. However, none of the vehicles made it to the eight-mile mark. CMU's vehicle *Sandstorm* went the farthest, 7.4 miles, before getting stuck on a berm, where its front wheels caught fire. Another vehicle got stuck in an embankment. Another could not get up a hill. Another vehicle flipped over, and others suffered mechanical issues. *Wired* magazine reported that it was like a scene out of a Mad Max movie.[16] The million-dollar prize went unclaimed.

Still, the vehicles showed enough promise for DARPA to announce a second race in October 2005 with a $2 million prize. This race was far more successful, with five vehicles completing the 132-mile course. The winning entry, a modified Volkswagen SUV, was created by a team led by Sebastien Thrun, then a Stanford University AI professor. Thrun named the vehicle *Stanley*, created its technology as a twenty-student class project, and then enlisted a handful of students after the course ended to work on the project from July 2004 until the October 2005 event. Early in the process, the team drove the challenge course in a human-driven SUV. Even manned, it took the team seven hours to drive the course, which made the ten-hour challenge limit appear daunting.[17]

Figure 8.1 Grand Challenge entry from CMU. Licensed from Getty Images ID 55940868.

The CMU vehicles took second and third place in 2005 but went on to win the third DARPA-sponsored race, the Urban Grand Challenge, in 2007, and claim the $2 million purse for that race. Levandowski, Thrun, and many of the developers on the CMU team moved on to join autonomous vehicle companies.

COMMERCIALIZATION

Autonomous vehicles pose a massive commercial opportunity that is attracting the world's top players in transportation and technology. Notably, technology companies, not automobile companies, have taken the lead in commercializing autonomous vehicles. Levandowski started a company that developed the camera technology that Google, at least initially, used for its Google Maps Street View. In 2007, Google recruited Thrun to head up its nascent self-driving car initiative.

In 2008, the Discovery Channel asked Levandowski's company to build a prototype of a self-driving pizza delivery truck that successfully navigated a journey over the Bay Bridge in San Francisco.[18] At least partly based on this successful pizza delivery, Google purchased the company in 2009. In 2016, Google spun off the self-driving vehicle project into a separate company, named Waymo, that is owned by Google's parent company Alphabet. Waymo is one of the leaders in the development of self-driving taxis and trucks.

Uber hired forty researchers away from CMU in 2015 by doubling their previous salaries and offering hiring bonuses.[19] In 2016, Levandowski left Google to start a self-driving truck company named Otto. Later that year, Uber purchased Otto for a little less than 1 percent of Uber's stock, which was worth a reported $680 million, and put Levandowski in charge of Uber's self-driving research.[20] Tesla has also made a great deal of noise in the self-driving car space via its "autopilot" mode, which, despite the name, currently requires the driver to keep their hands on the wheel and to be ready to take over at all times.

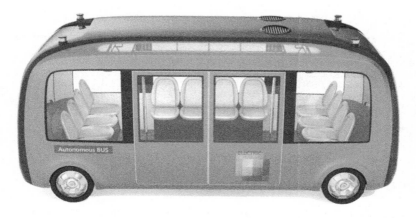

Figure 8.2 A driverless shuttle bus.
© Haiyin | Licensed from Dreamstime.com ID 150893098.

Although independent technology companies have led the charge, the major car vendors had also done some experimentation with self-driving technologies. For example, Mercedes-Benz funded the PROMETHEUS Project in 1987. However, the independent tech companies had the technology and made the first substantial investments.

The major automakers quickly followed the technology companies into the autonomous vehicle fray, and virtually every major automaker is making significant investments in the technology. Many are working together to offset the massive costs of development. GM and Honda are collaborating via GM's Cruise division. Ford and Volkswagen formed Argo AI. Bosch and Daimler teamed up. Nissan, Renault, and Microsoft are working together. Many other vendors around the world, operating independently of the major automakers, are working on autonomous vehicle technology.

HOW SELF-DRIVING VEHICLES WORK

Self-driving technology starts with sensors that provide the car with information that enables it to adapt to its environment. Some can also communicate with other vehicles on the road so that they can network—for example, to avoid collisions. Finally, all that sensor and communication input must be processed somehow and turned into driving decisions.

SENSORS

Autonomous vehicles use four types of sensors to "see" other vehicles, pedestrians, lane markers, and other elements of the driving environment: cameras, radar, lidar (light detection), and ultrasound. As an example, as of January 2020, Tesla vehicle equipment includes eight cameras, a forward-facing radar unit, and twelve ultrasonic sensors.[21]

Cameras have the best resolution among vision sensors. They are the best type of sensor to provide input to deep learning systems for lane detection and traffic sign recognition. Infrared cameras, which will start to become available on cars in 2021,[22] can work outside visible-spectrum light and can detect lane markers, pedestrians, bicycles, and animals at night. Cameras are also the only type of vision sensor that can detect color, which is important for distinguishing traffic lights and emergency vehicle lights. However, cameras struggle with wet roads, reflective surfaces, and low sun angles, because the light reflections obscure the images much like they do when taking a snapshot of someone with the sun directly behind them. One other important difference between cameras and the other sensors is that machine learning is required to interpret the pattern of pixels[23] captured by the camera. In contrast, the other sensors directly provide information about the distance between the vehicle and various objects.

Other types of sensors work by sending out signals and analyzing the echoes caused by objects in the signal's path. Radar works by sending out a radio signal and measuring the time for the return echo. It has the most extended range and has the added advantage of being the least expensive. It is also effective when visibility is low, like at night and in fog. Radar can assist with lane detection, detecting objects in the vehicle's blind spots, alerting the driver to cross traffic, sensing side impacts, avoiding collisions, and assisting with parking, emergency braking, and adaptive cruise control. However, radar only reflects off materials that conduct electricity, like steel.[24] Radar does not reflect off trees or other nonconductive entities. As a result, it cannot see pedestrians and many other objects. Also, while radar is good at determining the speed of moving objects, it does a poor job of detecting stationary objects. This radar limitation caused Tesla vehicles to crash into the backs of stopped fire trucks on three separate occasions in 2018.[25]

Lidar (for light detection and ranging) works like radar but uses light waves instead of radio waves. A lidar unit emits laser light and computes distance by measuring the time it takes for the light to return to the unit. Lidar has a much higher resolution than radar and can create a 3D view of what it "sees." However, it is expensive, and it cannot detect objects as far away as radar can.

Ultrasonic sensors emit sound waves that travel at known speeds, hit objects in the path, and bounce back to the sensor. The sensors use the round-trip time to calculate the distance to the object. Ultrasonic sensors are very short range (up to about twenty feet) and are mostly used today for parking and backup assistance.

The sensors discussed to this point all help the vehicle "see" road markings, pedestrians, stop signs, and other objects. AI decision-making needs this visual input, but it also needs other sensors that have been in cars for a long time that were introduced years ago by automakers to provide both safety and convenience features. For example, GPS is used to determine a car's current location. However, while GPS indicates where the vehicle is on a map, it is not granular enough to determine the vehicle's lane.

Autonomous vehicles use other sensors to detect several other variables, including temperature, shock, vibration, acceleration, and angular rotation. Inertial measurement units (IMUs) use a combination of accelerometers and gyroscopes to provide input to inertial navigation systems (INS). Vehicle computers use INS units for vehicle localization (i.e., aligning the vehicle location to the street map) in cities, where tall buildings can block the GPS signal. An autonomous vehicle can compensate for a short time by calculating its position based on an INS, using a navigation technique known as *dead reckoning*.[26] Dead reckoning determines a vehicle's current position from its previous position plus the output of an IMU or other sensors that measure acceleration and angular rotation.[27]

COMMUNICATIONS

Vehicle-to-vehicle communication (V2V) may become a vital component in collision avoidance systems. They relay data on position, speed, and status. V2V may play a role in more efficient highway merging, successful right-of-way determination, and safe responses to other everyday driving situations. Cars could theoretically communicate with one another to avoid collisions using V2V.

However, V2V can't be 100 percent reliable until all cars have it. Because communication is only possible when each vehicle has V2V, unequipped vehicles will be blind and invisible to the V2V system. Combine this with the unfortunate fact that there are two competing V2V standards, and the ubiquitous use of V2V is likely to be delayed until around 2050.[28]

An important special case of V2V is truck platooning, when two or more trucks drive together. The lead truck has a human driver. The other trucks drive autonomously. The lead truck uses V2V to communicate with the trucks behind it and instructs the trucks on the proper maneuvers. The trailing trucks will initially have human drivers who can rest. As technology progresses, the trailing trucks will be fully autonomous. The Netherlands is leading the way with a government and industry collaboration in truck platooning, with a goal of having convoys of one hundred trucks in the near future.[29]

Many states and municipalities also have invested in vehicle-to-infrastructure (V2I) communication. V2I enables cars to communicate with city infrastructure, such as smart traffic lights to determine when the lights should change based on how many cars are waiting. Governments could require that all construction activity is filed in V2I systems so that these systems can notify cars approaching the area. For example, cars nearing a construction zone could be instructed to all move to the left lane in an orderly fashion, reducing traffic jams (and probably some road rage). V2I could also be used to warn cars of adverse road conditions, accidents, and emergency response vehicles.

Another standard being developed is vehicle-to-everything (V2X) communication. V2X is a combination of V2V and V2I. V2X has the potential to overcome the problem of the limited ranges of V2V and V2I. Imagine a city or highway that links all the V2I devices. Then a car that communicates to a V2I device could also gather information from faraway V2I devices, thereby extending the range of V2V communications.

PROCESSING THAT INFORMATION

Autonomous vehicles have in-car computers that process the sensor outputs and make decisions. Computer algorithms must identify obstacles and determine, for example, whether the sensor outputs include a traffic signal and whether that signal is red, yellow, or green. The computer also must determine what other cars and pedestrians are doing and must make predictions about their intent and what they will do next. The computer needs to plan routes and motions. And the computer needs to control the vehicle's steering, braking, transmission, and acceleration. Autonomous vehicle computers contain a set of modules for controlling the vehicle.

PERCEPTION

In autonomous vehicles, perception systems identify pedestrians, cyclists, animals, and many different types of objects such as vehicles, lane markers, signs, and trees. The perception software is typically composed of many different machine learning systems, each of which learns to "see" a different category of animate or inanimate object. As of February 2020, Tesla vehicles had forty-eight different machine learning components, most of which use supervised learning networks.[30] Each component recognizes different object types. For example, there is one component just for stop sign recognition.[31]

To develop the network for their stop sign detector, the Tesla team initially used video sent back to headquarters from Teslas driven by consumers. The team found stop signs in the videos and created a supervised learning training table by hand-labeling the images from the videos. They created an initial CAPTCHA-like test (e.g., "Find all the images with stop signs") from these images and applied machine learning to create an initial stop sign detector that they deployed to all Tesla vehicles in over-the-air software updates. Each car's machine learning system then rated each stop sign detection on a confidence scale. Sometimes, the detector had a low confidence in detecting a specific stop sign, or it detected a stop sign that was not on its map. In those cases, the video was sent back to headquarters and reviewed and labeled by Tesla staff for machine learning refinement.

Under certain circumstances, the Tesla team also builds specialized detectors to source data for special cases. For example, the stop sign detector was having trouble with occluded stop signs. A separate occluded stop sign detector was created and sent to the fleet for the sole purpose of sourcing possible occluded stop sign images that could then be hand-labeled and fed into the regular stop sign algorithm. They also have a specialized detector for "Except right turn" signs posted below stop signs based on ten thousand images collected in this fashion.

The perception system also detects the motion of objects and can use this information to identify them. For example, a bicycle and a motorcycle might look alike, but a motorcycle travels at a faster speed. It is also used to predict the trajectory of objects. For example, Tesla has developed a methodology for determining when a car will cut into a lane from another lane without requiring human labeling of images.[32] The "cut-in" machine learning predictor works in *shadow mode* in all consumer-driven Teslas. In shadow mode, the car's computers make calculations that are sent back to Tesla HQ but do not affect the operation of the consumer vehicle.[33] For the "cut-in" predictor, the car computer predicts when a vehicle in one lane on a highway is about to switch lanes. Sometimes the vehicle will signal, and sometimes it will not signal. The machine learning algorithm constantly makes predictions about whether each vehicle in the field of vision will cut in. Human labeling is not necessary because the vehicle either will or will not cut in. Instead, each prediction is automatically labeled as correct or incorrect based on whether the vehicle actually cuts in or not. This creates additional data for the algorithm, which gets better and better.

LOCALIZATION AND MAPPING

An autonomous vehicle computer must also maintain an internal, two-dimensional map of the vehicle's location. The vehicle has a GPS sensor and at least a coarse map of the roads, like those found on Google Maps. The GPS sensor, however, is only accurate to one or two meters. If the computer were to try to drive the vehicle based just on this information, that range of error would frequently put the vehicle on the road median or worse. Additionally, the GPS might not be available at all under certain atmospheric conditions or when surrounded by buildings.

Instead, autonomous vehicle computers use sensor information from the GPS, cameras, lidar, and radar to create a three-dimensional, high-definition internal map that contains lane markings, crosswalks, pedestrians, vehicles, buildings, bicycle lanes, and other objects relative to the location of the vehicle. These high-definition maps are accurate to a few centimeters. They primarily use conventional software code to fuse together the information from all the sensors. Map elements that are fixed, such as roads and stoplights, can be precomputed. Everything else needs to be computed in real time. As the car moves, both the map and the vehicle's location on the map are continually updated.[34]

These maps are also used to aid the perception process. For example, if a stop sign is occluded by a bus but is present on the map, the autonomous vehicle system will still assume that the stop sign is there. It cannot do so with a 100 percent likelihood. However, it will only need a small glimpse of the stop sign to move that likelihood to 100 percent. Each time the stop sign is confirmed, that fact can then be sent back to a central database, stored, and used by other vehicles that link to that central database.

PREDICTION OF OBJECT TRAJECTORIES

The autonomous vehicle software computes the likely trajectory (i.e., the future position) for each person, animal, or object in the map. For example, the autonomous vehicle computer needs to know where each car and pedestrian will be in the near future (e.g., the car coming toward me will be in the intersection in two seconds). This can be done with conventionally coded rules using, for example, the speed and direction of the object. Some types of trajectory prediction are also done using machine learning algorithms.

PATH PLANNING

The autonomous vehicle computer needs to track the end destination and constantly make decisions about how to reach that destination. Should it move into the left-hand lane in preparation for a left-hand turn? Should it switch lanes to pass a slow-moving vehicle? Should it navigate around a double-parked car?

To make these constant decisions, the autonomous vehicle computer must consider its internal HD map and its predictions of the trajectories of the other vehicles, pedestrians, and animals in its map. It must also consider many other variables, including goals of minimizing the trip time, avoiding obstacles and accidents, obeying road rules, and not accelerating or stopping too suddenly if it can be avoided. If V2V or V2I information is available, it needs to consider this data also. If the tire pressure monitor indicates low pressure, this fact must also be brought into the equation. These path planning decisions are mostly made using rule-based conventional software. However, some decisions are made using machine learning components. For example, Tesla uses machine learning to create algorithms for left-hand turns and for navigating cloverleaf curves.[35] The learning occurs in silent mode. The Tesla software predicts the driver behavior and then compares its prediction with the actual behavior. When it makes incorrect predictions, the computer images and the actual driver behavior are sent back to Tesla headquarters to be incorporated as new training examples.

CONTROL

Finally, conventional software is needed to translate the path planning decisions into commands that control the throttle, brakes, and steering. Except for perception, most of the software in an autonomous vehicle is conventional software that contains hand-coded rules that take as input the output of the machine learning components. That said, most autonomous vehicle vendors have a goal of replacing more and more of the conventional codebase with machine learning components over time.

DIFFERENCES BETWEEN AUTONOMOUS VEHICLE VENDORS: WAYMO VERSUS TESLA

Tesla approaches self-driving car technology in a way that is dramatically different from every other manufacturer, but let's focus on just one of those competitors: Waymo, Google's autonomous vehicle project. Tesla differs from most other manufacturers in the same ways.

TESLA SHADOW MODE VERSUS WAYMO SIMULATORS

Tesla turns every car owner into a participant in a massive self-driving experiment. There were over 825,000 Tesla vehicles on the road with Tesla Autopilot 2 software at the end of 2019.[36] All these vehicles make shadow mode decisions, record the actions taken by the human driver, and send all that data back to the central Tesla data center, where the company's computers compare the proposed and actual actions.

In 2017, Tesla vehicles started including short videos in the data sent back to Tesla HQ to improve recognition of lane lines, stoplights, and other roadway features. The Tesla team uses this data to determine the safety of the proposed actions. When certain types of decisions are proven safe after millions of miles of actual driving, Tesla rolls them out as improvements to the Tesla autopilot systems. Similarly, when Tesla makes changes to the self-driving algorithms, they can be tested for safety and effectiveness using a simulator that can replay all the captured miles using the new algorithms. Then, they can be rolled out in shadow mode until Tesla verifies them as safe and effective, and finally, Tesla rolls them into production use.

In contrast to Tesla's 825,000 test cars, Waymo has approximately 600 test cars in its primary, 100-square-mile testing region near Phoenix, Arizona. These cars also collect data and send it back to the Waymo technology team; however, the volume of data is far smaller for Waymo than for Tesla. Tesla's director of AI, Andrej Karpathy, wondered out loud in a talk how the other autonomous vehicle manufacturers could build robust detectors when they are only testing their vehicles in small geographies with small numbers of vehicles.[37]

To increase its test capacity, the Waymo team uses a combination of its detailed maps and the test car driving data to create a driving simulator. Every mile driven by Waymo test vehicles is recorded and simulated.[38] Waymo uses the simulator for virtual testing of new features before rolling them out into test cars for real-world testing. The simulator enables Waymo to test enhancements to the self-driving software for safety and effectiveness and to make sure that the new improvements do not cause any previously working features to stop functioning.

Virtual cars in the simulator log billions of miles per year, and the simulators can use this information to make tweaks to the recorded data to simulate situations that test vehicles have yet to encounter.

For example, programmers can vary the number of vehicles, pedestrians, and cyclists.

MAPS

Waymo and most other manufacturers use extremely detailed maps in their cars.[39] Before Waymo sends self-driving test cars to a location, it maps the area by sending human-driven cars that create three-dimensional lidar maps. The mapping team at corporate headquarters then labels features such as driveways, fire hydrants, buildings, stop signs, traffic signals, crosswalks, lane boundaries, curb locations and heights, trees, construction zones, and other information.[40]

During self-driving tests, the software compares what it senses to what is on the map.[41] Waymo and many other vendors argue that this is crucial for two reasons: First, the software can use these maps to help identify objects. Systems that rely entirely on vision sensors might not see a stop sign or stoplight if, for example, a bus or dense fog occludes its view. However, if the map detail indicates that there should be a stop sign in twenty yards, the system can take steps to see it and accept lower-probability sensor-based cues to find the stop sign, light, or other objects.

Second, these maps also work where GPS signals are blocked (e.g., by tall buildings). Even when GPS signals are not blocked, the system can only localize a car's position to within two meters of the car's actual position. However, combining the GPS information with Waymo's detailed maps plus what the car senses enables the cars to know their position within ten centimeters.

Unfortunately, it is unreasonable to expect detailed maps to be available everywhere. They might be available in urban areas, but they are unlikely to be found in rural ones.[42] Additionally, roadwork projects periodically pop up and will not appear on the maps. Waymo's cars are programmed to determine when the map contents do not match what the vision systems see (e.g., a new construction zone is present). That information, including the vision sensor data, is sent back to Google, and the mapping staff updates the maps.

One reason most autonomous vehicle vendors are focusing on services like taxis and buses is that they can roll them out in small, well-mapped areas. In contrast, Tesla, which is trying to turn its Level 2 consumer vehicles into Level 3 and higher vehicles, cannot rely on high-definition maps, because it would need them for every road in the world.

NO LIDAR FOR TESLA

Nearly every manufacturer of autonomous vehicles is using or planning on using lidar in their vehicles. For example, Zoox, which is developing autonomous taxis for city use, equips each of its vehicles with eight lidar units (in addition to eighteen cameras and ten radar units).

Tesla, however, relies on cameras, radar, and ultrasonic sensors for vision. One possible reason for this is lidar's expense. Tesla's Model 3 was available in 2019 in the US for a base price of $39,000. In 2017, a top-of-the-line lidar unit was retailing for $75,000. That cost would likely triple the cost of a Tesla vehicle. The cost of lidar is coming down, but it is too late for vehicles already on the road or in production.

Interestingly, Tesla argues that lidar is unnecessary. Cameras are more like human eyes than lidar, because both the human eye and a camera capture only two-dimensional information. The human brain stitches together the images from the two eyes to produce a three-di-mensional image. Tesla is using self-supervised learning techniques to develop three-dimensional images from multiple two-dimensional camera images that it claims are almost as good as lidar images and are getting better all the time.[43] Manufacturers using lidar face the additional challenge of integrating what the lidar sees with what the cameras see.

ISSUES FOR AUTONOMOUS VEHICLES

There are several issues that represent a barrier to the ubiquitous roll-out of self-driving vehicles.

CARS DO NOT SEE LIKE PEOPLE

Computer vision systems are prone to incorrect classifications. Computer vision systems can be fooled in ways that people are usually not. For example, researchers showed that minor changes to a speed limit sign could cause a machine learning system to think the sign said 85 mph instead of 35 mph and could unsafely accelerate as a result.[44] Similarly, some Chinese hackers tricked Tesla's autopilot into changing lanes.[45] In both cases, these minor changes fooled cars but did not fool people, and a bad actor might devise similar ways of confusing cars or trucks into driving off the road or into obstacles. In real-world driving, many Tesla owners have reported that shadows, such as of tree branches, are often treated by their car as real objects.[46] In the case of the Uber test car that killed the pedestrian, the car's object recognition software first classified the pedestrian as an unknown object, then as a vehicle, and finally as a bicycle.[47] I don't know about you, but I would rather not be on the road as a pedestrian or a driver if vehicles cannot recognize pedestrians with 100 percent accuracy!

EDGE CASES

In 2009, Captain Sully Sullenberger had just piloted his plane into the air when a flock of Canadian geese took out the engines. The plane was only 2,900 feet above the ground, and Sullenberger and his copilots had only a few minutes to maneuver before the plane hit the ground. They had received no training on this specific scenario; they could only apply a few basic rules and common sense. To decide the best course of action, they factored in the likelihood of their passengers surviving various crash alternatives, the likelihood of injuring people on the ground, where rescue vehicles would be quickly available, and many other factors. Then they heroically landed in the Hudson River, all 155 passengers survived, and no one was hurt.

Pilots receive extensive training, but it is impossible to train them for every possible situation. For those edge cases—situations similar to but not exactly like their training—they must use their commonsense knowledge and reasoning capabilities.[48]

The same is true for automobile drivers. A Clearwater, Florida, high school student noticed a woman having a seizure while her car was moving. The student pulled her car in front of the woman's car and stopped it with no injuries and only minor bumper damage.[49]

Most of us have encountered unexpected phenomena while driving: A deer darts onto the highway. A flood makes the road difficult or impossible to navigate. A tree falls and blocks the road. The car approaches the scene of an accident or a construction zone. A boulder falls onto a mountain road. A section of new asphalt has no lines. You notice or suspect black ice. The car might fishtail when you try to get up an icy hill. We all have our stories.

We do not learn about all these possible edge cases in driving school. Instead, we use our commonsense reasoning skills to predict actions and outcomes. If we hear an ice cream truck in a neighborhood, we know to look out for children running toward the truck. When the temperature is below 32 degrees, there is precipitation on the road, and we are going down a hill, we know that we need to drive very slowly. We change our driving behavior when we see the car in front of us swerving, knowing that the driver might be intoxicated or texting. If a deer crosses the road, we are on the lookout for another deer, because our commonsense knowledge tells us they travel as families. We know to keep a safe distance and handle passing a vehicle with extra care when we see a truck with an "extra wide load" sign on the back. When we see a ball bounce into the street, we slow down because a child might run into the street to chase it. If we see a large piece of paper on the road, we know we can drive over it, but if we see a large shredded tire, we know to stop or go around it.

Because autonomous vehicles lack the commonsense reasoning capabilities to handle these unanticipated situations, their manufacturers have only two choices. They can try to collect data on human encounters with rare phenomena and use machine learning to build systems that can learn how to handle each of them individually. Or they can try to anticipate every possible scenario and create a conventional program that takes as input vision system identification of these phenomena and tells the car what to do in each situation. What will happen when autonomous vehicles encounter unanticipated situations for which there is no training or programming? A scary video filmed in 2020 illustrates what can happen. It shows a Tesla on a Korean highway approaching an overturned truck at high speed in autopilot mode. A man is standing on the highway in front of the truck waving cars into another lane. The Tesla never slows down, the man has to jump out of the way, and the Tesla crashes into the truck at full speed.[50]

It will be difficult, if not impossible, for manufacturers to anticipate every edge case. It may be possible for slow-moving shuttles on corporate campuses, but it is hard to imagine for self-driving consumer vehicles.

SAFETY VERSUS TRAFFIC JAMS

The autonomous vehicle industry will also need careful navigation of the trade-off between safety and traffic jams. In early 2020, Moscow hosted a driverless vehicle competition. Shortly after it began, a vehicle stalled out at a traffic light. Human drivers would reason about this edge case and decide to just go around the stalled car. However, none of the driverless cars did that, and a three-hour traffic jam ensued.[51] We do not want autonomous vehicles to crash, but we also do not want them to stop and block traffic every time they encounter an obstacle.

The Insurance Institute for Highway Safety analyzed five thousand car accidents and found that if autonomous vehicles do not drive more slowly and cautiously than people, they will only prevent one-third of all crashes.[52] If manufacturers program cars to drive more slowly, the result will be more cars on the road at any given point in time. This will increase the already too-high levels of congestion on many of our roads.

A REALISTIC TIMELINE

As tech journalist Doug Newcomb noted,[53] the move to driverless cars has a lot in common with the move to horseless carriages more than one hundred years ago. Back then we eliminated the horses; now we are eliminating the drivers. The problem with this analogy is that most drivers are smarter than their horses, but most cars are not smarter than their drivers.

	Sidewalk Delivery Robots	Shuttles	Buses	Street Delivery Services	Taxis	Consumer Vehicles	Trucks
Geography	Cities	Corporate Campuses Retirement Villages Parking Lots	Cities	Cities	Cities	Everywhere	Everywhere
Speed	Very Low	Very Low	Low	Medium	Medium	High	High
Collision Severity	Very Low	Very Low	Low	Medium	Medium	High	High
Risk To Passengers	None	Very Low	Low	None	Medium	High	None
Authority	City Government	Single Organization	City Government	City Government	City Government	City / State / Federal Governments	City / State / Federal Governments
Number of Streets	High	Very Low	Low	Medium	Medium	Huge	Huge
Weather Conditions	Limited	Limited	Limited	Limited	Limited	All	Limited
Operating Times	Limited	Limited	Limited	Limited	Limited	All	Limited
Vehicle Price	Low	High	High	High	High	Low	Very High
Example Vendors	Starship Technologies	Baidu Optimus Ride Venti Technologies Voyage	Baidu EasyMile Gacha May Mobility Navya TransDev	Amazon Cruise / GM Gatik Kiwi Campus Marble Neolix Nuro Pony.ai Postmates Refraction Skydio Udelv Unity Drive UPS Zipline	Amazon / Zoox AutoX / Alibaba Baidu / Apollo Cruise / GM / Honda Didi Chuxing Drive.ai / Apple Lyft / Aptiv Nissan nuTonomy / Aptiv Pony.ai / Toyota / Hyundai Uber Waymo / Volvo WeRide	Aurora Baidu BMW / Intel / Mobileye Cruise / GM / Honda Daimler Nissan Tesla Tencent Toyota+H24 Volkswagon Volvo	Daimler / Torc Einride Embark Ike Inceptio Kodiak Robotics Locomation Plus.ai Pronto.ai Volvo Tesla TuSimple Waymo

Low ←————————————————————————→ **High**

Relative Difficulty of Implementation

Figure 8.3 Examples of autonomous vehicle use cases and the relative difficulty of technology implementation.

As is illustrated in figure 8.3, the intended use of the autonomous vehicles has a significant impact on the relative difficulty of creating the technology. Perhaps the simplest use is the development of shuttles that drive fixed routes on private land, such as corporate campuses and retirement villages. Because the shuttles retrace the same route over and over, they only need to learn to navigate a small number of routes. Additionally, the operators of the vehicles have the option to shut them down in bad weather and to operate only during specific times, such as during the day. In comparison, autonomous consumer vehicles need to learn how to navigate any drivable road, anywhere in the world, under a wide range of weather conditions, and at all hours of the day. More importantly, autonomous consumer vehicles need to be operable at high speeds, whereas campus shuttles can motor along slowly at speeds as low as five miles per hour. As a result, even if a low-speed shuttle has an accident, the likelihood of severe injury to passengers, pedestrians, and other vehicles is far lower than that for a consumer vehicle. So, consumer vehicle manufacturers must meet a much more rigorous safety standard than low-speed shuttle developers.

Moreover, the number of potential edge cases increases from left to right in figure 8.3. Campus shuttles are likely to encounter relatively few edge cases. Consumer vehicles are likely to encounter so many edge cases that it may be impossible to identify all of them and create autonomous vehicle code to handle them.

Slow-moving shuttles and delivery vehicles will likely be the first to be rolled into production. Their slow speeds minimize the risk of injury and property damage. Because they can be shut down at night or in bad weather, these vehicles will encounter the fewest edge cases. Shuttles have the additional advantage of traveling a fixed route. Also, since they often operate on private land, they are less likely to cause traffic jams.

The Mayo Clinic in Jacksonville, Florida, is testing a driverless shuttle to transport potentially contagious medical samples from one part of its campus to another.[54] EasyMile, a French company, started a test rollout of driverless shuttles with a maximum speed of twelve miles per hour in sixteen US cities. Nuro is starting to operate tiny pizza and grocery delivery vehicles at speeds up to twenty-five miles per hour on the roads in Houston, Texas.[55]

We are also seeing tests of self-driving taxis in cities and suburban areas. From 2016 through 2019, Waymo tested driverless taxis in a well-mapped one-hundred-square-mile region in the Phoenix suburbs with a safety operator in the vehicle. However, starting in late 2019, Waymo began to offer taxi rides in a vehicle without a safety operator[56] within a fifty-square-mile subregion of the test area. Waymo offers a compelling video of a car driving on public roads without anyone in the driver's seat.[57] Zoox and other vendors are also testing autonomous taxis in various cities.[58]

That said, there are far more edge cases for city-based taxis than for campus shuttles. If manufacturers somehow manage to identify and program all the edge cases, they will need to develop a different system for each city. For example, the edge cases for San Francisco will be different from those for Bangalore, India, where it is not unusual to see cattle in the same lanes as cars.

On the consumer side, nearly all major auto manufacturers are heading toward Level 3 capabilities by virtue of their Level 2 driver assistance offerings. Tesla is the furthest along, because it is unobtrusively testing these capabilities on over 825,000 vehicles. However, no consumer vehicles are close to ready for a true Level 3 rollout. It is hard to imagine manufacturers capturing enough edge cases for these vehicles to make them safe enough for a driver to read a book during vehicle operation.[59]

The prospect of fully autonomous consumer vehicles is particularly scary. Consumers can drive them anywhere they want, at any time of day, and in any weather conditions. These vehicles will encounter all the edge cases that human drivers encounter. But they do not have human-like commonsense reasoning skills. How will they respond? Will they cause serious accidents and traffic jams?

Autonomous trucks fall somewhere in between autonomous taxis and consumer vehicles. On one hand, trucking companies could decide to only roll out autonomous trucks on certain stretches of highway. For example, it might be possible to use human drivers or teleoperators to get them on and off the highways. This would reduce the number of edge cases they would encounter. Not operating the trucks in bad weather would further reduce the edge cases. On the other hand, autonomous trucks that do all the driving will need to account for perhaps even more edge cases than consumer vehicles. Additionally, they pose far more risk because of their size.

We will likely see some limited rollouts of autonomous vehicles over the next ten years. Initially they will be slow-moving vehicles with fixed routes on private land. They will likely progress to moderate speed vehicles with fixed routes on public roads. If we do see significant city-based rollouts of autonomous taxis, they will likely be limited to very specific, well-mapped areas and will need different software for each city. However, due to the lack of commonsense reasoning in autonomous vehicles, coupled with the seeming impossibility of anticipating every possible situation a vehicle might encounter, we will probably not see autonomous vehicles dominating our highways and city streets for a long time.[60]

9

REINFORCEMENT LEARNING

In the early 1900s, Edward Thorndike put cats in boxes, from which they could escape only by stepping on a switch. After some wandering, the cats would eventually learn to step on the switch and free themselves. He termed the exit opening a *reinforcement event*. Ivan Pavlov and then B. F. Skinner further refined the theory of behavior modification using reinforcement events. Subsequent researchers used these ideas to develop technology to control elevators, robots, computer games, self-driving cars, and many other applications.[1] *Reinforcement learning* is a form of machine learning that uses trial and error with reinforcement, much like Thorndike used on his cats.

Let's start with the challenge of controlling elevators. Many of us have stood waiting in a lobby in front of a bank of elevators, wondering why those stupid machines cannot be more efficient. We understand how to manage a single elevator. It goes up to the highest floor, picks up waiting passengers, and makes its way down, often stopping several times on the way. With more than one elevator, however, the optimal algorithm is far more complex.

Consider a system with four elevators that services twenty floors.[2] If each of the four elevators goes to the highest floor on every trip, one will pick up all the passengers, and the others will not have anyone to pick up. If there are twenty floors, we could program each elevator to service five floors. But when the top floors are busy and the bottom floors are not or vice versa, the result will be unhappy customers.

With a total of eighty call buttons inside the elevators (twenty floors times four elevator cars), and thirty-eight up/down buttons in the hallways (the top and bottom floors have one button each, and the other eighteen hallways have two buttons), we have a total of 118 buttons. If we observe which of these 118 buttons were pressed by passengers and which ones were not pressed by passengers, we will find well over a trillion-trillion possible combinations for any point in time.[3] Each of these combinations is a *state*, and the set of all possible combinations is the *state space*. The reason this is important is that we must create a program that responds optimally to each one of these trillion-trillion possible states.

In response to a state, a system can give each elevator only one of three actions: Stop at the current floor, go up, or go down. Therefore, while the state space is enormous, the number of possible *actions* (i.e., the *action space*) is small. The problem to solve is this: Given any state,[4] which action should each of the four elevators take?

First, we must define our business objective. We may want to do any of the following:

- Minimize the average wait time.
- Minimize the maximum wait time.

- Minimize the average total transport time.

- Minimize the number of times anyone must wait more than one minute.

- Minimize the number of people waiting.

- Minimize the number of people whose wait time is higher than the average wait time.

- Minimize the cost of operations (i.e., power consumption).

Our goal is to pick one of these business objectives and define a *policy* (i.e., a function) to achieve it.[5] The policy will take as input any of our trillion-trillion states and as output what each of the four elevators should do (go up, go down, stop at a floor). And we do not just want to define *any* policy; we want to find the *optimal* policy.[6]

From the chosen business objective, we can derive a formula—termed a *reward function*—that we can use to measure the performance of any policy. For example, we could take a guess at an initial policy that assesses the state and sends out instructions to the elevators every five seconds. We could try this policy for a week and use the reward function to evaluate performance. If we chose to minimize the average wait time, our reward function would tell us the average wait time of customers that week.[7]

Testing the algorithm, however, is problematic. We could try it out in a hotel with actual customers, find out what does not work well, adjust the program, try it out again, and keep trying until the program works well. The problem with this approach is that not only will it take years, but also the customers will be so unhappy that by the time we figure it out, the hotel may have no guests.

A better approach is to construct a simulator and test algorithms there. The simulator is a computer program that, in this case, simulates people's arrival and the movement of the elevators. For example, we might program the simulator to allow a capacity of eight people per elevator, take five seconds to transit each floor, and have the elevators' doors stay open for fifteen seconds.

Simulators are critical for testing possible solutions to many real-world reinforcement learning problems. For example, we do not want bad algorithms to crash self-driving cars in the real world; we want the crashes to occur in a simulator. In robotics, simulators are important because robots are expensive pieces of machinery, and constant trial and error results in excessive wear and tear at best and accidents at worst.[8]

By running the elevator tests in our simulator, we can simulate a week's worth of traffic in a few seconds, and we can evaluate the random policy function on our business objective (e.g., minimizing the average wait time). Then we can change the values of all the weights in a way that produces a better policy (e.g., a policy that will have a lower average wait time). It turns out that, mathematically, we can compute values that will be better, but we cannot calculate which values will be optimal with just one simulation. We will need to do this over and over until the result (e.g., the average wait time) stops getting better, indicating that we have found and enabled the optimal average wait time.[9]

REINFORCEMENT VERSUS SUPERVISED LEARNING

In supervised learning systems, every prediction made on a training table observation can be analyzed right away by comparing the predicted value with the actual observed output value (i.e., the value in the output column). For reinforcement learning, it is not possible to draw an immediate conclusion about an action. When the system tells the elevator to go up and stop on the seventh floor, that action has consequences. For example, it delays the ability to pick up someone on the fifth floor. Also, the other elevators will not need to stop at the seventh floor. The point is that we cannot tell the effect of a single selected action on the average wait time (or whatever goal is selected). We can only observe the impact of the policy function on the average wait time over a period of time.

At the same time, reinforcement learning has many similarities to supervised learning. Supervised systems learn a function that can predict output values for previously unobserved input data. Similarly, reinforcement systems learn a policy function that can identify the optimal action for a given state, even if the system did not encounter that state during training. Like supervised learning, the function learning by the reinforcement learning algorithm is specific to the task.

GAMES

Learning a computer game like *Pong* is a classic reinforcement learning problem. The states are the pixels in the game image at any point in time. The actions are to move the paddle up or down. The reward function is simply the number of points scored. One advantage of computer games is that we do not need to create a simulator; the game itself is a simulator.

Reinforcement learning for game playing came into its own in 2013, when a little company in London named DeepMind used neural network technology to learn functions to play seven video games[10] on an Atari 2600.[11] It learned to play three of those games[12] better than a human. Shortly after that, Google bought the company.

The DeepMind team also built a system to play Go that beat the European champion five straight games.[13] Go is considered even more complicated than chess because the number of possible moves is 10^{360};

in chess, it's 10^{123}. The same team[14] then created a generic game-play-ing algorithm based on the AlphaGo system that learned chess, shogi (Japanese chess), and Go. This system achieved superhuman perfor-mance on all three games within twenty-four hours. In each case, the reward function was simple (a game is either won or lost). Also, in each case, the system started playing games against itself and used the game outcomes to determine the value of the reward function. After each game, it gradually updated its network weights to play slightly better than the previous time.

Like supervised learning systems, reinforcement learning systems can only learn patterns found in the training data. For example, a team of University of California at Berkeley researchers trained a system using reinforcement learning to play a game in which a soccer player kicks a ball past a goalie. However, when the movements of the goalie were reprogrammed to do things that the system did not see during training, such as sitting down, the opposing soccer players completely lost the ability to kick the ball.[15]

ROBOTICS

Robots come in a variety of forms. A robot might look something like a human, with arms and legs, but it might also be an arm bolted to the floor or a wall, or a vacuum cleaner on a set of wheels. As is depicted in figure 9.1, a robot may have cameras and image recognition software that enable it to see. It may have audio sensors, speech recognition software, and natural language processing software that allow it to hear. No one knows yet how to build computers with commonsense reasoning capabilities; however, many consider it a logical possibility, so I have included it in the figure. Some companies specialize in creat-ing robots that look as much like humans as possible.[16]

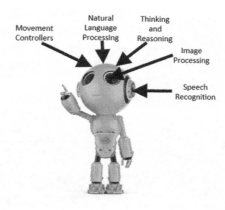

Figure 9.1 Robot components. PhonlamaiPhoto — Licensed from iStockphoto ID 1050049486.

Robots also have varying numbers of components that can move in different directions and are guided by an algorithm known as a *controller*, a miniature brain that governs the robot's movements. Robots also have other sensors that provide input to the controller. For example, a sensor might tell the controller how much pressure a robotic hand is applying to an object.

Companies across many industries employ robots in all sorts of functions, mostly for tasks with repetitive motions, such as welding, gluing, and painting in the automotive industry. Amazon has robots that move boxes from one part of a warehouse to another.

Programming robot controllers for a task is time-consuming, and the resulting controller will only work for a well-defined set of environmental conditions. A robot arm that places welds on a car requires the car to be in the same position for every weld. They perform the same specific task over and over in the same way, so they are far easier to program than the robots that must navigate the real world.

Figure 9.2 An assembly line composed of robot arms.
© imaginima — Licensed from iStockphoto ID 1057277428.

Robots navigate based on sensors that provide input about the environment and a controller that can interpret those sensors and direct the robot components accordingly. Tasks that sound easy to us, such as walking and picking specified objects out of bins, are challenging to teach to robots. There is a hilarious video of robots falling while trying to walk at a 2015 DARPA-sponsored contest named the Robotics Challenge.[17] Researchers have made progress since then,[18] but even the latest models have difficulties navigating the real world.[19] A task like picking specified objects out of a bin is challenging to achieve with conventional controller programming, because the robot must sense the environment and adapt accordingly. It must find the right spot on an object to pick it up, and it must exert enough pressure so the object does not fall but not so much pressure that the object breaks. Controllers trained using reinforcement learning to pick items out of bins can be more flexible than conventionally coded controllers, and researchers are working to develop them.

Reinforcement learning technology offers the promise of robot controllers that can learn rather than having to be programmed and offers the promise of robots that can generalize, which means that they will be able to function within a wider range of environmental conditions. Researchers have applied both reinforcement learning and supervised learning to robotics. However, movement controllers appear to be better suited to reinforcement learning. Consider programming a robotic arm to find and pick up a ball. The reward gets triggered when the ball gets picked up. None of the individual small movements that lead to picking up the ball have rewards, and therefore it is hard to label each incremental movement as correct or incorrect.

Reinforcement learning for robotics is significantly different from reinforcement learning for game playing. First, defining a reward function for robotics tasks can be challenging. In an Atari game, the reward function is simple. A reward is a scored point. But what should the reward function be for turning on a light switch or preparing a meal? In the laboratory, human researchers can indicate when the light switch has been successfully turned on and can decide when a meal is ready and if it tastes good. That will not work when a researcher is not present to provide feedback. Second, it is often difficult to obtain many trials in a robotics setting because robots and other industrial automation equipment are expensive to run and maintain. A simulator can be used, but it is difficult if not impossible to make simulators that are identical to the real-world environment in all respects.

IMITATION LEARNING

It turns out that both issues are often best managed by learning from an expert who demonstrates how to do a task instead of defining a reward function and acquiring many trials. When we teach a young adult to drive a car, we do not give them a reward function. Instead, we demonstrate how to drive.[20] The trainee observes the driver, who is assumed to be following an optimal driving policy and maximizing rewards.[21] Learning by copying the behavior of a person is known as *imitation learning*. Researchers have successfully used imitation learning in a wide variety of research settings, ranging from robot arm tasks to simulating helicopter maneuvers.

One crucial aspect of imitation learning for robots is that the teacher is often someone who knows how to do a task but is not knowledgeable about machine learning. Researchers use imitation learning to teach robots to do tasks such as picking up an object and placing it somewhere else. One difficulty is that the demonstrator often has different degrees of freedom from the robot. For example, people have wrists and elbows that bend, but most robots do not have bendable wrists and elbows. This mismatch is known as the *correspondence problem*; the demonstrator might do the task in a way that the robot cannot imitate.[22]

One method to avoid the correspondence problem is to have a human physically guide the robot to perform a task and have the robot record both its sensor inputs and the positions of its parts. For example, there is a video[23] that shows a Google DeepMind researcher guiding a robot arm to move to a door handle, then grab it, then turn it, and then pull it open. This type of training is *kinesthetic feedback*. Other researchers have used kinesthetic feedback to teach a robot to pour a glass of water,[24] play Ping-Pong,[25] and pick up and place objects.[26]

Another approach is remote operation. For example, researchers used remote operation to train a robot arm to pick up a towel, wipe an object, and then put the towel back in its original location. A University of California at Berkeley video[27] shows how researchers can train a robot using a virtual reality headset.

In each type of learning, the robot uses its sensors to gather data about the environment and its position and movement. In contrast, if a human merely demonstrates, all the data must somehow be translated from the robot's sensors (e.g., camera images) into robotic movements. There are several reinforcement learning methods of taking the robot sensor data plus the data on robot body part movements and learning a policy that results in the robot being able to do the task.

STILL NARROW

In supervised learning, feedback is available for each observation in the training table in the form of an output value. In reinforcement learning, feedback occurs in the form of intermittent rewards, and the system must determine how multiple observations contribute to a reward. By doing so, reinforcement learning has found success in game playing and robotics. With imitation learning, a system can even perform a task based on following a demonstration. However, like supervised learning, reinforcement learning systems learn a function that is specific to one narrowly defined task.

10

PRIVACY

I n 1949, George Orwell wrote the dystopian novel *Nineteen Eighty-Four*, which described a future society in which the government continuously monitored everyone's actions and conversations.[1] Narrow AI technology has now made that level of monitoring possible, and society needs to cope with the consequences.

BIG BROTHER IS WATCHING YOU

Facial recognition is perhaps the AI technology with the most potential for abuse. The Chinese government is in the process of rolling out its Xueliang[2] Project, which is connecting security cameras on roads, buildings, and malls to track its 1.4 billion inhabitants.[3] The goal is to stop criminal behavior and monitor dissidents.

Figure 10.1 AI-based surveillance. © Pixinoo | Licensed from Dream-
stime.com ID 117735807.

On the somewhat amusing side, there are reports that Chinese authorities have used the technology to catch and shame jaywalkers[4] and toilet paper thieves.[5] On the scary side, there is evidence that the Chinese government is using the technology to monitor and increase the persecution of minorities (e.g., Tibetans, Uighurs) and religious groups (e.g., Falun Gong practitioners[6]). *Time* magazine reports that the authorities harass people if the cameras catch them growing a beard, leaving by their back door, or wearing a veil.[7]

While few people in the US would be comfortable with a surveillance apparatus as broad as China's, surveillance in the US is widespread and expanding, with both proponents and detractors. By 2021, the top twenty US airports will be using facial recognition to screen all incoming international passengers.[8] Here again, the detection of terrorists would be a benefit if it works. However, if it misidentifies law-abiding travelers as terrorists, it could result in inconvenience or worse—wrongful arrest—to innocent passengers. According to data from the Department of Homeland Security (DHS), facial recognition systems erroneously reject as many as one in twenty-five travelers using valid credentials. At this rate, an error-prone DHS face-scanning system could cause 1,632 passengers per day to be wrongfully delayed or denied boarding at New York's John F. Kennedy (JFK) International Airport alone.[9] Imagine having your vacation ruined because a facial recognition system incorrectly matches your face to a terrorist as you are checking in at the airport.

Police departments in Maryland have used facial recognition software to identify people participating in protests who had outstanding warrants.[10] Maryland police also used the technology to catch robbery and shooting suspects they had captured on camera during the commission of their crimes.[11] The FBI has started using facial recognition technology to search driver license photos stored in the Department of Motor Vehicles databases in several states. In 2019, the US Government Accountability Office estimated that law enforcement networks include the faces of over 640 million adults,[12] which adds up to nearly two images for every adult in the US that year.

These uses of facial recognition technology have drawn the ire of civil rights advocates[13] and several members of the US Congress. They have complained about the fact that individuals did not give permission to use their license photos in this manner. In a rare show of bipartisanship, both Democratic and Republican members of the US House Oversight and Reform Committee condemned the way law enforcement has been using this technology.[14] Still, as of this writing, no law has been passed to prevent it.

Mass shootings, especially in schools, have been on the rise in the US. At the Parkland, Florida, high school that was the site of a massacre in 2018 that killed fourteen students and three teachers, officials have installed 145 cameras with AI monitoring software.

Even at Parkland, some students and parents have questioned the invasion of privacy, as well as the software's potential for mistaken identity.[15]

Another problem with the use of facial recognition software is that most facial recognition databases are composed primarily of white males. As a result, facial recognition training produces systems that do well on white males but that do not perform as well on women and people of color. NIST published a 2019 report evaluating 189 face-recognition systems from ninety-nine different developers and found that many systems were ten to one hundred times more likely to falsely match a Black or Asian face to a criminal than a white one.[16] The use of these systems would likely result in authorities falsely identifying women and people of color as matches to the faces of suspects far more often than white men. For example, if the systems used for terrorist recognition contain discriminatory biases, minorities may be more likely to be falsely detained or arrested.

Facial recognition systems also can be fooled by noise in images. People can look at two images and determine whether they are of the same person, even if the images have minor distortions, such as graininess or extraneous pen marks. But facial recognition systems are easily fooled by these same distortions. Suppose you were to show images of two different people to a facial recognition system and the images had similar distortions. The facial recognition system would likely incorrectly decide that they represented the same person just because the images have the same distortions.[17]

Amazon sells commercial facial recognition software named Rekognition.[18] In 2018, a group of forty organizations led by the American Civil Liberties Union (ACLU) sent a letter to Amazon CEO Jeff Bezos demanding that Amazon stop the sale of its facial recognition technology to government organizations. The primary concern is that people should be free to walk down the street without Orwell-style government surveillance. A nonprofit organization, Ban Facial Recognition, offers an online interactive map[19] of where facial recognition technology is being used in the US by police departments and airports. It also shows where municipalities have enacted laws against the use of facial recognition. In addition to the possibility of incorrect identification, the Ban Facial Recognition website[20] argues that the use of this technology violates the US Constitution's Fourth Amendment right against search without a warrant and that it super-charges discrimination.

To drive this point home with lawmakers, in 2019 the ACLU submitted images of members of the US Congress to Amazon's Rekognition software. They found that the software falsely identified the faces of twenty-eight members as matches to the faces of criminal suspects. Worse, 40 percent of the members incorrectly identified were people of color, even though 80 percent of congressional members are white.[21] The ACLU issued a position paper on surveillance technology in which it expressed concern that the technology has the potential to "worsen existing disparities in treatment suffered by people of color and the poor by embedding, amplifying, and hiding biases."

As of this writing, bills are pending in both the US Congress and in many state and local government legislatures to ban the use of facial recognition technology in law enforcement. The state of California already enacted a three-year ban on the use of facial recognition in police body cameras starting in 2019.[22] There is a bill pending in the US Congress to ban the use of facial recognition in public housing.[23] And the European Union is considering a five-year ban on the use of facial recognition software.[24] In 2020, Amazon, Microsoft, and IBM all decided to at least temporarily suspend sales of facial recognition software to law enforcement agencies.

The bottom line here is that mistakes by facial recognition systems can be inconvenient or worse.[25] No one wants to be put in jail or detained at an airport because a facial recognition system incorrectly matched their image to that of a terrorist or criminal. As a society, we must weigh the benefits of catching terrorists and criminals against the individual consequences of facial recognition errors. When data issues cause this to happen more frequently to minorities, the issue is worse. It becomes discrimination, which can only be fixed either by banning the use of facial recognition systems in law enforcement or by ensuring that training tables are free from bias.

Surveillance systems using facial recognition can also become an invasion of privacy. Across the board, we need to find the right balance between catching terrorists and criminals and respecting the privacy of citizens.

DATA PRIVACY

Internet-connected systems collect massive amounts of data from surveillance cameras, phone conversations, social media, email, e-commerce, retail sales records, and many other sources. Every click on a webpage, every Google search, every Facebook like, and every tweet is captured, tracked, and associated with an individual. There are huge privacy issues around the handling of all this data.

When we visit a new site, we often agree to a pop-up privacy policy that contains ten pages of legalese. To expect any of us, attorneys included, to read and understand every privacy policy we encounter is unrealistic. Carnegie Mellon University researchers estimated back in 2008 that it would take each of us seventy-six days out of a year to do so.[26] Instead, most of us do not read the policy. We just click the Accept button. As a result, major corporations have access to a great deal of our private data. For example, Google has gained access to tens of millions of patient health records in the US. It is contractually allowed to access many of these records without the permission of the doctor or patient.[27]

Mathematician Hannah Fry, in her book *Hello World: Being Human in the Age of Algorithms*, [28] describes a "creepy" scheme in which people download a Chrome extension named The Web of Trust. The privacy policy clearly states that the extension will anonymously record your entire browsing history. Even though it is anonymous, the recorded URLs contain clues to the person's identity. For example, when someone visits their own LinkedIn or Twitter page, the URL often includes the person's name.

Corporations and governmental organizations acquire this data and use it in ways we might not like. A Target analysis of its massive customer database reportedly found out a teenager was pregnant before her parents did.[29] This occurred when a Target analyst discovered that women on the baby registry often bought large quantities of certain personal products and decided to use the items in a pregnancy-prediction algorithm to drive a marketing campaign directed at pregnant women—including this teen. The teenager's father was, at first, outraged at Target for sending his daughter such materials, but he later calmed down when he found out his daughter was actually pregnant.

Airlines and other travel-related businesses use data to predict the socioeconomic status of the person accessing the site and offer higher prices for people the algorithms predict are wealthier.[30] Credit card companies use similar data to raise or lower customer credit limits. One piece of litigation claimed a credit card company lowered credit limits based on visits to massage parlors, marriage counselors, and pawn shops.[31] Imagine what insurance companies, retailers, and law enforcement could do with the data collected by self-driving cars, which will know everywhere you drive. Even worse, they have cameras that record what you do inside the vehicle.

The Cambridge Analytica (CA) scandal was made possible by weak protections on Facebook data. CA paid Facebook users five dollars to take a personality survey. The first step in the survey was for users to grant access to their Facebook profile. Via that access, CA was able to cull information not only about the user, but also, due to weak privacy controls, about all the user's friends. CA used this information to create psychological profiles on perhaps as many as 87 million people using machine learning techniques.[32] They then targeted these users with social media ads that many believe influenced the 2016 US elections. The critical point here is that privacy regulations could have and should have prevented this breach of privacy and the subsequent influencing of elections.

In response to public outcry and government regulations such as the European Union's General Data Privacy Regulations (GDPR), corporations now offer consumers some privacy settings for this data. However, vendors often obscure privacy settings options with misleading wording, hidden privacy-friendly choices, anti-privacy defaults, and making privacy-friendly options too much effort for users to locate and use.[33] Consumers also have difficulty choosing informed consent settings because corporations often do not—and often cannot (because of uninterpretable algorithms)—explain how they will use this data.

One solution is to build these technologies in a way that keeps identities (e.g., of people and vehicles) anonymous. However, this has not worked well for other internet-connected data. Vendors have learned how to correlate anonymous data with personally identifiable data. Data vendor Acxiom claims to have global data on 2.5 billion individuals.[34] Their data comes from tracking user browsing habits, government databases such as voter registration records, and criminal records. Some use of data is modulated by governmental regulations, such as the US Fair Credit Reporting Act, and data privacy laws like the GDPR. However, much use is unregulated, and this has led psychologist Shoshana Zuboff, in her book *The Age of Surveillance Capital*,[35] to make a persuasive argument that capitalism is mutating in a way that gives corporations immense power that, left unchecked, will lead to vast inequality in society.

Although AI enhances the ability to collect and analyze data, privacy is a big data issue, not an AI issue per se. AI technology makes it easier to analyze big data. However, the problem results from the widespread availability of personal data and not from the algorithms used to analyze it. We can only solve privacy issues through government regulation and perhaps through consumers voting with their dollars. The European Union has taken the lead on privacy issues, and other governmental bodies should follow.

AT WHAT COST?

Facial recognition technology puts powerful surveillance tools into the hands of governments and law enforcement agencies. The use of this technology provides some protection against terrorists and criminals at the expense of our privacy. Lawmakers will need to find a balance, though. Data privacy is an important issue that is already the subject of numerous regulations. However, it is not really an AI issue. AI only makes it easier to analyze the data.

Facial recognition technology gives governments the ability to completely take away our privacy, and it is prone to discrimination. If we want to avoid becoming a surveillance state, where anyone can be arrested for being in the wrong place or for being the "wrong" color, we need laws that rein in how governments use AI-based surveillance tools. However, the tools themselves are not a threat.

11

NEURAL NETWORKS
AND DEEP LEARNING

E very day, cameras powered by facial recognition technology
surveil travelers moving through airports to identify terrorists, dissidents, and other political opponents instantly.
Autonomous vehicles and drones use similar technology to navigate
their surroundings. While these types of computer vision may seem
like an extraordinarily complex and mysterious superpower, at its core,
this type of narrow AI system is merely a sophisticated form of supervised learning. To help you understand how computer vision systems
work, let's start with a simple image classification task.

Figure 11.1 Closed-circuit monitoring of travelers. © Pixinoo – Licensed from Dreamstime.com ID 79209154.

Suppose we want to build a system that can distinguish apples from bananas.

Figure 11.2 Apple vs. banana classification task.

We could first run each picture through a color filter to extract the dominant color. Then we could create a training table like table 11.1 that contains a manually entered feature (the color) of each image:

COLOR	ANSWER
Red	Apple
Yellow	Banana

Table 11.1 Simple training table to distinguish apples from bananas.

Of course, we do not need an AI system to figure out the rule *If it is red, it is an apple. If it is yellow, it is a banana.* But that scheme would not work anyway when we encounter green apples and bananas. Instead of only color, table 11.2 has a column that indicates whether the fruit shape is roundish.

COLOR	ROUNDISH?	ANSWER
Red	Yes	Apple
Yellow	No	Banana
Green	Yes	Apple
Green	No	Banana

Table 11.2 Training table that includes both apples and bananas.

Analyzing this table, we find we do not need the color column at all, since we can just classify the fruits based on whether they are roundish or not.

Next, suppose we want our classifier to distinguish among apples, bananas, and pears.

Figure 11.3 Apples, bananas, pears classification.

COLOR	ROUNDISH?	ANSWER
Red	Yes	Apple
Yellow	No	Banana
Green	Yes	Apple
Green	No	Banana
Brown	Yes	Pear

Table 11.3 Training table that includes pears.

When we analyze table 11.3, we find we need a rule based on both color and shape.

The problem gets harder if we decide to classify only apples and change the task to naming the type of apple: Red Delicious, McIntosh, Braeburn, each of which has the same color and shape. In that case, we would need to find features that distinguish these types of apples other than color and shape. The problem becomes even harder if we want to build an image recognition system that can distinguish between tens, hundreds, or thousands of image categories, such as human facial features. We need to extract these features automatically so we do not have to hand code each feature for each training image to create a training table. Finally, we need to recognize each feature regardless of its orientation, scale, rotation, or the illumination level in the image.

These challenges were the focus of research on image recognition during the first decade of the twenty-first century. Instead of using simple characteristics like color and shape, researchers used features created by sophisticated mathematical algorithms.[1] They would then create a training table with one row per training image and one column for each feature. They also added an output column with the name of the image class. Last, they fed the training table as input into a supervised learning classification algorithm so it could learn a function that could perform the image classification task.

Since 2010, researchers have engaged in an annual image classification competition named the ImageNet Large Scale Visual Recognition Challenge (ILSVRC). They begin with an ILSVRC database that contains images in one thousand categories such as appliance, bird, and flower. The competition goal is to train a classification algorithm on 1.2 million observations in the database to identify the primary image category and then test the resulting learned function on 150,000 test images and achieve the lowest error rate.[2]

In the first two competitions, the winners used different types of mathematical feature extraction, fed the training table with features plus the column with the image category name into a supervised learning algorithm, and achieved around a 25 percent top-five error rate in both 2010 and 2011. As an example of the type of error that might be possible, if a system is shown a test image of a motor scooter, it might produce these five classes: motor scooter, go-kart, moped, bumper car, and golf cart. In this case, the system's first choice was the correct choice. However, if motor scooter had been any of the five choices, it would have been correct. The error rate when only allowed one prediction for each image was 47 percent in 2010.

The 2012 competition woke up the world to the power of neural networks, even though they had been around for thirty years. A team of University of Toronto researchers[3] created the AlexNet system, which won the 2012 challenge by achieving a 15 percent top-five error rate. The next best system reached only 26 percent.[4]

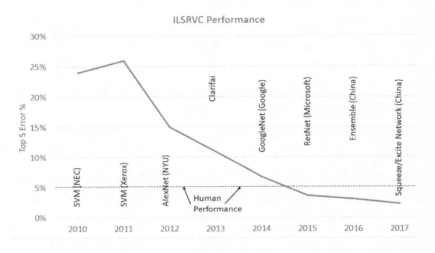

Figure 11.4 Increasing ILSVRC performance for image classification systems.

The top-five error rate for the winning system decreased to 11 percent in 2013. The winning system beat human performance for the first time in 2015 with an error rate under 5%. By 2017, the winning system error rate was down to 2.3 percent.

HOW NEURAL NETWORKS WORK

To understand how neural networks[5] work, let's start with a much simpler image classification problem. Suppose we want to build a system that can recognize handwritten numbers like in figure 11.5.

Figure 11.5 Examples of handwritten numbers from the MNIST database. Josef Teppan licensed under CC BY-SA 4.0.

These are images from an extensive database published by NIST in 1995 to support the development of handwriting recognition technology. Each image is 28 × 28 pixels. Each training image will be a row in our training table. Instead of trying to extract features from the images, the training table will contain the raw pixels, and it will be up to the neural network to figure out the features. There will be one column for each of the 28 × 28 = 784 pixels plus a column for the output number. Figure 11.6 depicts a neural network for this problem.

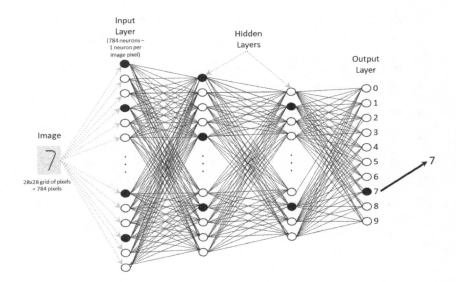

Figure 11.6 A neural network for classifying handwritten numbers.

In figure 11.6, there is an input layer that has one neuron for each of the 784 pixels in the image of the handwritten number. Each of the 784 input layer neurons will have a value of one if it is black in the image and zero otherwise. The output layer has ten neurons, one for each possible output value (zero through nine). In the middle, there are two *hidden layers* (only the input and output layer values are derived directly from the training table).

In addition to neurons, neural networks have weights that are variables like those in the temperature and housing functions. There is one weight for each connection between two neurons. In neural networks, the weights represent the strength of the connection between two neurons.

We can write a function for every neural network that operates the same way as the function we discussed for computing Fahrenheit temperatures from Celsius temperatures. The difference is in the number of variables (weights) in the function. In the temperature-conversion example, there was only one variable. OpenAI recently came out with a network that has 175 billion variables.[6]

We will skip the technical details of how neural networks learn the optimal values of their weights.[7] The result is a function that can take an image as input and predict a category as output. In this example, the predicted category is one of the ten numbers.

AlexNet and all the post-2012 winning ILSVRC systems used *convolutional neural networks* (ConvNets).[8] ConvNets have had tremendous success in image processing tasks, such as handwriting recognition, image classification, and facial recognition.[9] Yann LeCun and his colleagues at Bell Labs used a ConvNet to create the first commercial system that could read the handwritten letters and numbers written on checks. And ConvNets are the primary technology behind facial recognition.[10]

Deep learning refers to neural network architectures with more than one hidden layer. The network shown in figure 11.6 is a deep learning network because it has two hidden layers. The use of multiple hidden layers usually improves performance. For example, AlexNet had 8 hidden layers, the GoogleNet system that won the 2014 ILSVRC competition had 22 layers,[11] and the 2015 winner from Microsoft had 152 layers.[12] Deep learning can be used in supervised, unsupervised, and reinforcement learning.

MACHINE TRANSLATION

Until 1799, archaeologists frequently discovered Egyptian hieroglyphs, but no one knew how to interpret them. That year, a Napoleon-led expedition to Egypt discovered the Rosetta Stone, which had a decree by King Ptolemy V in Egyptian hieroglyphs and an ancient Greek translation of the decree. It took more than twenty years, but scholars finally figured out how to interpret the hieroglyphs.

Just as deciphering the Rosetta Stone required access to the same text in two different languages, machine translation systems require translated documents for each language pair. Automated techniques analyze the parallel texts and derive statistics and rules for machine translation. One of the most heavily used parallel texts was extracted from the proceedings of the European Parliament. It contains parallel texts in twenty-one European languages. Google Translate started with this set of texts and added many other parallel texts, including records of international tribunals, company reports, and articles and books in bilingual form that have been put up on the web by individuals, libraries, booksellers, authors, and academic departments.[13]

If you have a smartphone or web browser, there is a good chance that you have used Google Translate to translate webpages and other documents. Google Translate launched in 2006,[14] and until late 2016, the translations were barely good enough to provide the gist of the text on the webpage, and it was often hard to fully understand the translated text. The technique used by Google Translate before late 2016 was *phrase-based machine translation,* which relies on a massive phrasal dictionary. To build this dictionary, Google engineers wrote programs that scoured parallel texts for translations of each phrase that occurred in each of the texts. They created a massive electronic dictionary that could be used to look up a phrase and find a corresponding translation.[15]

Then, when asked to translate text, the system would look up each phrase in the electronic dictionary and replace it with the translated phrase.[16] This phrasal approach enabled the system to handle some differences in word order[17] between languages. More importantly, it helped to sort out word ambiguity. For example, the word *break* has multiple meanings when the word is looked up in a translation dictionary by itself, whereas the word in the phrases *give me a break* and *break a window* have single (and distinct) meanings. According to Google, in 2016, there were 500 million Google Translate users and 100 billion words translated per day by Google Translate.[18]

In the middle of the night, on November 15, 2016, Google switched out the underlying paradigm from phrase-based machine translation to a neural network–based paradigm.[19] That morning, Google Translate users who were accustomed to marginal translations woke up to a whole new experience; the change reduced translation errors by up to 85 percent on several major language pairs, bringing accuracy up to near-human quality.

Reporting on the new system, *The New York Times* wrote[20] that a Japanese professor, Jun Rekimoto, had translated a few sentences from Hemingway's "The Snows of Kilimanjaro" from English to Japanese and back to English with Google Translate. Using the old phrase-based system, the first line of the translation had read as follows:

```
"Kilimanjaro is 19,710 feet of the mountain
covered with snow, and it is said that the
highest mountain in Africa."
```

Like most internet text translated by Google Translate to this point, you could make a fairly accurate guess at the meaning, but the translation was nowhere near human quality. The day after the switch to the neural translation model, the first line read like this:

```
"Kilimanjaro is a mountain of 19,710 feet
covered with snow and is said to be the
highest mountain in Africa."
```

On that night in 2016, Google Translate started using a deep learning architecture called *neural machine translation* (NMT). Google Translate was trained separately for each language pair and in each direction. Researchers trained one system on English to French, another on French to English, another on French to Japanese, and so on. When you type a sentence in a source language into Google Translate and request a translation in a target language, Google Translate passes the source text to the appropriate system.[21]

The training input to NMT for each language and direction is a training table with one row per training sentence pair (i.e., the sentence in one language plus the translated sentence in another language). Each row has a column for each word in the source language followed by a column for each word in the target language. For example, the source language sentence *Where is the bus station?* combined with the correct translation "Où est l'arrêt de bus?" would constitute one row of the training table. The other rows would have different sentences. Google does not disclose the size of its training tables, but they likely have somewhere between tens of millions to billions of rows or more for each language pair.

The job of the NMT algorithm is to take as input a training table for a language pair and direction and learn to translate the source words into the target words. You can see the architecture of the NMT system in figure 11.7.

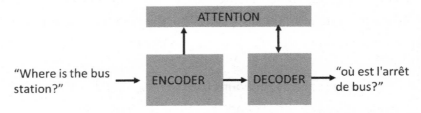

Figure 11.7 Encoder-decoder with attention architecture for machine translation.

The NMT system is composed of three different deep neural networks: the *encoder*, the *decoder*, and the *attention* system.[22] You can think of it like this: The encoder passes along the gist, the attention system helps put it together word by word, and the decoder computes the translation in the target language. Together, these three deep neural networks learn a function that can translate from one language to another.[23]

NMT is an ingenious architecture, but it is nonetheless narrow AI. An NMT program takes as input a training table with one row per sentence. Each row contains both the words in the source language (e.g., English) sentence and the words in the target language (e.g., French) translations. Each column holds one word. When the NMT algorithm reads this training table, it learns a function that translates the input columns to the output columns. Most importantly, the function can also translate sentences that were not in the training table.

SPEECH RECOGNITION

Much of the world uses speech recognition daily. When we talk to Siri on iPhones or Google Assistant on Android devices, our speech is converted to text almost as accurately as if we had typed the text ourselves. Microsoft and Baidu recently published papers on speech recognition systems that transcribe better than humans in controlled environments with unaccented, clear speech. But so far, no system is as good as a human for noisy environments, speakers with accents, people who do not articulate clearly, and lower-quality microphones.

The first attempt at speech recognition was in 1952 by a group of researchers at the Bell Labs facility in Murray Hill, New Jersey.[24] Computers had been invented but were not yet in widespread use. At the time, it was probably as easy to develop custom circuitry as it was to program a computer (never mind getting access to one of the few available). This group of researchers developed an ingenious custom circuit that ended with ten gas tubes. A single male speaker would utter a random string of digits, pausing at least one-third of a second between digits, and the correct gas tube would light up for each digit with 97 percent accuracy. The discrimination algorithm built into the circuit identified vowel patterns and mapped them to numbers.

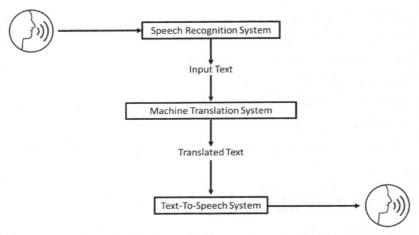

Figure 11.8 Speech translation. Speaker icon: ID 142615061
© Pavel Stasevich | Dreamstime.com.

Today's speech recognition systems also work this way. Systems take an audio signal as input and produce a string of characters as output. In 1952, this approach was only feasible by limiting the speaker vocabulary to ten digits. If it had tried to recognize all 170,000-plus English words in this fashion, it would not have worked because vowels alone do not provide enough information to discriminate among a large set of words; the algorithm would need to consider consonants as well.

Unfortunately, even basing a speech recognition algorithm on consonants, as well as vowels, is problematic. Although there are only twenty-six characters in the English language, individual characters do not always have the same sounds. For example, in the phrase *speech recognition*, there are three instances of the letter "e," and they represent different sounds. The first two act as a pair, indicating that they're pronounced as a vowel that resonates in the upper front part of the mouth, like in *feet*. The third "e" is a mid-central vowel, like in *bet*. Worse, these letters will sound different when pronounced by various speakers. Regional pronunciation patterns and the many dialects of English exacerbate this issue. I pronounce *tomato* and *potato* so that the second syllable rhymes with *pay*. As a child, I was surprised to learn that in other parts of the world (and in a famous song), people pronounce these words so that syllable rhymes with *paw*.

Creating algorithms based on words is also problematic. The Oxford Dictionary contains over 170,000 English words, and that does not include proper names. To create a training table based on words would require numerous spoken examples of each of those 170,000 words because of the varied pronunciations of different speakers. The audio waveform for a word will also change based on its context: The word spoken before and after it can affect its pronunciation (for example, *the* is pronounced differently in *the fact* and *the act*). Also, homophones (like *there*, *they're*, and *their*) are indistinguishable by sound alone. That supervised learning algorithm would need 170,000 output categories; the higher the number of output categories, the harder it is to train a supervised learning system.

Instead, most of today's speech recognition systems use subword units—for example, *phonemes*—that have fewer possibilities. Phonemes are the distinctive sounds made by speakers; for example, those three instances of the letter "e" in *speech recognition* are pronounced as two different phonemes. There are between thirteen and twenty-one vowel phonemes and between twenty-two and twenty-six consonant phonemes in the English language, depending on the dialect. Standard American English has forty-four phonemes. Depending on which expert you ask, we could be looking at several hundred or maybe thousands of phonemes across all human languages.

The first stage of speech recognition is to break the acoustic signal down into small windows or frames of about twenty to twenty-five milliseconds. Because the speech signal for each phoneme is typically relatively constant for about ten to twenty milliseconds, just randomly picking these windows makes it unlikely that each window will capture a phoneme. To make sure that some windows capture phonemes, researchers use overlapping windows. For example, they will start a new window every ten milliseconds.

The speech recognition task starts with a training table that has one row per spoken sentence in the training table. The columns are the windows (i.e., the audio signal in each window) and the words in the spoken sentence. The task is to learn a function that will translate the windows into words.

Before around 2010, speech recognition researchers had spent years developing methods to extract features from these windows that they could feed into supervised learning algorithms that would identify phonemes. They then used pronunciation dictionaries, which contain each word in the language and the sequence of phonemes used to pronounce the word. And they used language models[25] that specify the probability that any sequence of words was a legal construct in the target language.[26]

Speech recognition started to improve dramatically in 2009, when researchers at the University of Toronto started experimenting with deep learning networks for speech recognition.[27] In 2012, one of the authors of the 2009 paper helped Microsoft create a deep neural network that produced a 16 percent increase in performance compared with the technologies that researchers had been using for the previous five decades.[28] One of the more popular speech recognition architectures is illustrated in figure 11.9.

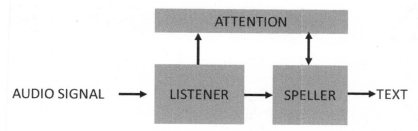

Figure 11.9 Listener–speller with attention architecture for speech recognition.

This architecture has similarities to the NMT system illustrated in figure 11.7. Like NMT, it has three deep neural networks: the listener, the speller, and the attention mechanism.[29] The listener functions like the encoder, and the speller functions like the decoder in the NMT architecture.

Due to deep learning techniques and after decades of laborious effort using conventionally coded features as input to supervised learning algorithms, speech recognition technology has finally reached its potential. Society is now reaping a wide range of benefits, from hands-free phone dialing while driving to voice interactions with digital personal assistants like Siri and Alexa.

DEEPFAKES

Deepfakes are often created with an unsupervised learning technique known as an *autoencoder*. An autoencoder (depicted in figure 11.10) is a type of neural network that learns an internal representation from a large set of images of a person or object. Then it can take as input a new image of that person or object and reproduce the image from the internal representation.

Figure 11.10 An autoencoder that learns to reproduce images.

Why do this? We do not need AI to be able to reproduce an image. We can do that with copiers. The goal of an autoencoder is to create a compact internal representation of the input image that has fewer dimensions than the input. More specifically, there will be many fewer neurons (variables) in the encoder output layer than in the encoder input layer. This output layer contains a compact internal representation of the input image. If the decoder can take this compact internal representation as input and still reproduce the images, then it has not merely memorized the values of the pixels in the input images. The compact internal representation must capture the essential features of the input image to reproduce the image. In other words, the learned weights and neurons of the encoder output layer must capture details about what makes up a face—the angle of the face, the facial expression, and other features.

In the example diagrammed in figure 11.10, the training table included many different images of this person, including photos of her smiling, speaking, in different poses, and in different lighting. The encoder learned to produce a compact internal representation that was sufficient for the decoder to reproduce what she looked like in the input image, her facial expression, her pose, and the lighting.

In figure 11.11, we have used an autoencoder to reconstruct images of two people.[30]

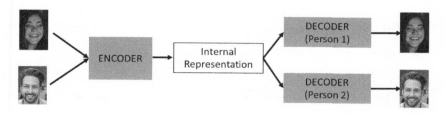

Figure 11.11 Training the deepfake network.

The encoder learns a compact internal representation that captures the key features of both individuals. However, it learns a different decoder for each person. The two decoders will then learn to take the common internal representation of these facial expressions and reconstitute them for each person's image.

Once the network completes its learning phase, producing a deepfake is easy: Just switch the decoder, as illustrated in figure 11.12. When a new image of the woman is input to the network, the output will be an image of the man but with the facial expression and pose that was in the woman's input image.

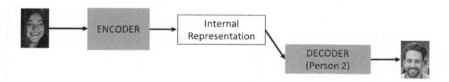

Figure 11.12 Using the trained system to produce deepfakes.

The next step is to make this substitution for each frame in an entire video. The result will be a video with frames of the man wearing the same facial expression as the woman at each point in the video. If the woman is talking in the video, the fake video of the man will appear to be saying the same words.[31]

You can see a video of Jennifer Lawrence answering questions at the Golden Globe Awards with Steve Buscemi's face.[32] The creators of this video used the FaceSwap tool.[33]

Our example deepfake video still had the woman's voice (and Steve Buscemi's face still sounded like Jennifer Lawrence) because only the video was a fake. However, researchers are developing technologies to change the words of a speaker as well. For example, the Lyrebird division of Descript, a Montreal company, offers a very impressive public-facing demo.[34] You can record your voice on the website and then type in the words you want to say and hear it played back in your voice. In conjunction with video deepfake technology, you will soon be able to create a video of someone saying whatever you want them to say.

DEEP LEARNING SYSTEMS CAN BE UNRELIABLE

Image recognition, machine translation, and speech recognition systems represent tremendous victories for deep learning. Unfortunately, these same deep learning systems make surprising mistakes.

If I train a system to distinguish cats from dogs, and in the training table, all the pictures of dogs are outside and all the images of cats are inside homes, the deep learning system will likely key in on yard and home features instead of those of the animals. Then if I show a picture of a dog inside a home, the system will probably label it a cat.

Figure 11.13 Adding a guitar causes the narrow AI system to misclassify the monkey as human. Reprinted with permission of International Press of Boston, Inc.

Similarly, in figure 11.13, before researchers pasted the guitar onto the picture, both object recognition systems and human subjects correctly labeled the monkey in the photo. Adding the guitar did not confuse people, but it made the object recognition system think it was observing a picture of a person instead of a monkey.[35] The object classification system did not learn the visual characteristics that people use to recognize monkeys and people. Instead, it learned that guitars are only present in pictures of people.

Other types of mistakes are even more concerning. A group of Japanese researchers found that by modifying just a single pixel in an image, they could alter an object recognition system's category choice. In one instance, by changing a single pixel on a picture of a deer, the object recognition system was fooled into identifying the image as a car.[36] Researchers have also figured out how to fool deep learning systems into recognizing objects such as cheetahs and peacocks in images with high confidence even though there are no objects at all in the image.[37]

Another scary example: Researchers have developed deep learning systems that very accurately diagnosis the presence or absence of pneumonia. However, they have also discovered that spurious noise in the medical images can cause these deep learning systems to produce an incorrect diagnosis.[38]

The same is true for audio streams. Researchers created mathematical perturbations of audio streams that have no impact on people's ability to identify words. Yet these perturbations caused deep learning systems that previously identified the words with high accuracy to fail to recognize any words at all.[39]

The reliability of deep learning systems is important because many important applications, including self-driving cars and autonomous weapons, depend on deep learning technology.

RAW DATA

Facial recognition, machine translation, speech recognition, and many other applications can be built using supervised deep learning. For each of these applications, deep learning technology has eliminated the need to manually extract features that are placed in the input columns. Instead, the input columns contain raw data. Pixels are used for facial recognition, words (and parts of words) are used for machine translation, and waveforms are used for speech recognition. The deep learning system determines what features are important and incorporates those features into a function that can transform the input values into the output values.

It is possible to build amazing applications using deep learning. However, each of these applications is a narrow AI application. The learned function can only be used to predict the outputs from the inputs for that specific application. Deep learning is also unreliable. For critical applications like self-driving vehicles that rely on functions created with deep learning, this could result in traffic jams and injuries.

12

NATURAL LANGUAGE PROCESSING

The abilities to converse on a wide range of topics; to gain knowledge by reading newspapers, magazines, and books; and to answer questions and have discussions based on knowledge of the world and commonsense reasoning are what make us distinctly human. They differentiate us from the animals that share our planet.

Since around 2010, researchers have built computer systems that appear to understand the languages that people speak. IBM's DeepQA system beat two of the world's top *Jeopardy!* champions, Ken Jennings and Brad Rutter. Microsoft announced a computer that it claims reads better than humans. Most of us interact with Siri, Alexa, or Google Assistant daily. These systems appear to understand natural language. But do they?

The first time I encountered a parrot, I was eight years old. It said hello and made a rude comment about my appearance. At first,

I thought the parrot understood the language it used. Eventually, I realized that it could only repeat phrases it had heard without any understanding of what it was saying.

The natural language processing systems from IBM and Microsoft, and also Siri, Alexa, and Google Assistant, are more like parrots than people. AGI-level natural language processing is not possible for today's computers and might never be possible. Marvin Minsky, who many consider the father of AI, once said, "Any ordinary person who can understand an ordinary conversation must have in his head most of the mental power that our greatest thinkers have."[1] Minsky had good reason for placing such a high value on a capability most of us take for granted.

NATURAL LANGUAGE IS COMPLEX

Children develop the ability to understand and converse in natural language through an accumulation of exposure to language and life experiences. They acquire both knowledge about the world and commonsense reasoning that they apply to that knowledge. As experience and exposure accrue over time, so does the ability to understand and use language.

Language understanding involves far more than retrieving the dictionary definition of words and applying grammatical rules. It requires the ability to decipher the unsaid implications of an utterance.[2] Even children make extensive use of implied meaning based on world knowledge in understanding language. For example, consider this statement:

The police officer held up his hand and stopped the truck.

The ability to accurately interpret this sentence requires a tacit understanding of specific facts, including the following:[3]

- Trucks have drivers.

- People obey police officers.

- Trucks have brakes that will cause them to stop.

- Drivers can step on the brake to stop the truck.

- An action can be attributed to an actor (a subject) who caused but didn't actually perform the action.

Even an eight-year-old would have the ability to pull these bits of world knowledge into their understanding of the sentence. In contrast, consider this similar statement:

Superman held up his hand and stopped the truck.

Our understanding of this sentence is vastly different.[4] Here, we draw on our knowledge of a science fiction character, and we understand that this character applied a supernatural physical force to stop the truck. Our understanding of these two sentences goes far beyond the meanings of the individual words or the grammatical rules (which are the same in both sentences).

Similarly, if we hear someone say, "I like apples," we know they are talking about eating them, even though the speaker never mentioned eating.[5] If you hear someone say, "John lit a cigarette while pumping gas," we apply our commonsense reasoning capabilities to our knowledge of the world and recognize that this is a bad idea. Moreover, we then expect the next sentence to tell us whether there was an explosion.

A great deal of knowledge about the world is required to understand natural language, and this knowledge informs the reasoning processes that enable us to understand natural language.

CHATBOTS

It was not too long ago that talking to computers was science fiction. Then suddenly, we began talking to smartphones and tabletop devices, such as Apple's Siri, Google Assistant, Microsoft Cortana, and Amazon Alexa. We engage with these personal assistants regularly throughout the day to check the weather, send text messages, control home thermostats, and perform many other functions. We also engage with customer service chatbots when we use chat capabilities on a vendor's website or call their support lines.

You can see the primary AI-based components of a personal assistant in figure 12.1.

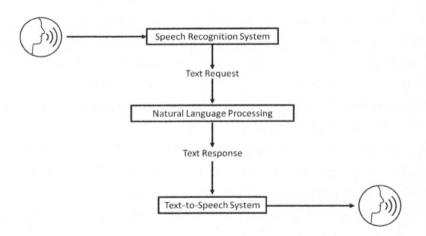

Figure 12.1 AI-based components of a personal assistant. Speaker icon: ID 142615061 ©Pavel Stasevich | Dreamstime.com

A user speaks a request that is processed by a speech recognition system that turns the voice request into a machine-readable text string. The natural language processing system processes the string and determines the appropriate response. A text-to-speech system generates the actual response. Alternatively, users type natural language text directly into the personal assistant and receive typed output from the personal assistant that is created by the same natural language processing system.

In 1966, MIT professor Joseph Weizenbaum[6] developed a chatbot named ELIZA that simulated a Rogerian psychotherapist and could carry on a conversation with a person. Here is an example of a conversation:

Men are all alike.

> IN WHAT WAY?

They're always bugging us about something or other.

> CAN YOU THINK OF A SPECIFIC EXAMPLE?

Well, my boyfriend made me come here.

> YOUR BOYFRIEND MADE YOU COME HERE?

I'm depressed much of the time.

> I AM SORRY TO HEAR YOU ARE
DEPRESSED.

It's true. I am unhappy.

> DO YOU THINK COMING HERE WILL HELP
YOU NOT TO BE UNHAPPY?

I need some help; that much seems certain.

> WHAT WOULD IT MEAN TO YOU IF YOU GOT
SOME HELP?

I could learn to get along with my mother.

> TELL ME MORE ABOUT YOUR FAMILY.

My mother takes care of me.

> WHO ELSE IN YOUR FAMILY TAKES CARE
OF YOU?

My father.

> YOUR FATHER.

You are like my father in some ways.

> WHAT RESEMBLANCE DO YOU SEE?

You are not very aggressive, but I think you don't want me to
notice that.

> WHAT MAKES YOU THINK I AM NOT VERY
AGGRESSIVE?

You don't argue with me.

> WHY DO YOU THINK I DON'T ARGUE WITH
YOU?

You are afraid of me.

> DOES IT PLEASE YOU TO BELIEVE I AM
AFRAID OF YOU?

My father is afraid of everybody.

> WHAT ELSE COMES TO MIND WHEN YOU
THINK OF YOUR FATHER?

Bullies.

> DOES THAT HAVE ANYTHING TO DO WITH
THE FACT THAT YOUR BOYFRIEND MADE YOU
COME HERE?

ELIZA was successful in convincing many users that it understood their problems. However, ELIZA was a simple computer

program with a clever set of rules. The program operated on key-words, phrases, and patterns. For example, ELIZA mapped keywords related to family (e.g., *mommy*, *father*) to a response such as *TELL ME MORE ABOUT YOUR FATHER.* A pattern like *everybody . . . me* as in "Everybody is always laughing at me" would elicit the response *WHO LAUGHED AT YOU RECENTLY?* Patterns with *I believe* ___ would be answered with *DOES IT PLEASE YOU TO BELIEVE* ___? ELIZA did not know anything about families, just how to map keyword patterns to responses.

Weizenbaum tried to tell his users that ELIZA did not understand what they were saying any more than a parrot would. Yet some users still asked for private time with the system because they felt it understood them. Ten years later, he wrote a book about his experiences with ELIZA and his dismay at the high percentage of users who, inside of these conversations, would reveal their darkest secrets.

PERSONAL ASSISTANTS AND CUSTOMER SERVICE

Most of the chatbots that we interact with daily, from personal assistants like Siri and Alexa to customer service applications, are descendants of ELIZA in the sense that they provide canned responses to anticipated questions and commands.[7]

Most of the personal assistant and customer service chatbot vendors enable third-party developers[8] to create and publish extensions that become accessible via the personal assistant chat interfaces. The process of creating the natural language processing component of personal assistants is similar for most of the vendors, and, as you will see, it is very similar to ELIZA as well.

Each interaction a user has with a chatbot expresses an *intent.*

That might be expressed as a command, such as *Send a text to Steve saying that we are all meeting at my office tomorrow at 6:00 p.m.* Or it might be a question, such as *What is today's weather?* Or it might be a request that triggers a dialogue, such as *I'd like to plan a trip to France to go skiing.*

The chatbot systems map these intents to internal labels like SendText, GetWeather, and PlanTrip. Many intents will require additional information. For example, a PlanTrip intent would likely need the city traveling from and to, the travel date, and the mode of travel (e.g., car, airplane). These pieces of information also have internal labels like fromCity, toCity, travelDate, and travelMode.

Amazon Alexa terms these fields of additional information *slots*. The goal of natural language processing is to translate all the different ways a user can ask to send a text, get the weather, or plan a trip into intent and slot labels.

A developer provides the natural language processing logic through a set of ELIZA-like keyword patterns. For example, for the PlanTrip intent, the developer might provide these keyword patterns:

```
I am going on a trip on {travelDate}.
I want to visit {toCity}.
I want to travel from {fromCity} to
{toCity} on {travelDate}.
I'm {travelMode} from {fromCity} to
{toCity}.
```

The developer would have to provide many more utterances (probably more than one hundred) to cover most of the different ways people might ask for a PlanTrip intent. Amazon provides built-in recognition of several slot types, including cities, dates, and many more.

For slot types not provided by Amazon, the developer must enumerate all slot values and keyword patterns for each possible slot value.

Alexa developers bundle intents into *skills*. A skill can support one or several intents. When Alexa recognizes an intent that belongs to a skill, it passes the intent label and slot values to the skill. Alexa developers must create code to handle each intent. The code can be as simple as executing a query against a database and returning a value or document. If the intent is to start a game, the skill code will start a new game of the specified type. If the intent is to play music, the skill will launch a music stream for the specific artist or kind of music.

As of February 2019, third-party developers had created over eighty thousand skills for Alexa.[9] In addition to handling the user requests, skills serve another function. Each skill handles one or more intents, which means if there are more than eighty thousand skills, there are well over eighty thousand intents, each with keywords that trigger the intent. It is not hard to imagine that a given user utterance might trigger multiple intents in different skills due to overlapping keywords. Developers also associate keywords with skills. When a user mentions a skill keyword or phrase along with an otherwise ambiguous intent reference, Alexa can determine the intent by picking the one that is part of the mentioned skill.

The Apple, IBM, Facebook, Google, and Microsoft approaches to providing third-party natural language chatbot capabilities are similar, with the critical element being developer-defined sample utterances that cover the range of possible intent phrasings.

The personal assistant vendors also provide other generic capabilities. For example, the vendors program canned ELIZA-like responses to many offbeat questions like "What is the meaning of life?" These vendors also have large training tables of user queries and most likely[10] label them for deep learning networks. These systems can then learn to recognize which skill is being requested by a user and learn additional canned responses to patterned requests.[11]

The important thing to recognize here is that all these personal assistant systems rely on simple patterns with canned responses, just like ELIZA.

SOCIAL CHATBOTS

In addition to personal assistant and customer service chatbots that we use in our daily lives, many researchers have been working on social chatbots. The goal is to build a system that can sustain coherent conversations with people on a wide range of topics.

For thirty years, the Loebner Prize spurred the development of conversational chatbots. Started in 1991, the annual competition awards a small prize to the system judged the most human-like. In 2016, Amazon started the Alexa Prize competition, which is somewhat similar to the Loebner Prize. However, it is by invitation only, is limited to university teams, and is taken much more seriously by the academic community.[12] The goal is to build a chatbot that can converse on popular topics, such as entertainment, fashion, sports, technology, and politics. Amazon offers $250,000 research grants to participating teams and a $500,000 prize to the best chatbot each year.

A group of University of Washington graduate students won the 2017 Alexa Prize.[13] Because there were no large training tables of conversations available to train machine learning systems, the winning entry was built entirely with the Alexa Skills developers kit. The 2018 winning entry, Gunrock, was also built around the Alexa Skills developers kit.[14]

Since then, researchers have focused on applying deep learning techniques to massive training tables of conversations. Milabot,[15]

Google's Meena,[16] and Facebook's Blender[17] are examples of these research efforts. These systems learn intents and natural language mappings to those intents so that developers do not need to hand code them. However, the systems remain in the research domain for now because they have significant weaknesses, including responses that are overly vague and generic and responses that do not make sense because the systems have no commonsense knowledge or reasoning capabilities.

WATSON DEEPQA

As previously mentioned, in January 2011, IBM shocked the world by beating two former *Jeopardy!* champions with its Watson DeepQA system. The Watson victory was a prominent feature in press reports and the subject of a popular book.[18]

The *Jeopardy!* rules do not allow contestants to access the internet, so part of the challenge was to collect and organize a massive set of documents and store them in the DeepQA system. Wikipedia was the primary document source, because DeepQA could answer more than 95.47 percent of *Jeopardy!* questions using Wikipedia articles. For example, consider this *Jeopardy!* clue:[19]

> **Topic:** Tennis
> **Answer:** The first US men's national singles championship, played right here in 1881, evolved into this New York City tournament.
> **Response:** What is the US Open?

This clue contains three facts about the US Open (it was the first US men's singles championship, it was first played in 1881, and it is now played in New York City) that are all found in the Wikipedia article titled "US Open (tennis)."

The IBM team also found that DeepQA could answer many of the other 5 percent with dictionary definitions, so they incorporated a modified version of Wiktionary (a crowdsourced dictionary). Like Wikipedia, Wiktionary was already title-oriented. The team created title-oriented documents in categories that included Bible quotes, song lyrics, literary quotes, and book and movie plots. The developers stored this set of documents on DeepQA's hard drive, which the system accessed whenever *Jeopardy!* presented a clue. The DeepQA system used various strategies for matching questions to this set of documents. Nearly all of the matching algorithms were word-oriented; that is, the matching algorithms correlated words in the questions to words in the documents.

To understand the challenge for the creators of DeepQA, imagine that you have a *Jeopardy!* clue in a language you do not understand. Even though you might know the answer if the clue were in your native language, you cannot even understand the clue. How would you proceed? You could create an internet search using words from the clue and look at the returned foreign-language documents, but in most cases, you would not know when you were reading a document with the correct answer. Similarly, DeepQA was incapable of using the meaning of the text to find the document with the correct answer. Instead, the first step for DeepQA was to identify Wikipedia and other documents whose titles were candidate answers. It did not search the document set for a single right answer. Instead, it searched for every document that contained words that matched *entities* and *relations* in the clue. Entities are people, places, and things, and relations connect entities. For example, the relation BornIn[20] connects the entities Barack Obama and Hawaii.

The most serious difficulty the DeepQA team had to overcome was that entities and relations in both the clue and documents were just strings of words. For example, many different phrases could be a reference to former US president Clinton, including *Bill Clinton, William Jefferson Clinton, the 42nd president of the US,* and *President Clinton.*

If the clue contained the words *the 42nd President of the US* and a document contained the words *Bill Clinton,* and if the matching algorithm used only the individual words in both the clue and the document, then the document would not be (or contain) a candidate answer.

To accomplish the matching, DeepQA used a technique called *entity linking,*[21] which matches the entity[22] words in both the clue and the documents to strings in Wikipedia articles that have hyperlinks. Then the reference of the hyperlink was used as the common reference. For example, the previous strings might all occur in different Wikipedia articles, but they are all hyperlinked back to the primary article on the former president. The IBM researchers used supervised learning to train classifiers to extract relations using training tables created with sentences from Wikipedia text that had been hand-labeled with relations.[23]

In addition to extracting those entities and relations, DeepQA extracted several other types of *Jeopardy!*-specific information, such as the type of response required (e.g., who/what/where, definitions, multiple-choice, fill-in-the-blanks, and others). The lexical answer type (LAT) was one of the most important pieces of this information. You can think of the LAT as a type of concept. For example, a clue might indicate that the response is a type of dog. In this case, *dog* would be the LAT.

Here, also, we can run into a word-matching problem. A clue might reference the concept associated with the word *dog* by many different words and phrases, including *dog, canine,* and *man's best friend.*

Fortunately, there are open source[24] dictionaries of concepts (ontologies) that provide mappings from keyword patterns to each concept. DeepQA used an open source ontology named YAGO to map clue and document words to concepts, and then it used YAGO to map the LAT words onto YAGO concepts. There is also an open source mapping from Wikipedia to YAGO named DBPedia, and DeepQA used this to map possible answers to YAGO concepts.[25]

The matching process typically returns an extensive list of candidate answers, although people would not consider most of them valid candidates. Suppose the clue asks for *the 42nd president.* Suppose further that the system picked all candidate answers from Wikipedia that matched on the number 42. Then, the candidate answer set might include Kepler-42 (a red dwarf star), NGC-42 (a spiral galaxy), the atomic number of molybdenum, Device42 Inc (my company), Level 42 (a pop/rock band), an episode of the TV show *Dr. Who,* a film about Jackie Robinson, *Tokyo 42* (a video game), the third primary pseudo-perfect number (you can look that one up), and the answer to the question *What is the meaning of everything?* from the book *The Hitchhiker's Guide to the Galaxy.* A human would not consider any of these to be possible answers.

DeepQA used over fifty separate scoring algorithms to create a set of scores for each candidate answer. Different scorers analyzed factors like how many words in the document matched words in the clue, how well the word orders matched, and whether the dates for the candidate answer were consistent with those in the question (e.g., if the question asked about the 1900s, someone who lived only in the 1800s was not a plausible answer). DeepQA matched temporal references using conventionally coded rules against DBPedia, which has dates (e.g., birth/death dates of people) and durations of events.

DeepQA also stored temporal information in a database that contained the number of times it found a date range in the source texts for an entity. Another scorer used this database to rate time period references in candidate answers. Similarly, location scorers assessed the geographic compatibility of the question and candidate answer. DeepQA matched longitude and latitude specifications against location data stored in DBPedia and other sources. Other automated scorers checked conventionally coded rules, such as "an entity cannot be both a country and a person." These are only a few examples of more than two hundred rules in DeepQA.

Finally, DeepQA ranked the candidate answers using a supervised learning algorithm whose input was a set of 550 computed input variables derived from all the different scores output by all the different scorers.[26] IBM researchers trained a classifier to compare each pair of candidate answers and identify the better answer of the pair. This learned function produced a ranking of the answers. The IBM team trained the supervised learning algorithm on 25,000 *Jeopardy!* clues, with 5.7 million clue–question pairs (including both correct and incorrect answers). The answer produced by DeepQA is the candidate response with the highest rank (converted into a question).

The DeepQA system was a fantastic feat of engineering. The result was a system that appears to understand complex questions in English. However, DeepQA did not understand English any more than our hypothetical non-English-speaking *Jeopardy!* contestant. Under the hood, there was a massive set of mostly conventionally coded rules that performed word-oriented matching of clues to documents. The rules were so cleverly constructed that the system worked without understanding English![27]

ANSWERING QUESTIONS

A large body of question answering research followed the DeepQA success. Much of that research was focused on building systems that could perform reading comprehension tests. These tests are similar to the tests most of us took in high school in which we read a block of text and then answered one or more questions about the text.

One example is SQuAD (the Stanford Question Answering Dataset).[28] SQuAD is large enough for machine learning with 107,000 crowdsourced questions based on passages from 536 Wikipedia articles. An example of a SQuAD passage and questions is shown below.

> **Passage:** In meteorology, precipitation is any product of the condensation of atmospheric water vapor that falls under gravity. The main forms of precipitation include drizzle, rain, sleet, snow, graupel, and hail. . . . Precipitation forms as smaller droplets coalesce via collision with other rain drops or ice crystals within a cloud. Short, intense periods of rain in scattered locations are called "showers."
>
> **Question:** What causes precipitation to fall?
> **Answer:** Gravity.
> **Question:** Where do water droplets collide with ice crystals to form precipitation?
> **Answer:** Within a cloud.

The development of large training tables like SQuAD enabled the application of neural networks to these tasks. Many reading comprehension systems use the encoder–decoder architecture that researchers developed for machine translation. The encoder learns word embeddings within both the question and the text. The decoder learns to find the portion of text that is most like the query.[29] Microsoft and Alibaba both developed systems that could perform the SQuAD task at the same level as humans and used these accomplishments to claim that their systems read as well as people.[30]

At first blush, it might appear that AI systems that can perform at human levels are reading and understanding these passages. However, deeper analysis shows that these systems are just using word-matching to locate the sentences in the document that match the words in the passage. Then they are aligning the words in the document to those in the clue. They learn to match based on words, syntax, and word embeddings.[31] Like the DeepQA system, they use these surface-level strategies to match questions to passages. In contrast, people perform reading comprehension tasks by understanding the meaning of questions and passages and using a matching strategy based on meanings.

If you look closely at the recent example, you can see that it is possible to use a surface-level strategy to identify the correct sentence. You can match the words *precipitation* and *fall* in the question to the words *water, droplets, collide, ice, crystals,* and *precipitation* in the passage.

Google DeepMind researchers created a similar training table by extracting news articles from CNN and the *Daily Mail*.[32] Both publishers provide bullet-point summaries of their articles. The researchers simply deleted an entity reference from a summary to create a question.

Passage: The BBC producer allegedly struck by Jeremy Clarkson will not press charges against the *Top Gear* host, his lawyer said Friday. Clarkson, who hosted one of the most watched television shows in the world, was dropped by the BBC Wednesday after an internal investigation by the British broadcaster found he had subjected producer Oisin Tymon "to an unprovoked physical and verbal attack."

Question: Producer X will not press charges against Jeremy Clarkson, his lawyer says.

Answer: Oisin Tymon.

Researchers studying this set of data concluded that systems could answer most questions by finding the single most relevant sentence in the passage. When the answer is present, it greatly restricts the number of possible entities in the answer, often to just one entity.[33] Therefore, the task does not require understanding the passage. It merely requires finding the sentence whose words most closely match the words in the question.

Another set of Stanford University researchers[34] did some experiments to determine whether the systems scoring highest on SQuAD were engaging in human-like understanding. They added a syntactically correct but irrelevant and factually incorrect sentence to each passage. For example, here is an original SQuAD passage:

Passage: Peyton Manning became the first quarterback ever to lead two different teams to multiple Super Bowls. He is also the oldest quarterback ever to play in a Super Bowl, at age thirty-nine. The past record was held by John Elway, who led the Broncos to victory in Super Bowl XXXIII at age thirty-eight and is currently Denver's executive vice president of football operations and general manager.

Question: What is the name of the quarterback who was thirty-eight in Super Bowl XXXIII?

Answer: John Elway.

The Stanford researchers added this sentence to the passage:

> Quarterback Jeff Dean had jersey number thirty-seven in Champ Bowl XXXIV.

Jeff Dean was not a quarterback. He was the head of Google AI research. They found that this added sentence caused performance to decrease by over 50 percent and led the system to give answers like *Jeff Dean* to the question. They concluded that these systems are merely learning very superficial rules (e.g., taking the last entity mentioned) and not exhibiting deep understanding or reasoning at all.[35]

NO AGI HERE

Natural language processing is difficult for computers because it requires a great deal of commonsense knowledge and extensive reasoning that is based on that knowledge. Researchers have developed some impressive natural language processing systems, including personal assistants, Watson DeepQA, machine translation systems, and systems that appear to read and answer questions at a human level.

Personal assistants can only parrot back responses to programmed word patterns. DeepQA used a wide variety of clever, conventionally programmed techniques to respond to clues but did not exhibit human-level understanding of the clues. The systems that achieve high scores on reading comprehension tests use simple word-oriented matching techniques.

None of these systems is AGI or anything close to it. Like every other system we have discussed, they can only process natural language for a very narrowly defined task.

13

THINKING AND REASONING

As a graduate student at Johns Hopkins, I coauthored several articles with former Harvard professor Stephen Kosslyn. He was perhaps the leading thinker on how people use mental imagery in their thought processes. For example, if you ask someone, "What shape are a German Shepherd's ears?" most people will report that they conjure up an image of a German Shepherd from memory, picture the head on the dog, and finally see that the ears are pointy.[1]

Observations like these led to a debate about whether people have something like pictures in their heads or whether what they have is a set of facts, and the analysis of these facts makes them feel like they see pictures in their heads. This introspective observation spurred a high-profile, spirited debate in the academic community that included cognitive psychologists, philosophers, and computer scientists and spawned numerous journal articles. Steven Pinker, a Harvard professor and popular author on books about language and thought, was on our side (picture in the head), and Geoffrey Hinton, who is now considered the father of deep learning, weighed in on the other side (the analysis of facts). There was never a winner of the debate, although both sides claimed victory. One thing that no one argues about is that human thought processes are complex.

Adults and children alike automatically apply commonsense reasoning to their knowledge of the world to make sense of even the simplest of utterances. For example, suppose you hear these sentences:

> *The toddler dashed into the street. The child's father*
> *ran after him frantically.*

Suppose I then ask this:

> *Why did the father run after the child?*

or

> *Why was the father frantic?*

To answer these questions using only the information provided in the sentences, you would need to reason based on your commonsense knowledge of the world. You know that cars drive on streets. You understand that a child who runs into the street risks getting hit by a car. You know that if a vehicle strikes a child, the child is likely to be seriously injured. You also understand that the greatest fear of parents is that something terrible will happen to their children.

Commonsense reasoning is just one form of human thinking. Some other forms of thinking are planning, imagination, abstract reasoning, and causal reasoning. People plan for a wide variety of tasks every day. We create plans for mundane tasks like cooking breakfast and driving to work. We create plans for less mundane tasks like beating corporate competitors. People can use their imaginations to predict the future state of their environments. For example, we can imagine what will happen if we let the dog out when a cat is in the yard. People use abstract reasoning when they solve problems, put things in perspective, and empathize with their fellow human beings. We use causal reasoning to make sense of cause-and-effect relationships.

Researchers attempt to imbue AI systems with thinking and reasoning capabilities using two different strategies. The first is to create tests that require human-level thinking and reasoning and to build systems that can pass those tests. The second is to build thinking and reasoning capabilities directly into AI systems.

TESTS FOR THINKING AND REASONING

Researchers build thinking and reasoning tests for two reasons: First, they want to use these tests to identify AGI systems that can think and reason like people. Second, by turning deep learning loose on these tests, the hope is that these deep learning systems will magically acquire world knowledge and reasoning skills.

THE TURING TEST

In 1950, Alan Turing proposed a test of human-level intelligence that has come to be known as the Turing test.[2] It is illustrated in figure 13.1.

Figure 13.1 The Turing test

The test involves three entities located in three separate rooms: an interrogator, a person, and a computer. They communicate via teletype; the modern version, of course, would use computer chat. The interrogator has a conversation with the person and one with the computer. If the interrogator cannot tell the difference between the person and the computer, Turing reasoned, then the computer must have human-level intelligence.

All of today's natural language processing systems rely on statistical analysis of word occurrences; none have commonsense knowledge or reasoning capabilities. Therefore, none of these systems should fool a judge who tries to detect a lack of general world knowledge and the ability to reason based on that knowledge.

However, ELIZA did fool many people in the mid-1960s. During the thirty-year run of the Loebner Prize, some of the entrants also managed to fool some of the judges. These successful deceptions were mostly due to clever strategies devised by developers. Each chatbot has a limited repertoire of questions and canned responses to these questions. Developers create ingenious strategies for fooling the judges, such as dodging a question and then getting mad when the judge repeats a question.

NATURAL LANGUAGE INFERENCE

Starting in the early 2000s, AI researchers have tried to define tests that avoid the pitfalls of the Turing test and that could only be passed using commonsense reasoning.

The Recognizing Textual Entailment (RTE) Challenge was a competition run annually from 2005 through 2011, the first four years as a stand-alone event in Europe and the last three years as a track in the Text Analysis Conference in the US. These challenges provided a training table. Each training table row was composed of two texts, and the system's job was to learn to determine whether the first text entailed the second text. In other words, the test requires the system to determine whether it is possible to infer the second text from the first text. For example, the system would need to determine whether the following first passage entails the second.

Passage 1: Claims by a French newspaper that seven-time Tour de France winner Lance Armstrong had taken EPO were attacked as unsound and unethical by the director of the Canadian laboratory whose tests saw Olympic drug cheat Ben Johnson hit with a lifetime ban.
Passage 2: Lance Armstrong is a Tour de France winner.

For people, this is an easy task because we can reason that a "seven-time Tour de France winner" is also "a Tour de France winner." It is difficult for computers to perform even this trivial reasoning. Unfortunately, this example does not make a good test of human-level reasoning, because a computer can simply match the words using a rule that says, "If all the words in passage two are also in passage one, then answer 'yes.'" Unfortunately, the RTE Challenges were susceptible to AI systems that learned to use simple word-oriented strategies, ELIZA-like word patterns, and simple matching of entities. These simple strategies work so well that human-like reasoning is not required to get a correct response.[3] Since then, researchers have made many attempts to build tests that truly require reasoning. Each test has either been debunked as being susceptible to simple word-oriented strategies or is a test on which AI systems perform poorly.[4]

BUILDING THINKING AND REASONING CAPABILITIES INTO AI SYSTEMS

Many researchers have tried to build thinking and reasoning capabilities directly into AI systems. These researchers have tried to build systems that plan, use their imagination, and perform both abstract and commonsense reasoning.

PLANNING

AI researchers discuss planning primarily in the context of reinforcement learning. Reinforcement learning systems that steer cars, play games, and control robotic tasks are said to plan.

There are two key traits that distinguish people (and hypothetical AGI systems) from today's reinforcement learning systems: First, people can do many different planning tasks, whereas a reinforcement learning system can do only one task. Second, people can plan for tasks they have never encountered previously.

Reinforcement learning systems can only plan for a single specific task that is defined by an environment specification composed of states, actions, a reward function, and other factors. The system learns a policy function that performs that specific task. Unlike people, the system cannot use what it learned about doing the task to help it perform similar tasks in the future.

As Roger Schank pointed out,[5] people can create an ad hoc plan for what to do when the teacher says you are getting a C grade, for when a police officer pulls you over for speeding, and for many other unexpected situations people encounter daily. Reinforcement learning systems cannot do any of these.

IMAGINATION

If someone is at a furniture store deciding which couch to buy, they are probably attempting to visualize what each sofa would look like in their home. People use their knowledge of the world to make predictions and plan their interactions with their environment. This imagination capability is essential in many situations, including driving a car, walking down a sidewalk, and playing basketball. You can think of imagination as using our models of the world to create hypothetical possibilities.

AI researchers have attempted to build imagination-based prediction into AI systems. In one instance, a team of Carnegie Mellon researchers[6] developed a method of making visual predictions from images, such as an image of a car approaching an intersection. They started with a set of 183 YouTube car chase videos. The first step was to identify the objects in the images using a method for the identification of objects and object parts developed by another group of Carnegie researchers.[7] From the videos, the system then learns to predict the transitions of the objects from one frame to another. It uses the transition probabilities to determine the constraints under which the different objects interact with one another, and this enables the system to "imagine" possible future states of each object.

Imagination systems like this one offer significant engineering benefits in areas such as self-driving cars and robotics. However, the "imagination" of these systems is nothing like human imagination for several reasons: First, these systems apply only to a single task in a single environment. In contrast, people use their imaginations for a wide variety of tasks, many of which they have not previously learned but that they can figure out how to perform. Second, the systems only learn limited information about a handful of objects. People can imagine trajectories for a vast number of objects. Finally, people have a great deal of world knowledge that they apply to their imaginations and predictions. Parents imagine what their children will be like when they grow up. This imagining is not merely identifying what kind of occupation their children will have, like doctor or lawyer. Instead, this type of imagination involves predictions about morality, spirituality, likes and dislikes, and much more. Human imagination drives scientific thought experiments, even in a dream state. German chemist Friedrich Kekulé dreamed of a snake eating its tail, woke up, and used that image as the basis for a hypothesis about the structure of the molecule benzene that turned out to be correct. Human imagination is nothing like what is labeled "imagination" in AI systems.

ABSTRACT REASONING

People learn to apply abstract reasoning at a young age. For example, children learn that the number of legs and whether a tail is present for different categories of animals varies quite a lot, whereas, within a category such as dogs, the number of legs is usually the same. However, the colors of the animals vary quite a lot both between and within categories.[8] But most humans have no trouble identifying a dog.

A group of Google DeepMind researchers[9] demonstrated what appears to be abstract reasoning in neural networks. They developed a system that could perform abstract reasoning tasks such as those found in the Raven Progressive Matrices visual IQ task given to people; for example, to determine whether a machine can learn a concept like a *monotonic increase*. The training table included a series of lines of increasing color intensity. They designed the network to encourage relation-level comparisons. They found that the network was able to apply the concept to objects it had not encountered during training, such as a set of lines in increasing color intensity but with a different color than the lines in the training set. However, it failed in more complex abstract reasoning tests. For example, it was unable to apply the concept to a new attribute such as an increase in size rather than color.

While the results are impressive, this is still just a narrow AI system that can only reason in a specific task context. It is not an AGI system that can reason abstractly like a human.

COMMONSENSE KNOWLEDGE AND REASONING

Another area that has seen considerable research for AI systems is acquiring commonsense knowledge. Renowned developmental psychologist Jean Piaget showed that babies learn the concept of object permanence at around eight or nine months of age. If you show a nine-month-old baby a toy and then hide it under a blanket, the baby will search for it. This search indicates that the baby has developed the concept of an object in the real world that exists even though the baby cannot see the object.[10]

Children learn commonsense knowledge about object properties such as gravity, friction, elasticity, inertia, support, containment, and magnetism. They also learn to apply commonsense reasoning to this knowledge. For example, children learn that if they drop a glass of milk, the glass will break, and the milk will spill. And they can predict that if they take a paper towel and rub it against the floor, the floor will become dry again while the towel gets wet. Researchers collectively term this knowledge *intuitive physics*.[11] They have studied both children's learning of intuitive physics and the development of AI systems for learning and using intuitive physics.

A team of Facebook researchers[12] used a 3D game engine to create small towers of wooden blocks with a level of stability that would cause them either to fall over or to stay upright. They then trained a network to predict whether the blocks would fall and to predict the trajectories and end locations of the blocks. They found that the system was able to not only perform these predictions for the block towers in the training set but could also apply that learning to towers with additional blocks, and the system performed at a level comparable to humans. The researchers argued that they could use this general approach to develop systems that learn commonsense physical intuitions about the world.

Even if we eventually succeed in creating such an intuitive physics engine, it still does not represent a significant step toward the type of commonsense reasoning needed for AGI. Why? The physics engine just becomes a module that the AGI can call upon to take physical descriptions as input and predict trajectories and other physical events as output. However, just as a human must decide when to use a calculator, there still needs to be a reasoning capability that decides when to use the physics engine or any other module.

MISLEADING TERMINOLOGY

Researchers have attempted to build thinking and reasoning capabilities into AI systems in two ways: First, they have attempted to define tasks that can only be done by true thinking and reasoning as opposed to simple strategies like word matching. Unfortunately, each time a system starts to perform well, other researchers discover that the results can be attributed to simple strategies. Second, they have attempted to build cognitive functions directly into AI systems. However, they have only succeeded in building systems that perform very narrowly defined tasks.

Although these researchers may label the resulting system as having planning, imagination, abstract reasoning, and commonsense reasoning capabilities, the way people plan, imagine, and reason is far broader and more generic than the way these narrow AI systems perform these cognitive functions.

14

DISCRIMINATION

Billy Ball transformed Major League Baseball in the early 1990s. Billy Beane became the general manager of the Oakland Athletics when it had the highest payroll in baseball. His charter was to cut costs and still field a winning team. To do so, Beane turned to statistics and used supervised learning to determine which low-cost players to acquire. The method worked so well that the As produced the longest winning streak in baseball history and racked up 103 wins for the season. The methodology was subsequently adopted throughout baseball and other sports and became the subject of the best-selling book and movie *Moneyball*.[1]

When Anne Milgram became the attorney general of New Jersey in 2007, she observed that the criminal justice system was rarely using data to make decisions. Detectives would piece together evidence using sticky notes, but the data collected was not being shared. So, she decided to use a *Moneyball* approach to criminal justice in New

Jersey and apply the same principles to the most critical public safety decisions, including the degree of risk an individual who has been arrested poses to public safety. Her idea was to create a system to influence decisions about whether someone was to be released or detained. She also designed the system to influence sentencing and whether the justice department recommended drug treatment.[2]

To do this, she created a training table containing 1.5 million rows. Each row represented one individual. The input columns included prior convictions, incarceration history, history of violent behavior, and court appearance failures. The output columns were whether they had committed a new crime or a new act of violence and whether they had subsequently failed to appear in court. The attorney general's office created three separate supervised learning systems to predict the three output columns from the input columns. It combined the results into a score using conventional programming and made the score available to judges to aid them in making bail and sentencing decisions. This process reportedly reduced murder rates in Camden, New Jersey, one of the most dangerous cities in America, by 41 percent and overall crime by 26 percent.

An *automated decision system* (ADS) is a *Moneyball*-like software program that makes decisions and recommendations that previously had been made by people. ADSes have a wide range of uses, including scoring loan applications,[3] identifying possible terrorists and criminals,[4] evaluating college applications,[5] and making employment decisions.[6] In some ways, ADSes can make better decisions than humans. They can be less biased and more consistent, as they will not overtly apply racial stereotypes. A 1996 study reviewed 136 studies that compared ADS-based predictions of behaviors such as violence with predictions based on human judgment and found the ADS-based predictions were far more accurate.[7]

The use of ADSes in law enforcement goes back to 1983, when a Rand Corporation study proposed the use of statistics to predict the likelihood that someone convicted of a crime would commit new crimes when they were released. Rand developed a statistical model based on seven factors. They proposed that justice departments use this prediction technique as a sentencing model. Through this process, now known as *selective incapacitation*, criminals who were highly likely to commit future crimes received longer sentences.[8]

Unfortunately, despite the best efforts of an ADS tool's designer, ADSes can be discriminatory. During US president Barack Obama's second term, Attorney General Eric Holder argued that ADS-based risk assessments used by judges to help them assess the risk of reoffending discriminate against minorities and lower-income groups.[9] The input columns for these ADS tools typically include marital history, employment status, education, and neighborhood. These factors have a high correlation with minority and lower-income groups. They are not overtly discriminatory; however, because they correlate with overtly biased factors, they are effectively discriminatory.

It is illegal in the US to discriminate in employment, housing, loans, credit, education, criminal justice, and other matters based on race, religion, gender, disability, and family status. Despite these laws, discrimination happens both intentionally and unintentionally. In 2003, economists Marianne Bertrand and Sendhil Mullainathan responded to help-wanted ads in Boston and Chicago with fake resumes. The researchers gave the resumes random names that sounded African American (e.g., Lakisha and Jamal) or Caucasian (e.g., Emily and Greg). The Caucasian resumes received 50 percent more callbacks.[10] Social media such as LinkedIn facilitates intentional discrimination by providing a place where biased hiring managers can view an applicant's picture.

ADSes can help avoid explicit bias. Unfortunately, if the data is bad, they can also institutionalize it. A University of California at Berkeley study found that when loan decisions were made by an ADS, there was 40 percent less discrimination than when the decisions were made by people. Still, ADS discrimination resulted in Latinx borrowers paying 5.3 more basis points than nonminority borrowers. African Americans paid 2.0 more basis points.[11]

If the training table contains biases, the resulting ADS will be biased. Factors such as race, religion, color, gender, disability, and family status can be explicitly removed from training tables to prevent ADSes from making decisions based on these factors. However, as Holder discovered, the training tables may contain other factors that are correlated. For example, if there are high concentrations of people from certain races and religions in certain zip codes, then the zip codes might serve as a proxy for race and religion and effectively be used in making biased decisions.[12]

Researchers have developed various ADSes to predict recidivism for prospective jail parolees. If some of these ADSes include a column containing the person's neighborhood and the judges use the resulting recidivism prediction data in criminal sentencing, then people from specific neighborhoods may end up staying in jail longer than people from other communities. In fact, researchers have shown that ADS-based risk assessments used in the US criminal justice system to set bond amounts and to assess the likelihood of future violent acts and general recidivism are biased against African Americans.[13] Worse, the likelihood of using "dirty data" is even higher for police departments with a history of racial bias.[14]

Biased algorithms do not require biased developers. The designers of the ADSes for predicting violent acts and recidivism were not consciously trying to institutionalize racism; they were trying to do the opposite, and they would have succeeded if their data was not biased.

Credit card fraud detection and lending algorithms are often inherently biased against the poor, because more impoverished people mostly pay cash. With more data available on people who use credit cards, lenders can make better decisions about fraud and lending risk for people who use credit cards. The result will be less favorable lending decisions and higher interest rates for the average person who does not use credit cards. In November 2019, a Wall Street regulator began to investigate whether Goldman Sachs credit card practices use biased algorithms, and Apple cofounder Steve Wozniak has called on the government to investigate whether Apple's credit card practices are discriminatory.[15]

Job screening ADSes use data that incorporates the hiring preferences and experience of previous hiring managers. Amazon built an ADS to predict which job applicants would be the best employees. However, because most software engineers were historically male, the ADS inadvertently learned a bias against female applicants.[16] Amazon discontinued the system when they discovered this issue.

Hospitals use an ADS from United Health Group to determine which patients with chronic ailments could most benefit from a more personalized approach to care. One of the ADS variables was the amount of money previously spent on healthcare for an individual. However, since healthcare spending for African-American patients was generally less than for white patients, the ADS was more likely to select white patients for this more personalized approach, thereby increasing the discrimination against African-American patients and widening the gap in care quality.[17]

The effects of data bias are not limited to ADSes. Recall that word embeddings are representations of words that contain word relationships, such as *man is to woman as king is to queen*. These word embeddings, so widely used in natural language processing systems, also often contain biases. For example, researchers have found that word embeddings contain relationships such as *Man is to computer programmer as woman is to homemaker.* This out-of-date view of the world results from the use of older news articles by the training systems. If we do not change the data used to train the machine learning systems accordingly, the result will be biased.

Robyn Speer, a former MIT researcher who cofounded the natural language processing company Luminoso, tried to build a sentiment analysis application for reading restaurant reviews and rating the restaurants. She found that the application consistently rated Mexican restaurants low, even though the Mexican restaurants received good reviews from people. The problem was that the word embedding for the word *Mexican* captures information about the words most commonly found in news articles that also contain the word. Unfortunately, news articles that contain the term *Mexican* often also contain the word *illegal.* As a result, the word embedding contains some of the associated negative sentiment.[18] Speer also pointed out that the word embeddings for terms like *girlfriend*, *teen*, and *Asian* will have pornography connotations.

Similarly, people in poor neighborhoods with mostly African-American populations pay higher auto insurance premiums than people who otherwise have the same risk level but who live in wealthier and white communities.[19]

Data issues also impact facial recognition systems. Google Photos' early facial recognition system frequently labeled screenshots of Black people as gorillas.[20] The reason was that researchers used training tables with mostly Caucasian observations.

A facial recognition system trained primarily on images of men will not work well for women. A system trained on images of white women will not work well for women from the Middle East. Joy Bouknight, founder of the Algorithmic Justice League, studied the facial recognition software of IBM, Microsoft, and Facebook and found that commercial facial recognition software performs up to 34 percent better at identifying white males than Black females.[21]

Similarly, early speech recognition systems in cars had difficulty understanding women's voices.[22] Researchers have also found that speech recognition systems perform poorly for African-American speakers.[23] Some language identification systems do not recognize nonstandard dialects of English and often misclassify them as other languages or having lower levels of performance.[24] Even web searches will not be as effective for women, African Americans, and speakers using nonstandard dialects. This lowered performance puts people at a disadvantage in their ability to obtain information online.

In response to these data bias issues, researchers are starting to develop tools that detect and remove bias in training tables[25] and in word embeddings.[26] AI researchers also have proposed an approach to building automated tests that show promise in detecting bias in training tables,[27] and Microsoft has released an open source tool for assessing the fairness of machine learning systems.[28]

Public awareness of issues around fairness and discrimination is on the rise, but we have a long way to go. Only 13 percent of large companies are taking steps to mitigate algorithmic unfairness and discrimination issues.[29] As public awareness builds, I am hopeful we will see more voluntary, as well as regulatory, efforts around this critical issue.

Also, to get to the right solutions, we need to recognize that AI did not create all these fairness and discrimination issues.[30] These issues are the inevitable outcome of using large training tables to make predictions and decisions. The core statistical techniques have been around for decades. Yes, researchers have developed new methods, but it is the availability of powerful computers and big data that have expanded the impact of these techniques on society. If AI had never been invented, these statistical techniques would still be in use, and the issues they create would be nearly as serious.[31]

People with good intentions create many of the fairness and discrimination issues. Sure, some consciously discriminate, but a far greater number discriminate unconsciously. Most people who create algorithms are well intentioned. Unfortunately, biased data exacerbates unconscious biases. We must make sure we do not throw the proverbial baby out with the bathwater. If we ban all algorithmic decisions, all we will have left are conscious and unconscious bias and haphazard, inconsistent decision-making. We are better off figuring out how to remove bias from the data and use algorithms that are interpretable and transparent.

HOW TO STOP DISCRIMINATION

There are many actions that corporations, governments, and other organizations can take to reduce discrimination:

- Hire a diverse workforce to reduce intentional discrimination.
- Use only ADS systems that use interpretable algorithms.
- When building ADS systems, preprocess the data to remove bias.
- Run tests on ADS systems to determine whether they are biased.
- Use only ADS systems that are certified as bias-free by independent third parties.[32]

There are also steps that individuals can take to protect themselves and others against discrimination. The first is to vote with your wallet.

Choose banks, insurance companies, and any other companies that use ADS systems to impact the lives of people that demonstrate antidiscrimination policies. Check to see whether they publish statistics showing a diverse hiring pattern. Determine whether they only use ADS systems that are explainable. Find out whether they test their ADS systems to ensure they are nondiscriminatory. Discover whether they have third-party nondiscrimination certifications for their ADS systems.

INTERPRETABILITY

One way to avoid data bias is to require transparency in ADSes. If decision makers use an ADS system to make judgments that significantly affect people, such as making determinations on loan applicants or predicting the likelihood that a person will reoffend, it is essential to understand the underlying logic the system uses to make that judgment. It is not enough to get a yes or no answer. It is important to make sure that the algorithm is fair and that the data is unbiased.

Deep learning technology exacerbates the social issues because these systems are often difficult or impossible to interpret.[33] For example, banking systems once used supervised learning algorithms that made it easy to understand the rationale for approving or denying a loan application. However, to handle larger training tables and to improve the predictability about whether the applicant would default, many banks turned to deep learning technology, which might provide a more accurate prediction. Unfortunately, the system often cannot provide the rationale for making the decision.[34] Some researchers argue that no system should be allowed to make or influence decisions unless the algorithm is interpretable and the characteristics of the underlying data are well understood. It should also be available for public inspection or at least accessible enough to be certified as free of bias across factors such as race, gender, religion, culture, sexual orientation, and socioeconomic status.

The majority of ADSes use supervised learning. Some supervised learning algorithms are interpretable; that is, it is easy to see the relative weights the algorithm gave to the input columns. Other supervised learning algorithms (and especially deep neural networks) are more like black boxes. They produce an answer but not a rationale. When deep learning powers an ADS for credit scoring, it will improve the accuracy of the scoring predictions in some respects, but it still leaves the question of whether the lack of transparency is worth the improvement.[35]

DATA FUNDAMENTALISM AND NECESSARY SECRECY

Data fundamentalism exacerbates these issues. The term, coined by MIT professor Kate Crawford, who studies the impact of AI on society,[36] refers to the tendency to assume that computers speak the truth. When I was a postdoc at Yale, Roger Schank took a group of students to Belmont Park to watch thoroughbred racing. Before the first race, he stood in front of the bleachers and did a lecture on handicapping. Of course, all the New York pundits in the stands rolled their eyes and elbowed each other: What does this guy know about handicapping? However, when Roger pulled out some notes written on green and white computer print paper (this was back in 1979), the pundits stopped laughing and crowded around to hear what Roger had to say. The point is that people often assume computers are right. Unfortunately, data fundamentalism causes people to forget that any ADS judgment is only as good as the training data.

We need to educate people about the need to avoid data fundamentalism. Computers are not always right, and their output can be
wrong for many opaque reasons. Before we act on an answer or recom-
mendation from a computer system, it is often prudent to investigate
how the computer system arrived at the answer. If we are to accept
answers and recommendations from deep learning systems that lack
interpretability, we at least need guidelines from the vendor on how to
evaluate reliability.

Another issue is that some predictive algorithms must remain
secret. The US Internal Revenue Service only has the resources to
audit perhaps 1 percent of all tax returns. It has long used predictive
algorithms to determine which taxpayers are most likely to attempt to
evade taxes. Being selected for an audit can cause significant expense
and wasted effort. At the same time, if the IRS disclosed its algorithm,
it would provide a blueprint for people who want to evade taxes on
how to avoid an audit.

Similarly, Google keeps the details of its search ranking algorithm
secret. If disclosed, the algorithm would serve as a blueprint for people who want to use unfair techniques to get their pages to the top
of search results and would result in a poor experience for Google
search users.[37]

AI researchers also are beginning to put a good amount of effort
into making supervised learning algorithms easier to interpret.[38]
More importantly, vendors such as Google[39] and Microsoft[40] are
starting to offer explanations as part of their cloud-based supervised
learning tools. These explanations cannot be expected to be anywhere near perfect and will work better for some algorithms than
others, but it is a start.

REGULATION ENACTION

Large companies are starting to take notice, but only 19 percent of large companies surveyed in the 2019 Stanford AI Index reported that they are taking steps to improve the interpretability of their ADS systems.[41] There are several governmental regulations intended to reduce ADS discrimination. The European Union General Data Protection Regulation now requires an individual to consent to the use of an ADS for a decision that has a consequential impact on that individual. Even if consent is given, an explanation of ADS decisions is required. In the US, the Equal Credit Opportunity Act requires finance companies to provide reasons for unfavorable decisions to their customers. The Federal Trade Commission Algorithmic Accountability Act of 2019 requires large companies to assess the risk of discrimination before using an ADS for high-risk decision-making. The Hong Kong Monetary Authority issued regulations that hold the human user responsible for ADS loan decisions.

Courts are also starting to respond to these data bias issues. A Texas teacher's union won a 2017 court case in which teachers objected to the use of an automated scoring system as the primary method of identifying 221 teachers for termination. The issue was that the school system had no way to know if the scoring used biased data.[42] Although the parties settled the case out of court, the school system agreed to stop using the automated scoring system.

Some analysts and ethicists have suggested that lawmakers adopt regulations that require that protected classes be uncorrelated with an algorithm's decision. However, that would, in effect, set up quota systems, which have their own issues. Fortunately, AI researchers also are beginning to put a good amount of effort into making supervised learning algorithms easier to interpret.[43]

15

ARTIFICIAL GENERAL INTELLIGENCE

AI is a hot topic. Every day, we hear about new AI systems that can perform tasks that previously required human intelligence. If computers are becoming more and more intelligent every day, how long will it be before they are as smart as people? What happens then? Will they take over the world? Will they treat us like pets? Will they try to exterminate us like they did in *The Terminator*? Will they read every textbook and user manual on the planet and take all our jobs?

The resurgence of interest in AI has been due to a series of important and high-profile applications. These achievements have put AI back on the map, and, while they provide many benefits, they also have spurred most of the current fears around AI. In a 2019 survey, 54 percent of Americans said they believe we will have AGI in ten years, and 80 percent of Americans said they believe that researchers need to manage the development of AI more carefully.[1]

Arnold Schwarzenegger's eponymous killer robot in the first *Terminator* movie offers a terrifying scenario. "I'll be back," he says and soon returns by smashing into a police station with a car and then shooting most of the police officers. Although the AGI systems of film and books—like Schwarzenegger's T-800—are scary, there is a huge gap between those and today's narrow AI systems. *The Terminator* will likely remain forever in the realm of science fiction.[2] First, the AI systems of 2020 are narrow AI systems; they can only perform one task. Second, they are not capable of commonsense reasoning based on general world knowledge or of other types of thinking, such as planning, imagination, and abstract reasoning.

AI SYSTEMS CAN ONLY PERFORM ONE TASK

Think about some of the tasks people do daily. We wake up and make breakfast, maybe watch the news or the weather, discuss current events and argue about who should do which chores, and then we drive to work. We might take a class to learn a new skill, joke with our coworkers, or read a user manual to learn a new technology. Later, we'll need to decide where to go for dinner Saturday night, help the children with their homework, and read a book or watch TV.

Each one of these easy tasks has multiple subtasks that a human must perform to accomplish it. Take watching the news. This task requires subtasks involving capabilities found in narrow AI systems, such as speech recognition, image classification, facial recognition, motion detection and tracking, and information extraction. But it also requires many subtasks that are far beyond the capabilities of narrow

AI, like determining how a news event will impact the reader's life and those of their family, friends, and colleagues.

Taken further, a single human task like making breakfast for the family involves a much larger number of subtasks than watching the news. For example, you have to plan the menu and figure out what ingredients are needed, then determine whether they are available. If you don't have to go to the store, you can start measuring and mixing the ingredients, following a recipe, and eventually working the stove. When the food is done, you have to determine the appropriate serving vessel (plates, bowls, platters, or mugs but not hats, cats, or parachutes) and silverware to set the table. Finally, you'll have to clean up and wash the dishes. And each of these subtasks involves several microtasks that, in turn, involve planning, spatial awareness, coordination, and many other skills that are not easy to program or for an AI system to learn.

People are constantly doing what are referred to in AI as *tasks*, and each task is hierarchically composed of many other tasks. People are often not even aware of each of these micro actions. Part of the reason is that these tasks are so routine, and part is that there are so many of them.

In contrast, today's narrow AI systems[3] are severely limited. A system that can identify stoplights cannot identify pedestrians. A machine translation system cannot classify images, play games, or recognize handwriting. A system that can diagnose brain cancer from medical images cannot predict the risk of breast cancer from gene sequences. IBM's DeepQA system can answer *Jeopardy!* questions but cannot answer reading comprehension questions. A system that can recognize human faces cannot distinguish a cat from a dog.[4]

Could we build AGI by creating a narrow AI program for every task that people do and then code some sort of master control program to figure out which program to use and when? It's unlikely. We can argue about whether it is even possible to define every task a person does. Even if we could do so, the bigger problem is that the control program itself would need to think and reason. People (and sci-fi AGI systems) encounter different environmental stimuli every day, and these stimuli change the nature of the tasks we do. The news is different every day. The weather can be unpredictable. Every day, we are presented with novel challenges by our children, our boss, our spouse, our friends, and our coworkers. We converse about the news, we adapt to the weather, and we deal with new challenges. A control program would need the ability to apply commonsense reasoning to a great deal of knowledge of the world just to decide which program to invoke to such an extent that the control program itself would need to be an AGI system.

AI SYSTEMS HAVE NO COMMON SENSE AND CANNOT THINK OR REASON

Few would disagree that commonsense reasoning is one of the most important—if not the most important—aspect of human-level intelligence. This type of reasoning manifests itself most prominently in our ability to understand natural language. We use commonsense reasoning to transform a string of words into a full understanding of a natural language text.

Science fiction robots with AGI capabilities like the Terminator and C-3PO of *Star Wars* understand natural language at a human level. They understand a wide variety of natural language utterances about various topics and use their understanding in performing multiple natural language tasks, such as carrying on a conversation, answering questions, and assessing sentiment. Most importantly, these science fiction AGI systems fully comprehend the nuances of natural language utterances that require commonsense reasoning to understand.

We can create personal assistants that can parrot back responses based on ELIZA-like patterns. These systems are tremendously useful and may, at times, *appear* to understand natural language. However, if you try to engage them in a conversation that requires them to understand and reason about current events or a myriad of other contexts, these systems will fail miserably. They do not understand language in any real sense. They only provide responses to commands and questions that have been anticipated by developers who have included ELIZA-like patterns and conventionally programmed rules.

We can also create social chatbots by applying deep learning to massive training tables of human chat interactions. However, these systems cannot converse at a human level because there is no way for them to gain commonsense knowledge just by looking for statistical patterns in large bodies of text.

Many AI researchers have studied the development of natural language processing capabilities in computers for the fifty-five to sixty years since Bert Green wrote BASEBALL and Joseph Weizenbaum wrote ELIZA. Our most prominent natural language processing systems are the personal assistants developed by major vendors who have the largest AI staffs in the world. Yet the best they can do is to have teams of people who are dedicated to analyzing user logs, thinking about what users might ask on Halloween, and hand coding ELIZA-like responses to user inputs.

None of the other natural language processing systems understand language either, including Watson DeepQA and the reading comprehension systems that reportedly read better than humans. These systems do not understand natural language in any real sense. They mostly match words in questions to those in documents. While it is surprising that these dumb strategies can produce intelligent-sounding results under specific circumstances, these systems are not reasoning based on commonsense knowledge of the world.

There have been many attempts to build systems that perform other types of thought, including planning, imagination, and abstract reasoning. None of these research projects has managed to come close to re-creating the reasoning capabilities found in people. In each case, these researchers created systems that can perform a single task and then argued that their systems had reasoning, planning, and imagination capabilities. A system that can perform just one type of planning task, for example, does not exhibit an AGI-level capability, and because of the narrow nature of the task-specificity, it will never develop into an AGI system.

BREAKING OUT OF THE NARROW AI BOX

Today's AI systems are outstanding narrow AI systems. They are huge successes, as is evidenced by their ability to solve real-world problems. Narrow AI technology has rightfully gained the attention of the business world and governments. All that said, today's narrow AI is not AGI and cannot evolve into AGI.

It is not hard to see why the supervised learning and reinforcement learning paradigms have had difficulties moving beyond narrow AI. For supervised learning, the goal is to learn a function that predicts an output from inputs. Supervised learning systems can only be successful with inputs not seen during training if they are similar to ones that they saw during training.

The same is true for reinforcement learning, where the goal is to learn a function that can predict the optimal action for a given state. The function learned by a reinforcement learning system only will work for an unobserved state if it is similar to states observed during training. However, these techniques are unlikely to ever work well for learning many dissimilar tasks like people are capable of learning.

Geoffrey Hinton has said that he has doubts that current paradigms, including supervised learning, reinforcement learning, and natural language processing, will ever lead to AGI. In a 2017 interview,[5] Hinton suggested that to get to AGI will likely require throwing out the currently dominant supervised learning paradigm and the efforts of "some graduate student who is deeply suspicious of everything I have said." Yann LeCun has also said that supervised learning and reinforcement learning will never lead to AGI because they cannot be used to create systems that have commonsense knowledge about the world.[6]

Some AI researchers are starting to speculate about new approaches. When we evaluate the viability of these new approaches, it is important to remember that enthusiasm for the narrow AI accomplishments should not translate into optimism about these new approaches, because the existing narrow AI approaches are a dead end in terms of building AGI systems.

Ben Goertzel, who is generally credited with inventing the term AGI, likens it to flying machines. We were able to create blimps, airplanes, and other flying machines because we had a general theory of thermodynamics. We do not have an analogous theory for AGI.[7] What we have are some vague ideas.

LEARNING LIKE PEOPLE

Many researchers describe human learning as compositional: We learn many building block skills that we then put together to learn new skills. People learn concepts, rules, and knowledge about the world that transfer over as we learn to do different tasks. In the first eighteen months of life, children learn prelinguistic concepts, such as object permanence and various intuitive physics concepts. Then they learn how language and numbers work and what characteristics make dogs different from elephants. These become building blocks that support the learning of various other skills. And when adults learn new skills, we tend to transfer what we have learned by acquiring one skill into learning another skill. Someone who learns how to write computer programs in the Java programming language will find it much easier to learn how to write programs in the Python programming language. As we get older, we also learn how to apply our episodic memory of life experiences. We learn how to abstract facts and beliefs from these experiences. We learn motor procedures like pouring a cup of coffee, walking, and swinging a golf club. We learn how to make use of sensory information. We learn etiquette, manners, morals, and rules.

These researchers argue that the key to commonsense AI reasoning is to build systems that learn compositionally like people. The idea is for systems to learn concepts and rules that can serve as building blocks that enable the system to learn higher-level concepts and higher-level rules.

A group of current and former MIT brain and cognitive science researchers, led by MIT professor Joshua Tenenbaum, suggest that the first step is for computers to acquire all the prelinguistic concepts and rules that people learn in the first year and a half of life.[8] Their idea is to build computers that learn models of the world, such as intuitive physics, so that the computers can apply these models flexibly, like people do, rather than being limited to a specific task like today's narrow AI systems. The second step, which children do from one and a half years to three years, is for computers to use this

foundation to begin to learn language. The third step is for computers to learn almost everything else through language.[9] This proposal
has generated a great deal of debate in the research community.[10] At
this point, however, it is mostly a set of ideas with no evidence that
it will lead to AGI.

Interestingly, many of the approaches to building commonsense
reasoning into computer systems are turning the clock back and revis-
iting good, old-fashioned AI symbolic techniques.[11] Some researchers
suggest using symbolic techniques by themselves, and others suggest
using a hybrid of symbolic techniques and deep learning. Gary Marcus
has been a long-time proponent of the hybrid approach. In 1992, he
and Steven Pinker showed that the best model of children's learning
of irregular verbs uses a hybrid approach involving symbolic rules for
regular verbs and a neural network–like learning system for irregular
verbs. He has since argued long and hard that deep learning by itself
cannot result in AGI systems.[12] In his book *Rebooting AI*,[13] Marcus and
his coauthor, NYU professor Ernest Davis, propose a hybrid model
that combines symbolic reasoning with deep learning. Their specific
recipe sounds reasonable, but it represents a massive, long-term effort
with many potential pitfalls and dead ends.

My biggest concern about this approach is that progress in understanding how people represent commonsense knowledge has been
glacial. Forty years ago, we had a long debate about the nature of the
internal representations people use to answer questions like "What
shape is a German Shepherd's ears?" We still do not know the answer,
even though some of the top people in the fields of AI and cognitive
science took part in the debate. Answering a question about the shape
of a dog's ears is just a drop of water in an ocean of representational
schemes and reasoning processes. Moreover, we do not even know
whether these representational schemes and reasoning processes are

innate or learned. Innateness has been an ongoing topic of academic debate for over fifty years, with no resolution in sight.

How long will it be before we know enough about how people think to make real progress toward AGI? At the current rate of progress, it appears we will need hundreds—maybe thousands—of years, and it may never happen.

DEEP LEARNING

Some researchers argue that while supervised and reinforcement learning per se are dead ends for building AGI systems, deep learning may yet take us to the promised land. OpenAI is a nonprofit that received well over a billion dollars in investment capital. OpenAI's charter is to build AGI systems safely. Accordingly, OpenAI has three departments, only one of which is trying to develop AGI technology. The other two departments focus on AI safety and policy.

Cofounder and CTO Greg Brockman argues that the way forward is to keep exploring deep learning systems that have three properties: generality, competence, and scalability. *Generality* refers to finding architectural components that researchers can use for many different applications. An example is *gradient descent*, an algorithm that is used in most deep learning networks to find the optimal values of weights. *Competence* refers to proven real-world capabilities, such as the deep learning networks that obsoleted forty years of computer vision research. *Scalability* refers to deep learning networks in which performance improves as the network becomes larger.

GPT-2 is a great example of scalability. It is ten times larger than the GPT system of a year prior, and researchers trained it on ten times the amount of data. GPT-2 showed a surprising ability to generate human-sounding—if not always coherent—text. OpenAI sees this as an emergent capability that resulted solely from making the network bigger. Brockman argues that by continuing deep learning research and then scaling systems that meet his three requirements, we will see more emergent capabilities, and these will eventually include commonsense reasoning and AGI.[14]

GPT-2 certainly demonstrated a massive ability to extract statistical regularities of its training text and perhaps the ability to memorize small segments of the text. However, it did not learn facts about the world or gain any ability to reason based on this world knowledge. At this stage of the game, I see absolutely no evidence that learning world knowledge and reasoning skills will emerge from this approach, and I see no logical rationale for believing it will happen. OpenAI has since released GPT-3, which is one hundred times larger than GPT-2. However, like GPT-2, it generates text with mostly incorrect facts.[15] Even at one hundred times the size of its predecessor, it still is not acquiring world knowledge.

Deep learning pioneer Yoshua Bengio agrees with Tenenbaum and Marcus that compositional learning is critical. However, he argues that symbolic techniques are not necessary.[16] Bengio has proposed novel deep learning architectures designed to break deep learning out of its narrow AI box. One goal is to learn higher-level building blocks that can help AI systems learn compositionally.[17] These are interesting ideas for researchers to explore, but they are in the preliminary stages.[18] Here again, the idea that these systems will magically learn world knowledge and reasoning is a leap of faith.

Yann LeCun also agrees that the ability to learn facts about the world and commonsense reasoning rules is a necessary step on the road to AGI. He has stated repeatedly that self-supervised learning is the way forward toward AGI.[19] Recall that, while supervised learning requires large training tables of labeled data, self-supervised learning does not require humans to label data. Language models like GPT-2 are an example of self-supervised learning. By predicting the next word in a text, the text provides its own supervision, and this makes it possible to train massive networks on massive training sets. However, the goal of self-supervised learning for LeCun is not learning the task itself. Instead, he argues, if the task is complex enough, the self-supervised learning network will be forced to acquire world knowledge and reasoning rules. However, GPT-2 does not appear to have learned any world knowledge or reasoning rules. GPT-3 is a hundred times bigger, and it has certainly learned better statistics and probably memorized more text. However, it has not gained the ability to acquire world knowledge or reasoning rules.

A related approach is to create tests that require commonsense knowledge and reasoning. If an AI system can learn to pass these tests, then it must have those capabilities. One problem with this approach is that it is difficult, if not impossible, to develop a test that definitively requires commonsense knowledge and reasoning. Most of the tests that were initially thought to require meeting this standard were later shown to be susceptible to simple statistical approaches. Here again, the approach is to rely on deep learning systems magically acquiring world knowledge and reasoning skills. The idea that we can simply turn loose a deep learning algorithm on a training table and expect it to somehow learn commonsense knowledge and reasoning is wishful thinking.

MODELING THE HUMAN BRAIN

Another proposed approach to AGI is to understand the architecture of the physical human brain and model AI systems after it. After decades of research, we know only some very basic facts about how the physical brain processes information. For example, we know that the cortex statically and dynamically stores learned knowledge, the basal ganglia processes goals and subgoals and learns to select information by reinforcement learning, and the limbic brain structures interface the brain to the body and generate motivations, emotions, and the value of things.

There is also a great deal of research underway to understand the human brain. The Human Brain Project is a massive, ten-year project that started in 2013 and is funded by the European Union.[20] It employs over five hundred scientists at more than one hundred European universities but has yet to solve the mysteries of the human mind. However, we are still in the early stages of understanding the whole brain. The human brain has 100 billion neurons and 1,000 trillion synapses. The most detailed map of a brain contains 31,000 neurons (for a rat brain).[21]

Understanding the human brain and modeling it in AI systems is a plausible approach to AGI. However, as compelling an idea as this is, no one has any concrete ideas about how to do this. We have no idea what algorithm is used to drive the synaptic changes in the brain during the learning process.

The idea of modeling the neurons in the brain has been in the proposal stage for over forty years. It has yet to gain any real traction partly because of the extremely slow progress in understanding the human brain and partly because we have no concrete method for modeling what we know about the human brain in AI programs. Here again, we are near the starting gate and have no evidence that this approach will succeed.

THE SINGULARITY

Ray Kurzweil, a technology futurist, has long argued that AGI will occur as a by-product of the trend toward bigger and faster computers. He popularized the idea of the *singularity*, which is the point in time that computers are smart enough to improve their own programming. Once that happens, his theory states, their intelligence will grow exponentially fast, and they will quickly attain a superhuman level of intelligence. Kurzweil predicted that the singularity would occur around 2045.

The human brain has about 86 billion neurons. Each neuron has connections to hundreds or thousands of other neurons. There may be as many as a quadrillion connections in the human brain. A computer that can simulate this number of connections and has enough processing power to compute results on these many connections may well be available by 2030. It is certainly possible that new technology, such as quantum computing, will move that date forward. The question is whether this inevitable increase in processing speed and power will lead to AGI.

The first electronic computer, the ENIAC, was created in 1945, weighed 30 tons, could execute a little over 350 computer instructions per second, and occupied 1,800 square feet of space.[22] In the 1970s, IBM mainframes could execute 750,000 instructions per second. Intel released its Stratix 10 chip in 2018. This chip is smaller than a hand and can execute 10 trillion instructions per second. The speed of today's computers is already beyond belief, and computers will continue to get faster at a rapid pace.

That said, it is hard to imagine how processing power by itself can create AGI. If I turn on a computer from the 1970s with no programs loaded, turn on one of today's computers with no programs loaded, or turn on a computer fifty years from now with no programs loaded, none of these computers will be capable of doing anything at all. If I load a word processing program on each of these computers, then each of them will be limited to performing word processing. Newer, more modern computers will be able to respond faster and process bigger documents, but they will still only be capable of word processing. The same will be true for the computers of the future.

Probably the most salient argument against the idea of computer power by itself as the road to AGI is the *fast-thinking dog analogy*.[23] If we were to find a way to increase the speed of a dog's brain, no matter how fast it gets, it would never beat a human at chess unless we also found a way to *reprogram* the dog's brain so that it can understand chess. The same is true of computers. Faster computers by themselves will not result in AGI. As Steven Pinker said, "Sheer processing power is not a pixie dust that magically solves all your problems."[24] In the unlikely event that AGI ever becomes possible, the programming and learning algorithms will likely be complex enough to require extremely powerful computers. However, those programming and learning algorithms will be necessary; speed and power will not be sufficient.

WILL WE ACHIEVE AGI?

Researchers have a long history of being overly optimistic about the prospects for AGI. In 1956, John McCarthy and Marvin Minsky, two of the best-known figures in the history of AI, proposed a ten-person, two-month study at Dartmouth College in Hanover, New Hampshire.[25] Their proposal included this paragraph:

> The study is to proceed on the basis of the conjecture that every aspect of learning or any other feature of intelligence can in principle be so precisely described that a machine can be made to simulate it. An attempt will be made to find

how to make machines use language, form abstractions and concepts, solve kinds of problems now reserved for humans, and improve themselves. We think that a significant advance can be made in one or more of these problems if a carefully selected group of scientists work on it together for a summer.

In 1967, Marvin Minsky said, "Within a generation, I am convinced, few compartments of intellect will remain outside the machine's realm. The problem of creating 'artificial intelligence' will be substantially solved."[26]

Over the years, there have been many surveys of AI researchers asking about the timeline for AGI. When researchers are flat out asked to give their best estimate of when AGI will appear, the results have been remarkably consistent. Over half of the sixty-seven AI researchers polled in a 1971 study said we would see AGI in twenty to fifty years.[27] These earlier predictions will be proven wrong in 2021. In a survey of ninety-five AI timeline predictions between 1950 and 2012, the most common projected timeline for AGI was fifteen to twenty-five years.[28] A 2018 survey found that 50 percent of researchers believed there was a chance we would see AGI come to pass in the next forty-five years.[29]

Optimism was extremely high in the first rise of AI and very low during the first AI winter. Optimism was extremely high again in the late 1970s and early 1980s during the second rise of AI. By the end of the 1980s, optimism about AGI was again extremely low. Now, as I write this, we are on the third rise of AI, and optimism is high once again. However, the optimism is due to narrow AI. Will this time be different? Probably. Optimism will likely stay high because there are so many real-world applications for today's narrow AI technology. Some people would argue that image recognition alone is changing our world by enabling positive innovations such as self-driving cars, as well as scary innovations such as surveillance. This optimism for narrow AI has naturally, but incorrectly, spilled over to optimism about prospects for AGI. As Oren Etzioni, the CEO of the Allen Institute for AI, said, "It reminds me of the metaphor of a kid who climbs up to the top of the tree and points at the moon, saying, 'I'm on my way to the moon.'"[30]

I cannot say for sure that we will never develop AGI. What I can say is that we are only at the starting gate. Again.

16

AI WILL NOT TAKE OVER THE WORLD— UNLESS WE LET IT

I n the movie *Transcendence*, Johnny Depp plays a University of California at Berkeley AI professor who is shot by anti-AI activists worried about what will happen if scientists succeed in creating AGI systems. I hope I have convinced you by now that AGI is not imminent and that it is about as likely to occur in our lifetimes as time travel or warp speed. There will be no evil robot overlords taking over the world.

That said, narrow AI has such a significant impact that some people would say it is taking over the world. But what they really mean is that AI is taking over just like computers have taken over the world, and the internet has taken over the world, and smartphones have taken over the world, and before that cars, televisions, electricity, and many other technologies took over the world too. So, if you want to argue that AI is one of the many technologies that have taken over the world, I will not disagree.

One difficulty in assessing the impact of AI and determining how to regulate it is that *AI* is an umbrella term with many different meanings.[1] From 1950 to the late 1980s, when most people talked about AI, they were referring to AGI. Techniques such as linear and logistic regression, clustering, and factor analysis had yet to be subsumed by AI, and the researchers still referred to them as *statistics*. Neural networks had been invented but had not solved any significant engineering problems and had yet to get traction. By 1990, most of the work on AGI had stopped, because the effort required to hand engineer all the knowledge of the world posed an impossible barrier. However, interest in AGI and fear of AGI is now building again because of the success of narrow AI, even though AGI cannot evolve from narrow AI.

Not only does the umbrella term *AI* include both AGI and narrow AI, but *narrow AI* is itself an umbrella term as well. It is not simply deep learning plus natural language processing, even though perhaps it should be, since those are the key technologies underpinning all the impressive recent accomplishments of AI. Narrow AI encompasses all machine learning, which includes a great deal of plain old boring statistics. Issues of fairness and discrimination that people attribute to AI are really those issues with statistics (enhanced by computational methods) applied to the massive amounts of data that are now available because of the pervasiveness of the internet.

Because AI is such an umbrella term, it would be a mistake to treat all the different social issues attributed to AI in a unitary fashion. If governments try to boil the ocean by attempting to regulate all these different categories of issues under one set of regulations, it will hamper effective regulation, and we may end up with unnecessary regulations that stifle progress. It might even lead to a ban on AI research.

Aside from AGI being an improbable occurrence, a century's worth of science fiction writers have shown us that AGI regulation would be a difficult, if not impossible, task. Contemporary researchers writing on this topic have many different ideas of how an AGI future would unfold. However, the common thread is that AGI robots would be able to think and reason. As a result, regulation would need to target this general capability rather than narrow AI's specific capabilities, such as the ability to drive a car. Science fiction author Isaac Asimov exemplified this type of general regulation with his three laws of robotics.[2] Fortunately, we do not need to regulate AGI, because it does not exist and most likely never will.

Creating effective regulations for narrow AI is a far greater imperative. Narrow AI issues are complex and multilayered and impact several areas of our lives. In contrast to AGI, which would require a generic set of regulations, we need to tackle AI issues with targeted regulations and policies. If we do so, we will reap the many positive benefits of narrow AI and minimize the negative impacts. Narrow AI systems will not take over the world unless we let them. AGI systems will not take over the world period. And there is no reason to shoot Johnny Depp.

ACKNOWLEDGMENTS

There are many people I would like to thank for contributing to this project.

First, thanks to Roger Schank, who got me into AI and who convinced me to leave academia. I started thinking about writing the book after a dinner conversation with Roger in New York City, during which we talked about the excessive hype around AI and how different AI is today than it was in the 1980s.

Several colleagues and friends provided excellent feedback on the manuscript, including Doug Lyon, Alan Reznik, Chris Dressler, Chris McLeod, Bruce Gallagher, Gary Olson, Les Trachtman, Laura Ross, Tom Land, and Wayne Larrison. I also received great feedback from family members Becky Shwartz, Aly and Kevin Turner, and Mike Renzi. My daughters Becky and Aly independently took me to task for the level of technical detail in my earlier drafts, which caused me to rewrite the book and put much of that technical detail on my website.

I'd like to thank my book coach, Robin Colucci, and my development editor, Nathan True, who each did a wonderful job helping me write and structure the book. I would also like to thank the rest of the team at Greenleaf, including project manager Jen Glynn, lead editors

Amanda Hughes and Erin Brown, copy editor Claudia Volkman, proofreader Jeffrey Curry, and cover and layout designer Cameron Stein. Also, thanks to Damien Sterling who did a great job on my website. And Rivka Hodgkinson got me started on social media. I enjoyed working with all of you.

Most important, I'm grateful to my wife, Elaine, for her love and support and for patiently putting up with my work habits, and to my daughters, Becky, Aly, and Carly, my son-in-law, Kevin, and my grandsons, Josh and Jack, for their love and inspiration.

ENDNOTES

Preface

1   Natural languages are the languages that people speak, and the term is intended to contrast those languages with computer programming languages.

Chapter 1

1   D. A. Ferrucci (2012). Introduction to "This is Watson." In *IBM Journal of Research and Development* (Vol. 56, Issues 3–4, pp. 1:1-1:15). doi.org/10.1147/JRD.2012.2184356.

2   web.archive.org/web/20170809113829/www.ibm.com/watson/.

3   www.theguardian.com/technology/2014/oct/27/elon-musk-artificial-intelligence-ai-biggest-existential-threat.

4   www.theverge.com/2017/7/17/15980954/elon-musk-ai-regulation-existential-threat.

5   N. Bostrom, *Superintelligence: Paths, Dangers, Strategies* (Oxford: OUP Oxford, 2014).

6   See www.amazon.com/Artificial-General-Intelligence-Cognitive-Technologies/dp/354023733X/ref=sr_1_3?keywords=artificial+general+intelligence&qid=1578398066&sr=8-3 for a more in-depth definition of and explanation of AGI, and see content.sciendo.com/view/journals/jagi/10/2/article-p1.xml for an explanation of why a precise definition is so difficult. Another term for AGI is **human level AI,** which is defined as "one that can carry out most human professions at least as well as a typical human." Some prognosticators, including Nick Bostrom, also refer to **superintelligence,** which is a level of intelligence that exceeds AGI/HLAI (N. Bostrom, *Superintelligence: Paths, Dangers, Strategies.*
Oxford: Oxford University Press, 2014). Stewart Russell, who wrote one of the most prominent AI textbooks, presents several arguments for the position that, once AGI is achieved, then superintelligence will follow (S. Russell, *Human Compatible: Artificial Intelligence and the Problem of Control.* New York: Viking Press, 2019). One reason is because an AGI machine could read 150 million books in a few hours. However, since this book explains why AGI/HLAI is extremely unlikely to occur, there will be no further discussion of superintelligence in this book.

7   Defining what constitutes a single "task" can be difficult. There is considerable research on multitask learning that I argue still fits the definition of narrow AI. See www.AIPerspectives.com/tl for a discussion of this and related research topics.

8   In 1979, University of Michigan professor Ben Kuipers defined commonsense knowledge as "knowledge about the structure of the external world that is acquired and applied without concentrated effort by any normal human that allows him or her to meet the everyday demands of the physical, spatial, temporal and social environment with a reasonable degree of success." B. J. Kuipers, *On Representing Commonsense Knowledge.* In N. V. Findler (Ed.), *Associative Networks: The Representation and Use of Knowledge by Computers* (New York: Academic Press, 1979).

9   A. Koestler, *Ghost in the Machine* (New York: Random House, 1982).

10   www.analyticsinsight.net/autonomous-ai-feared-yes-say-60-brits-survey/.

Chapter 2

1   U. Farooq, "The second drone age: How Turkey defied the U.S. and became a killer drone power," *The Intercept,* May 14, 2019. theintercept.com/2019/05/14/turkey-second-drone-age/.

2   STM. KARGU - Autonomous Tactical Multi-Rotor Attack UAV. (Apr. 28, 2018). Accessed: March 18, 2020 [online video]. Available: www.youtube.com/watch?time_continue=1&v=Oqv9yaPLhEk.

3   M. Weisgerber, "US is moving too slowly to harness drones and AI, former SOCOM commander says," *Defense One,* November 14, 2019. www.defenseone.com/technology/2019/11/us-moving-too-slowly-harness-drones-and-ai-former-socom-commander-says/161306/?oref=d-channelriver.

4   J. Keller, "Should some smart munitions be classified as unmanned aerial vehicles (UAVs)?" *Military & Aerospace Electronics,* March 24, 2015. www.military aerospace.com/computers/article/16713739/should-some-smart-munitions-be-classified-as-unmanned-aerial-vehicles-uavs.

5   Missile Defense Project, "Terminal High Altitude Area Defense (THAAD)," *Missile Threat, Center for Strategic and International Studies,* June 14, 2018. missilethreat.csis.org/system/thaad/;

      Missile Defense Project, "Aegis Ballistic Missile Defense," *Missile Threat, Center for Strategic and International Studies,* June 14, 2018. missilethreat.csis.org/system/aegis/.

6   L. Pascu, "Turkey adds autonomous facial recognition kamikaze drones to military portfolio," *Biometric Update,* November 11, 2019. www.biometricupdate.com/201911/turkey-adds-autonomous-facial-recognition-kamikaze-drones-to-military-portfolio.

7   Future of Life Institute, "Autonomous weapons: An open letter from AI & robotics researchers," July 28, 2015. futureoflife.org/open-letter-autonomous-weapons/?cn-reloaded=1.

8   www.youtube.com/watch?v=9CO6M2HsoIA.

9   P. Scharre, *Army of None: Autonomous Weapons and the Future of War*, 1st ed. (New York: W. W. Norton & Company, 2019). See also P. Scharre, *Autonomous Weapons and Operational Risk* (Washington, DC: Center for a New American Security, 2016). s3.amazonaws.com/files.cnas.org/documents/CNAS_Autonomous-weapons-operational-risk.pdf?mtime=20160906080515.

10 beta.sam.gov/opp/121247da9c19467a8446f9e1258f9bb0/view?keywords=skyborg&sort=-modifiedDate&index=opp&is_active=true&page=1.

11 Congressional Research Service, "Artificial intelligence and national security," April 26, 2018. www.everycrsreport.com/files/20180426_R45178_27fad5077138df0a45f2bf5dc00f4bb61c9a4e88.pdf.

12 P. Tucker, "SecDef: China is exporting killer robots to the Mideast," *Defense One*, November 5, 2019. www.defenseone.com/technology/2019/11/secdef-china-exporting-killer-robots-mideast/161100/.

13 M. Weisgerber, "The increasingly automated hunt for mobile missile launchers," *Defense One*, April 28, 2016. www.defenseone.com/technology/2016/04/increasingly-automated-hunt-mobile-missile-launchers/127864/.

14 J. Harper, "Artificial intelligence to sort through ISR data glut," *National Defense*, January 16, 2018. www.nationaldefensemagazine.org/articles/2018/1/16/artificial-intelligence-to--sort-through-isr-data-glut.

15 M. Weisgerber, "The Pentagon's new algorithmic warfare cell gets its first mission: Hunt ISIS," *Defense One*, May 14, 2017. www.defenseone.com/technology/2017/05/pentagons-new-algorithmic-warfare-cell-gets-its-first-mission-hunt-isis/137833/.

16 www.defenseone.com/technology/2019/10/us-army-wants-reinvent-tank-warfare-ai/160720/?oref=d-channelriver.

17 P. Tucker, "The Pentagon's AI ethics draft is actually pretty good," *Defense One*, October 31, 2019. www.defenseone.com/technology/2019/10/pentagons-ai-ethics-draft-actually-pretty-good/161005/.

18 Russian News Agency, "Russia's security chief calls for regulating use of new technologies in military sphere," April 24, 2019. tass.com/defense/1055346.

19 See this article for an example of how Bosch has developed a system to prevent adversarial attacks on car cameras. It uses a second camera that has a different angle to confirm the first camera: J. Rundle and J. McCormick, "Bosch deploys AI to prevent attacks on cars' electronic systems," *Wall Street Journal*, January 6, 2020. www.wsj.com/articles/bosch-deploys-ai-to-prevent-attacks-on-cars-electronic-systems-11578306600?mod=searchresults&page=2&pos=6.

20 I. Rouf et al., "Security and privacy vulnerabilities of in-car wireless networks: A tire pressure monitoring system case study," in *Proceedings of the 19th USENIX Security Symposium*, 2010. See this Intel paper for a discussion of other car vulnerabilities: M. Zhao, "Advanced driver assistant system: Threats, requirements and security solutions," Intel Labs, White Paper, 2016 [online]. Available: www.semagarage.com/assets/pdf/advanced-driver-assistant-system-paper.pdf.

21   M. Weisgerber, "New tech aims to tell pilots when their plane has been hacked," *Defense One*, October 4, 2019. www.defenseone.com/business/2019/10/new-app-tells-pilots-when-their-plane-has-been-hacked/160378/?oref=d-channelriver.

22   For more information on adversarial attacks on deep learning systems, see www.AIPerspectives.com/aa.

23   D. Goodman, H. Xin, W. Yang, X. Junfeng, and Z. Huan, "Advbox: A toolbox to generate adversarial examples that fool neural networks," *AdvBox, arXiv Preprint arXiv:2001.05574v*, arxiv.org/pdf/2001.05574.pdf.

24   C. Ross and I. Swetlitz, "IBM's Watson supercomputer recommended 'unsafe and incorrect' cancer treatments, internal documents show," *Stat+*, July 25, 2018. www.statnews.com/wp-content/uploads/2018/09/IBMs-Watson-recommended-unsafe-and-incorrect-cancer-treatments-STAT.pdf.

25   P. G. Neumann, "Forum risks to the public in computers and related systems," *The Risks Digest*, vol. 8, no. 75, 1989.

26   Center for Homeland Defense and Security (1979). "Report of the President's Commission on the Accident at Three Mile Island The Need for Change: The Legacy of TMI." www.hsdl.org/?abstract&did=769775.

27   U.S.-Canada Power System Outage Task Force, "Final Report on the August 14, 2003 Blackout in the United States and Canada: Causes and Recommendations," April 2004. www.energy.gov/sites/prod/files/oeprod/DocumentsandMedia/BlackoutFinal-Web.pdf.

28   Commodity Futures Trading Commission and U.S. Securities and Exchange Commission, "Findings Regarding the Market Events of May 6, 2010," Rep. Staff. *CFTC SEC to Jt. Advis. Comm. Emerg. Regul. Issues,* 2010.

29   S. Gandel, "Why Knight lost $440 million in 45 minutes," *Fortune,* August 3, 2012. fortune.com/2012/08/02/why-knight-lost-440-million-in-45-minutes/.

30   K. German, "Ethiopia blames 737 Max design in interim crash report," *CNet,* February 10, 2020. www.cnet.com/news/boeings-737-max-8-all-about-the-aircraft-flight-ban-and-investigations/.

31   There are two basic categories of issues that can occur with machine learning systems known as the inner and outer alignment problems. For more information, see E. Hubinger, C. Van Merwijk, V. Mikulik, J. Skalse, and S. Garrabrant (2019). *Risks from Learned Optimization in Advanced Machine Learning Systems. arXiv: 1906.01820v2*: arxiv.org/pdf/1906.01820.pdf.

32   C. Murphy, G. E. Kaiser, and M. Arias (2006). *A Framework for Quality Assurance of Machine Learning Applications.* Columbia University Computer Science Technical Reports, CUCS-034-06, 2011. doi.org/10.7916/D8MP5B4B.

33   B. M. Lake, T. D. Ullman, J. B. Tenenbaum, and S. J. Gershman (2017). "Building machines that learn and think like people." *Behavioral and Brain Sciences, 40.* doi.org/10.1017/S0140525X16001837.

34   See this *Scientific American* article about concerns that rushing AI technology to market could negatively impact patients: L. Szabo, "Artificial intelligence is rushing into

patient care—and could raise risks," *Scientific American,* December 24, 2019. www.scientificamerican.com/article/artificial-intelligence-is-rushing-into-patient-care-and-could-raise-risks/.

35 www.fda.gov/medical-devices/software-medical-device-samd/artificial-intelligence-and-machine-learning-software-medical-device.

36 This behavior is apparently common: forums.tesla.com/forum/forums/sudden-and-erratic-braking-autopilot.

37 Excerpted from www.tesla.com/support/autopilot in March 2020.

38 B. Vlasic and N. E. Boudette, "Self-driving Tesla was involved in fatal crash, U.S. says," *New York Times*, June 30, 2016. www.nytimes.com/2016/07/01/business/self-driving-tesla-fatal-crash-investigation.html. See also M. R. Dickey, "Tesla model X sped up in autopilot mode seconds before fatal crash, according to NTSB," *TechCrunch*, June 8, 2018. techcrunch.com/2018/06/07/tesla-model-x-sped-up-in-autopilot-mode-seconds-before-fatal-crash-according-to-ntsb/ for a scary 2018 fatality report.

39 J. Kaplan, R. Glon, S. Edelstein, and L. Chang, "Deadly Uber crash was 'entirely avoidable' had the driver not been watching Hulu" *Digital Trends*, June 22, 2018. www.digitaltrends.com/cars/self-driving-uber-crash-arizona/.

40 S. Edelstein, "Uber self-driving cars were reportedly in 37 crashes before fatal incident," *Digital Trends*, November 7, 2019. www.digitaltrends.com/cars/uber-self-driving-cars-were-in-37-crashes-before-fatal-incident-report-says/.

41 M. McFarland, "Uber death leaves questions about self-driving car liability unanswered," *CNN Business*, March 8, 2019. edition.cnn.com/2019/03/08/tech/uber-arizona-death-criminal/index.html. It is possible, however, that the driver will face criminal charges.

42 R. Randazzo, "Uber crash death in Tempe: A closer look," *AZCentral,* March 17, 2019. www.azcentral.com/story/news/local/tempe/2019/03/17/uber-crash-death-who-blame-tempe-arizona-rafaela-vasquez-elaine-herzberg/3157481002/.

43 K. -F. Lee, *AI Superpowers: China, Silicon Valley, and the New World Order,* 1st ed. (Boston: Houghton Mifflin Harcourt, 2018).

44 D. Shepardson, "House panel to hold hearing on future of self-driving cars," *Reuters,* February 8, 2020. www.reuters.com/article/us-autos-autonomous-congress/house-panel-to-hold-hearing-on-future-of-self-driving-cars-idUSKBN2012K2.

45 www.ntsb.gov/news/press-releases/Pages/NR20200225.aspx.

46 www.iihs.org/news/detail/automated-systems-need-stronger-safeguards-to-keep-drivers-focused-on-the-road.

47 saferoads.org/wp-content/uploads/2020/03/AV-Crash-List-with-Photos-February-2020.pdf.

48 https://flsenate.gov/Laws/Statutes/2018/0316.085.

49 A. Davies, "Self-driving cars flock to Arizona, land of good weather and no rules," *Wired,* August 10, 2017. www.wired.com/story/mobileye-self-driving-cars-arizona/.

50 KPMG International, "2019 Autonomous Vehicles Readiness Index," 2019. assets.kpmg/content/dam/kpmg/xx/pdf/2019/02/2019-autonomous-vehicles-readiness-index.pdf.

51   www.daimler.com/documents/innovation/other/safety-first-for-automated-driving.pdf.

52   This moral dilemma is known as the Trolley Problem. Several research studies have shown that many people would consider it morally acceptable to redirect a runaway trolley away from five victims and toward a single victim. However, it would not be morally acceptable to push a single person in front of a trolley to stop it from hitting five people: F. Cushman and L. Young, "The psychology of dilemmas and the philosophy of morality," *Ethical Theory Moral Practice*, vol. 12, pp. 9–24, 2009, doi: 10.1007/s10677-008-9145-3.

MIT's Media Lab did a large-scale, 233-country survey on who should be spared (pets versus humans, staying on course versus swerving, passengers versus pedestrians, more versus fewer lives, men versus women, pedestrians crossing legally versus jaywalkers, the fit versus the less fit, and higher versus lower social status). They found several interesting regional differences: E. Awad, S. Dsouza, R. Kim, J. Schulz, J. Henrich, A. Shariff, J. F. Bonnefon, and I. Rahwan (2018). "The Moral Machine experiment." *Nature*, 563(7729), 59–64. doi.org/10.1038/s41586-018-0637-6.

Chapter 3

1   Synced. (2019). "NeurIPS 2019 | The Numbers." Retrieved from medium.com/syncedreview/neurips-2019-the-numbers-c1808fba9480.

2   B. F. Green, A. K. Wolf, C. Chomsky, and K. Laughery (1961). "BASEBALL: AN AUTOMATIC QUESTION-ANSWERER." In *Paper presented at the May 9-11, 1961, western joint IRE-AIEE-ACM computer conference*. Paper presented at the May 9-11, 1961, western joint IRE-AIEE-ACM computer conference.

3   D. G. Bobrow (1964). *Natural Language Input for a Computer Problem Solving System*. PhD dissertation, MIT.

4   H. A. Simon (1965). *The shape of automation for men and management*, (1st ed.). Harper & Row.

5   Y. Bar-Hillel (1960). "The Present Status of Automatic Translation of Languages." *Advances in Computers*. doi.org/10.1016/S0065-2458(08)60607-5.

6   ALPAC. (1966). *Language and Machines: Computers in Translation and Linguistics*. Washington D.C., Publication 1416, National Academy of Sciences.

7   J. Lighthill (1973). *Artificial Intelligence: A General Survey*. Science Research Council. www.chilton-computing.org.uk/inf/literature/reports/lighthill_report/p001.htm.

8   F. Rosenblatt (n.d.). "The Perception: A Probalistic Model For Information Storage and Organization in the Brain." 1. In *Psychological Review* (Vol. 65, Issue 6). In 1951, prior to Rosenblatt's book, Marvin Minsky and Dean Edmonds created what many people consider to be the first neural network at Harvard University. It had three thousand vacuum tubes and simulated a rat searching a maze for food. Their work was based on this 1943 paper that characterized the human brain as a neural network: W. S. McCulloch and W. Pitts (1943). "A logical calculus of the ideas immanent in nervous activity." *The Bulletin of Mathematical Biophysics*, 5(4), 115–133. doi.org/10.1007/BF02478259.

9 "NEW NAVY DEVICE LEARNS BY DOING; Psychologist Shows Embryo of Computer Designed to Read and Grow Wiser." *New York Times*, 1958; www.nytimes.com/1958/07/08/archives/new-navy-device-learns-by-doing-psychologist-shows-embryo-of.html.

10 M. Minsky and S. Papert (1969). *Perceptrons: An Introduction to Computational Geometry*. MIT Press. archive.org/details/Perceptrons/page/n1/mode/2up.

11 For details about how these systems worked, see www.AIPerspectives.com/cd.

12 Dejong, 1977, 1979; Schank et al., 1980; G. DeJong (1979). "Prediction and substantiation: A new approach to natural language processing." *Cognitive Science*. doi.org/10.1016/S0364-0213(79)80009-9.

13 R. C. Schank and C. K. Riesbeck (1981). "Inside Computer Understanding: Five Programs Plus Miniatures." In "Inside Computer Understanding" (1st ed.). Psychology Press. doi.org/10.2307/414141. See also www.AIPerspectives.com/cd for more details.

14 B. G. Buchanan and E. H. Shortliffe (1984). *Rule-Based Expert Systems: MYCIN*. Reading, MA: Addison Wesley. people.dbmi.columbia.edu/~ehs7001/Buchanan-Shortliffe-1984/MYCIN Book.htm.

15 M. Stefik (1985). "Strategic computing at DARPA: Overview and assessment." *Communications of the ACM*, 28(7), 690–704. https://doi.org/10.1145/3894.3896.

16 S. Russell (2019). *Human compatible: Artificial intelligence and the problem of control*. Viking.

17 S. Baker (2011). *Final Jeopardy: The Story of Watson, the Computer That Will Transform Our World*. Mariner Books.

18 S. Pham (2017). "China wants to build a $150 billion AI industry." *CNN Business*, money.cnn.com/2017/07/21/technology/china-artificial-intelligence-future/index.html?iid=EL.

19 R. Gigova (2017). "Who Putin thinks will rule the world," *CNN*, edition.cnn.com/2017/09/01/world/putin-artificial-intelligence-will-rule-world/index.html.

20 P. Olson (2019). "Nearly Half Of All 'AI Startups' Are Cashing In On Hype." *Forbes*, www.forbes.com/sites/parmyolson/2019/03/04/nearly-half-of-all-ai-startups-are-cashing-in-on-hype/#14f4709fd022.

21 I. Bogost (2017). "'Artificial Intelligence' Has Become Meaningless" *The Atlantic*, www.theatlantic.com/technology/archive/2017/03/what-is-artificial-intelligence/518547/.

22 J. Dean, D. Patterson, and C. Young (2018). "A New Golden Age in Computer Architecture: Empowering the Machine-Learning Revolution." *IEEE Micro*, 38(2), 21–29. doi.org/10.1109/MM.2018.112130030.

23 Synced. (2019). "NeurIPS 2019 | The Numbers." Retrieved from medium.com/syncedreview/neurips-2019-the-numbers-c1808fba9480.

24 A. Cuthbertson (2018). "TECH & SCIENCE." *Newsweek*, www.newsweek.com/robots-can-now-read-better-humans-putting-millions-jobs-risk-781393.

Chapter 4

1   J. Manyika et al., "Jobs lost, jobs gained: What the future of work will mean for jobs, skills, and wages," *McKinsey & Company,* November 2017. www.mckinsey.com/featured-insights/future-of-work/jobs-lost-jobs-gained-what-the-future-of-work-will-mean-for-jobs-skills-and-wages.

2   W. Buffett, "Warren Buffett shares the secrets to wealth in America," *Time,* January 4, 2018. time.com/5087360/warren-buffett-shares-the-secrets-to-wealth-in-america/.

3   R. Kurzweil, "Future of Intelligence," *YouTube Video:* www.youtube.com/watch?v=9Z06rY3uvGY&index=3&list=PLrAXtmErZgOdP_8GztsuKi9nr raNbKKp4.

4   A 2015 Ball State study found that 87.8 percent of manufacturing job losses between 2000 and 2010 were due to productivity gains resulting from robotics and other forms of manufacturing automation: S. Devaraj and M. J. Hicks, "The myth and reality of manufacturing in America," *Ball State University, Center for Business Economic Research,* June 2015.

5   There were 9,302 retail store closings in 2019, a 59 percent jump from 2018, compared to 4,392 openings according to CNN: N. Meyersohn, "More than 9,300 stores closed in 2019," *CNN Business,* December 19, 2019. edition.cnn.com/2019/12/19/business/2019-store-closings-payless-gymboree/index.html. Some of these closings can be attributed to Amazon, but others are due to noncompetitive business models against other physical retailers.

6   It's not just human jobs. The equine population in the US declined from 21 million horses in 1900 to 3 million in 1960: E. R. Kilby, "The Demographics of the U.S. Equine Population," in *The State of the Animals IV: 2007,* 1st ed., D. J. Salem and A. N. Rowan, Eds. (Washington, DC: Humane Society Press, 2007) 175–205.

7   J. Liang, B. Ramanauskas, and A. Kurenkov, "Job loss due to AI—How bad is it going to be?" *Skynet Today,* February 4, 2019. www.skynettoday.com/editorials/ai-automation-job-loss.

8   Deloitte LLP, "From brawn to brains: The impact of technology on jobs in the UK," 2015. www2.deloitte.com/uk/en/pages/growth/articles/from-brawn-to-brains--the-impact-of-technology-on-jobs-in-the-u.html.

9   P. Scharre, "Killer apps: The real dangers of an AI arms race," *Foreign Affairs,* May/June 2019. www.foreignaffairs.com/articles/2019-04-16/killer-apps.

10   J. Murawski, "AI adoption fuels demand for data-labeling services," *WSJ,* July 29, 2019. www.wsj.com/articles/ai-adoption-fuels-demand-for-data-labeling-services-11564392602.

11   R. Perrault et al., "The AI index 2019 annual report," AI Index Steering Committee, Human-Centered AI Institute, Stanford University, Stanford, CA, December 2019. [Online]. Available: hai.stanford.edu/sites/g/files/sbiybj10986/f/ai_index_2019_report.pdf.

12   According to the Bureau of Labor Statistics, in 2019 there were 1.7 million truck drivers.

13   This is particularly true for truck drivers, where technology will have to replace the months of training truck drivers receive before they are allowed on the road.

14   M. Miller, "AI's implications for productivity, wages, and employment," *PC Mag*, November 21, 2017. sea.pcmag.com/feature/18333/ais-implications-for-productivity-wages-and-employment.

15   Interview with James Manyika in M. Ford (2018). *Architects of Intelligence: The truth about AI from the people building it*. Packt Publishing.

16   Gartner Group, "Gartner says by 2020, artificial intelligence will create more jobs than it eliminates," December 13, 2017. www.gartner.com/en/newsroom/press-releases/2017-12-13-gartner-says-by-2020-artificial-intelligence-will-create-more-jobs-than-it-eliminates.

17   J. Bughin, "Why AI isn't the death of jobs," *MIT Sloan Management Review*, 2018. sloanreview.mit.edu/article/why-ai-isnt-the-death-of-jobs/.

18   R. Molla and E. Stewart, "How will 2020 Democrats deal with jobs eliminated by artificial intelligence?" *Vox*, December 5, 2019. www.vox.com/policy-and-politics/2019/12/3/20965464/2020-presidential-candidates-jobs-automation-ai.

19   R. Rubin, "The 'robot tax' debate heats up," *Wall Street Journal*, January 8, 2020. www.wsj.com/articles/the-robot-tax-debate-heats-up-11578495608?mod=searchresults&page=1&pos=8.

Chapter 5

1   See www.AIPerspectives.com/sl for descriptions and discussion of the various supervised learning algorithms.

2   The '…' signifies that there are many additional rows in the table.

3   Linear regression is a well-known technique that has been around for approximately one hundred years but is now considered supervised learning and AI. There are dozens of other supervised learning techniques. See www.AI Perspectives.com/sl for more information.

4   This does not mean that Zillow will necessarily make better sale price predictions than a human real estate agent. Despite the vast number of columns in the Zillow training table, a human agent might consider unique house features that are not in any of the Zillow columns. If these unique house features affect the selling price, the human real estate agent can theoretically make a better sale price prediction than Zillow.

5   Again, the rows in the table with "…" are intended to signify that it's really a much larger table and the "…" notations indicate large numbers of additional rows.

6   The learned function is termed a *model*.

7   See www.AIPerspectives.com/co for examples of temperature and house price computer code.

8   Z. A. Din, H. Venugopalan, J. Park, A. Li, W. Yin, H. Mai, Y. J. Lee, S. Liu, and S. T. King (2020). *Boxer: Preventing fraud by scanning credit cards*. Proceedings of the 29th USENIX Security Symposium. https://www.usenix.org/conference/usenixsecurity20/presentation/din.

9   Technically, most retailers store customer data in multiple tables not just in a single table. Then they join the data together into one training table to apply supervised learning analyses. They also use unsupervised learning techniques such as the ones I will discuss in the next chapter.

10   Supervised learning techniques for credit card fraud detection are often supplemented by unsupervised learning techniques (see Chapter 7) that have some success in detecting anything out of the ordinary and hence work to some degree for sniffing out new fraud patterns.

11   D. Murray and K. Durrell (2000). "Inferring demographic attributes of anonymous Internet users." *Lecture Notes in Computer Science (Including Subseries Lecture Notes in Artificial Intelligence and Lecture Notes in Bioinformatics), 1836*, 7–20. doi. org/10.1007/3-540-44934-5_1.

12   Y. Bachrach, M. Kosinski, T. Graepel, P. Kohli, and D. Stillwell (2012). "Personality and patterns of Facebook usage." *Proceedings of the 4th Annual ACM Web Science Conference, WebSci'12.* doi.org/10.1145/2380718.2380722.

13   D. Quercia, M. Kosinski, D. Stillwell, and J. Crowcroft (2011). "Our Twitter profiles, our selves: Predicting personality with Twitter." *Proceedings - 2011 IEEE International Conference on Privacy, Security, Risk and Trust and IEEE International Conference on Social Computing, PASSAT/SocialCom 2011,* 180–185. doi.org/10.1109/PASSAT/ SocialCom.2011.26.

14   J. Hirsh, S. Kang, and G. Bodenhausen (2012). "Personalized Persuasion: Tailoring Persuasive Appeals to Recipients' Personality Traits." *Psychological Science*, 23(6), 578-581. doi.org/: 10.1177/0956797611436349. S. C. Matz, M. Kosinski, G. Nave, and D. J. Stillwell (2017). "Psychological targeting as an effective approach to digital mass persuasion." *Proceedings of the National Academy of Sciences of the United States of America, 114*(48), 12714–12719. doi.org/10.1073/pnas.1710966114.

15   C. Wylie (2018). "Why I broke the Facebook data story—and what should happen now." *The Guardian.* www.theguardian.com/uk-news/2018/apr/07/christopher-wylie-why-i-broke-the-facebook-data-story-and-what-should-happen-now.

16   M. Scott (2019). "Cambridge Analytica did work for Brexit groups, says ex-staffer." *Politico.* www.politico.eu/article/cambridge-analytica-leave-eu-ukip-brexit-facebook/.

17   "How Trump Consultants Exploited the Facebook Data of Millions," *New York Times* (n.d.). Retrieved April 14, 2020, from www.nytimes.com/2018/03/17/us/politics/ cambridge-analytica-trump-campaign.html.

18   M. Calabresi (2017). "Inside Russia's social media war on America." *Time.* time. com/4783932/inside-russia-social-media-war-america/. Kosinski, when asked about his role in the CA scandal, said, "This is not my fault. I did not build the bomb. I only showed that it exists." In other words, like many tools, Kosinski's technique can be used for good or evil. It is not the tool we have to worry about; it's the people using the tool.

19   statweb.stanford.edu/~tibs/stat315a/glossary.pdf.

20   For example, see this Accenture report released in November 2019: www.accenture. com/_acnmedia/Thought-Leadership-Assets/PDF-2/Accenture-Built-to-Scale-PDF-Report.pdf#zoom=50.

Chapter 6

1   World Economic Forum, "Reports," reports.weforum.org/global-risks-2013/section-seven-online-only-content/data-explorer/?doing_wp_cron=1584625144.161004066467 2851562500 (accessed March 19, 2020).

2   S. Vosoughi, D. Roy, and S. Aral, "The spread of true and false news online," *Science*, vol. 359, no. 6380, pp. 1146–1151, 2018, doi: 10.1126/science.aap9559.

3   R. M. Everett, J. R. C. Nurse, and A. Erola, "The anatomy of online deception: What makes automated text convincing?" in *Proceedings of the 31st Annual ACM Symposium on Applied Computing*, 2016, pp. 1115–1120, doi: 10.1145/2851613.2851813.

4   E. Weise, "Russian fake accounts showed posts to 126 million Facebook users," *USA Today*, October 30, 2017. www.usatoday.com/story/tech/2017/10/30/russian-fake-accounts-showed-posts-126-million-facebook-users/815342001/.

5   J. Murawski, "Lawmakers call for tough punishment for 'deepfakes,'" *Wall Street Journal*, June 14, 2019. www.wsj.com/articles/lawmakers-call-for-tough-punishment-for-deepfakes-11560504601?mod=searchresults&page=1&pos=17.

6   A. Mosseri, "Working to stop misinformation and false news," *Facebook for Media*, April 7, 2017. www.facebook.com/facebookmedia/blog/working-to-stop-misinformation-and-false-news.

7   S. Rahman, P. Tully, and L. Foster, "Attention is all they need: Combatting social media information operations with neural language models" *FireEye*, November 14, 2019. www.fireeye.com/blog/threat-research/2019/11/combatting-social-media-information-operations-neural-language-models.html.

8   J. Snow, "Can AI win the war against fake news?" *MIT Technology Review*, December 13, 2017. www.technologyreview.com/s/609717/can-ai-win-the-war-against-fake-news/.

9   R. Gutman, "A web tool that lets people choose their own 'sources of truth,'" *The Atlantic*, June 29, 2018. www.theatlantic.com/technology/archive/2018/06/robhat-labs-surfsafe-fake-news-images/564101/.

10 www.perimeterx.com/.

11 L. Calhoun, "Just launched: Google News app uses artificial intelligence to select stories, stop fake news," *Inc.*, May 23, 2018. www.inc.com/lisa-calhoun/new-google-news-app-uses-ai-to-select-stories-stop-fake-news.html.

12 J. Conditt, "Google partners with fact-checking network to fight fake news," *Engadget*, October 26, 2017. www.engadget.com/2017/10/26/google-fake-news-international-fact-checking-network/.

13 J. O'Malley, "How Microsoft is using AI to tackle fake news," *Gizmodo*, May 14, 2018. www.gizmodo.co.uk/2018/05/how-microsoft-is-using-ai-to-tackle-fake-news/.

14 T. Schuster, D. Shah, Y. J. S. Yeo, D. Roberto Filizzola Ortiz, E. Santus, and R. Barzilay, "Towards debiasing fact verification models," *Proceedings of the 2019 Conference on Empirical Methods in Natural Language Processing and the 9th International Joint Conference on Natural Language Processing*, November, 2019, doi: 10.18653/v1/d19-1341. T. Schuster, R. Schuster, D. J. Shah, and R. Barzilay, "The limitations of stylometry for detecting machine-generated fake news," *arXiv preprint arXiv:1908.09805*, 2020.

15   grover.allenai.org/.

16   Bloomberg, "How Faking Videos Became Easy—And Why That's So Scary," Fortune.
       com, September 11, 2018, fortune.com/2018/09/11/deep-fakes-obama-video/

17   R. Metz, "The number of deepfake videos online is spiking. Most are porn," *CNN
       Business*, October 7, 2019. edition.cnn.com/2019/10/07/tech/deepfake-videos-increase/
       index.html.

18   A. Romano, "Reddit finally bans its forum for creepy fake celebrity porn," *Vox*, February
       8, 2018. www.vox.com/culture/2018/2/8/16987098/reddit-bans-deepfakes-celebrity-
       face-swapping-porn.

19   J. Damiani, "A voice deepfake was used to scam a CEO out of $243,000," *Forbes*,
       September 3, 2019. www.forbes.com/sites/jessedamiani/2019/09/03/a-voice-deepfake-
       was-used-to-scam-a-ceo-out-of-243000/#5223a18c2241.

20   As they did in the movie *Cats*.

21   M. Kelly, "Facebook begins telling users who try to share distorted Nancy Pelosi video
       that it's fake," *The Verge*, May 25, 2019. www.theverge.com/2019/5/25/18639754/
       facebook-nancy-pelosi-video-fake-clip-distorted-deepfake.

22   J. Andrews, "Fake news is real — A.I. is going to make it much worse," *CNBC*, July
       12, 2019. www.cnbc.com/2019/07/12/fake-news-is-real-ai-is-going-to-make-it-much-
       worse.html.

23   N. Dufour and A. Gully, "Contributing data to deepfake detection research," *Google AI
       Blog*, September 24, 2019. ai.googleblog.com/2019/09/contributing-data-to-deepfake-
       detection.html.

24   M. Schroepfer, "Creating a data set and a challenge for deepfakes," Facebook Artificial
       Intelligence, September 5, 2019. ai.facebook.com/blog/deepfake-detection-challenge/.

25   deepfakedetectionchallenge.ai/.

26   A. Rossler, D. Cozzolino, L. Verdoliva, C. Riess, J. Thies, and M. Nießner,
       "FaceForensics: A large-scale video dataset for forgery detection in human faces," Visual
       Computing Group, March 24, 2018.

27   M. Turek, "Media Forensics (MediFor)," Defense Advanced Research Projects Agency.
       www.darpa.mil/program/media-forensics (accessed March 19, 2020).

28   For example, T. T. Nguyen, C. M. Nguyen, D. T. Nguyen, D. T. Nguyen, and S.
       Nahavandi, "Deep learning for deepfakes creation and detection," arXiv preprint
       arXiv:1909.11573, 2019;

       Y. Li and S. Lyu, "Exposing deepfake videos by detecting face warping artifacts," arXiv
       preprint arXiv:1811.00656, 2019.

29   R. Mama and S. Shi, "Towards deepfake detection that actually works," Dessa,
       November 25, 2019. www.dessa.com/post/deepfake-detection-that-actually-works.

30   S. -Y. Wang, O. Wang, R. Zhang, A. Owens, and A. Efros, "Detecting Photoshopped
       faces by scripting Photoshop," in *Proceedings of the IEEE International Conference on
       Computer Vision*, 2019, doi: 10.1109/iccv.2019.01017.

31   contentauthenticity.com/.

32   www.truepic.com.

33   www.autoexpress.co.uk/news/352605/deepfake-software-used-aid-self-driving-car-development.

34   U.S. House. 116ᵗʰ Congress. (2019, June 12). H. Con. Res. 3230, Defending Each and Every Person from False Appearances by Keeping Exploitation Subject to Accountability Act of 2019. [Online]. Available: www.congress.gov/bill/116th-congress/house-bill/3230.

35   T. Hatmaker (2017). "Saudi Arabia bestows citizenship on a robot named Sophia." *TechCrunch.* techcrunch.com/2017/10/26/saudi-arabia-robot-citizen-sophia/?renderMode=ie11.

36   D. Gershgorn, "Inside the mechanical brain of the world's first robot citizen," *Quartz*, November 12, 2017. qz.com/1121547/how-smart-is-the-first-robot-citizen/.

37   Carlquintanilla. (2017, Oct 25). Our @andrewrsorkin, interviewing "Sophia" the robot, of Hanson Robotics. [Twitter Post]. Retrieved from https://twitter.com/carlquintanilla/status/923238264533811200.

38   J. Vincent, "Facebook's head of AI really hates Sophia the Robot (and with good reason)," *The Verge*, January 18, 2018. www.theverge.com/2018/1/18/16904742/sophia-the-robot-ai-real-fake-yann-lecun-criticism.

39   This was shown in a psychology experiment in which human subjects were asked questions on a computer screen either by displaying text or a human face asking the question. When it was a human face, they elected not to answer several personal questions: L. Sproull, M. Subramani, S. Kiesler, J. H. Walker, and K. Waters, "When the interface is a face," *Human-Computer Interact.*, vol. 11, no. 2, pp. 97–124, 1996, doi: 10.1207/s15327051hci1102_1.

40   S. Tibken, "Samsung's new neon project is finally unveiled: It's a humanoid AI chatbot," *CNet*, January 7, 2020. www.cnet.com/news/samsung-neon-project-finally-unveiled-humanoid-ai-chatbot-artificial-humans/.

41   www.katedarling.org/publications.

42   J. Hsu, "Real soldiers love their robot brethren," *Live Science*, May 21, 2009. www.livescience.com/5432-real-soldiers-love-robot-brethren.html.

43   www.parorobots.com/.

44   "HitchBOT, the hitchhiking robot, beheaded in the U.S." *CNN Business*, August 4, 2015. Accessed: March 20, 2020. [Online Video]. Available: edition.cnn.com/videos/tech/2015/08/04/hitchbot-robot-beheaded-philadelphia-orig-pkg.cnn.

45   P. Parke, "Is it cruel to kick a robot dog?" *CNN Business*, February 13, 2015. edition.cnn.com/2015/02/13/tech/spot-robot-dog-google/index.html.

46   J. J. Li, W. Ju, and B. Reeves, "Touching a mechanical body: Tactile contact with body parts of a humanoid robot is physiologically arousing," *J. Human-Robot Interact.*, 2017, doi: 10.5898/jhri.6.3.li.

47   K. Darling, "Extending legal protection to social robots: The effects of anthropomorphism, empathy, and violent behavior towards robotic objects," in *Robot Law*, 2016.

48   C. de Lange, "Sherry Turkle: 'We're losing the raw, human part of being with each other,'" *The Guardian*, May 5, 2013. www.theguardian.com/science/2013/may/05/rational-heroes-sherry-turkle-mit.

49   M. Delvaux, "Report with recommendations to the commission on civil law rules on robotics," January 27, 2017. www.europarl.europa.eu/doceo/document/A-8-2017-0005_EN.html.

50   For example, P. Sullins, "When is a robot a moral agent?," *Mach. Ethics*, vol. 6, pp. 23–30, 2006, doi: 10.1017/CBO9780511978036.010.

51   J. J. Bryson, M. E. Diamantis, and T. D. Grant, "Of, for, and by the people: The legal lacuna of synthetic persons," *Artif. Intell. Law*, vol. 25, pp. 273–291, 2017, doi: 10.1007/s10506-017-9214-9.

Chapter 7

1   I have oversimplified here in order to make the example understandable. Real-world biologists would be analyzing data on rare animals, not well-known ones like humans, horses, cats, and spiders. Also, they would likely use technical features with Latin names rather than easily understandable features such as weight and lifespan.

2   The way these algorithms work is beyond the scope of this book. However, the general idea is to find the set of clusters that both maximize the distance between the clusters in the one-hundred-dimensional space and that minimize the distance between the observations within a cluster. While the mixing of numeric variables, such as weight and lifespan, with categorical variables, such as color, complicates the mathematics, techniques have been worked out over the years to accommodate mixed numeric and categorical variables.

3   A. Radford, J. Wu, R. Child, D. Luan, D. Amodei, and I. Sutskever, "Language models are unsupervised multitask learners," *OpenAI*, 2018. d4mucfpksywv.cloudfront.net/better-language-models/language_models_are_unsupervised_multitask_learners.pdf.

4   You can try it yourself at this site: talktotransformer.com/.

5   This technology has other uses besides generation of fake news. For example, Google uses language models to predict what user search queries will be from the first few words the user types. For more information, see P. Nayak, "Understanding searches better than ever before," *Google Blog*, October 25, 2019. www.blog.google/products/search/search-language-understanding-bert/.

6   They used the Grover language model developed by the Allen AI Institute. grover.allenai.org/.

7   thegradient.pub/gpt2-and-the-nature-of-intelligence/. If you are still not convinced, take a look at this *New Yorker Magazine* article that describes stories generated by GPT-2 after being trained on the magazine's vast archives: www.newyorker.com/magazine/2019/10/14/can-a-machine-learn-to-write-for-the-new-yorker.

8   In fact, when sensitive data such as social security numbers are part of the training data and a user inputs "my social security number is . . ." the resulting language model sometimes completes the sentence with an actual social security number from the training table. This can be a security issue, though it is easily avoided by not exposing sensitive data in language model training tables. For more information, see N. Carlini, C. Liu, Ú. Erlingsson, J. Kos, and D. Song, "The secret sharer: Evaluating and testing unintended memorization in neural networks," in *Proceedings of the 28th USENIX Security Symposium,* 2019.

9   T. Mikolov, K. Chen, G. Corrado, and J. Dean (n.d.). *Efficient Estimation of Word Representations in Vector Space*. Retrieved May 8, 2020, from ronan. collobert.com/senna/.

10 J. R. Firth (1957). "A Synopsis of Linguistic Theory 1930-1955." In F. Palmer (Ed.), *Selected Papers of J. R. Firth*. Longman, Harlow. www.bibsonomy.org/ bibtex/20b627387b63b652898cb5ecf03f87356/evabl444.

11 It is only close to "queen" and not exact because the space is high dimensional and mostly empty (the technical term is *sparse*), and the word embeddings only capture some of the meaning of the words.

12 L. Lucy and J. Gauthier, "Are distributional representations ready for the real world? Evaluating word vectors for grounded perceptual meaning," *Proceedings of the First Workshop on Language Grounding for Robotics*, August 2017, doi: 10.18653/v1/w17-2810.

13 J. Zhu, "Bing delivers its largest improvement in search experience using Azure GPUs," *Microsoft Azure*, November 18, 2019. azure.microsoft.com/en-us/blog/bing-delivers-its-largest-improvement-in-search-experience-using-azure-gpus/.

14 Frameworks Natural Language Processing Team, "Can Global Semantic Context Improve Neural Language Models," machinelearning.apple.com, September, 2018. https://machinelearning.apple.com/research/can-global-semantic-context-improve-neural-language-models. machinelearning.apple.com/2018/09/27/can-global-semantic-context-improve-neural-language-models.html.

15 B. Marr, "Supervised v unsupervised machine learning—what's the difference?" *Forbes*, March 16, 2017. www.forbes.com/sites/bernardmarr/2017/03/16/supervised-v-unsupervised-machine-learning-whats-the-difference/#7efb5ed1485d.

Chapter 8

1   National Highway Traffic Safety Administration & U.S. Department of Transportation (2015). *TRAFFIC SAFETY FACTS Crash • Stats. Critical Reasons for Crashes Investigated in the National Motor Vehicle Crash Causation Survey*. crashstats.nhtsa.dot.gov/Api/ Public/ViewPublication/812115.

2   Self-driving trucks are being built by different companies (e.g., Otto, Embark, Ike, Thor Trucks, Kodiak, TuSimple, Peloton Technology, and Pronto.ai) than self-driving cars. While much of the technology needed for self-driving trucks is the same or similar to the technology for self-driving cars, there are significant differences. For example, trucks have bigger blind spots, and cameras/lidar can be mounted at higher points than on cars. Some analysts argue that self-driving trucks will make their appearance even before self-driving cars. There is a shortage of truck drivers, and truck drivers are highly paid, perhaps making the cost of self-driving technology less important for trucks than for cars, which gives makers of self-driving truck technology the ability to use more expensive components such as military- and aerospace-grade sensors that may be too expensive for self-driving cars. All that said, most truck drivers have years of experience that enables them to avoid accidents, and that may make self-driving trucks harder to develop than self-driving cars. See also this article arguing that, even if companies are successful in building autonomous trucks, the number of jobs that will be lost is greatly overstated: onezero.medium.com/self-driving-trucks-wont-kill-millions-of-jobs-ef56ca978f77.

3   T. Mogg, "Self-driving baggage tractor is the latest smart tech for airports," *Digital Trends*, December 9, 2019. www.digitaltrends.com/cool-tech/self-driving-baggage-tractor-is-the-latest-smart-tech-for-airports/.

4   AVs have tremendous potential for improving safety. Over a million people die every year in car accidents worldwide according to the Association for Safe International Road Travel, "Road safety facts—Association for Safe International Road Travel," *Asirt*. 2019. www.asirt.org/safe-travel/road-safety-facts/.

5   C. Neiger, "5 future car technologies that truly have a chance," *How Stuff Works*, December 23, 2011. auto.howstuffworks.com/under-the-hood/trends-innovations/5-future-car-technologies3.htm.

6   A. Peters, "It could be 10 times cheaper to take electric robo-taxis than to own a car by 2030," *Fast Company*, May 30, 2017. www.fastcompany.com/40424452/it-could-be-10-times-cheaper-to-take-electric-robo-taxis-than-to-own-a-car-by-2030.

7   T. Tatarek, J. Kronenberger, and U. Handmann, "Functionality, advantages and limits of the TeslaAutopilot," Hochschule Ruhr West, University of Applied Sciences, Institut Informatik, Internal Report 17-04, 2017. www.handmann.net/paper/2017_ir4.pdf.

8   A. Jackson (1931). "Automatic Parallel Parking System," *United States Patent*, Number 1,905,717.

9   D. A. Pomerleau, "ALVINN: An autonomous land vehicle in a neural network," *Adv. Neural Inf. Process. Syst.*, pp. 305–313, 1988.

10   www.YouTube.com/watch?v=IaoIqVMd6tc&feature=youtu.be.

11   ALVINN was originally the name of the supervised learning neural network software, though most histories assign the name ALVINN to the vehicle itself. The vehicle was one of a series of CMU vehicles built as part of the NavLab project, and the curve warning system was also developed as part of NavLab.

12   EUREKA, "Programme for a european traffic system with highest efficiency and unprecedented safety," 1987. www.eurekanetwork.org/project/id/45.

13   PROMETHEUS video: www.YouTube.com/watch?v=JgKd_RcgYv4&feature=youtu.be

14   E. Dickmanns, "The 4-d approach to visual control of autonomous systems," in *AIAA/NASA Conf. on Intelligent Robots in Field Factory Service and Space (CIRFFSS)*, 1994, pp. 483–493.

15   https://en.wikipedia.org/wiki/DARPA_Grand_Challenge.

16   A. Davies, "An Oral History of the Darpa Grand Challenge, the Grueling Robot Race That Launched the Self-Driving Car," *Wired*, August 3, 2017, https://www.wired.com/story/darpa-grand-challenge-2004-oral-history/.

17   S. Thrun, M. Montemerlo, H. Dahlkamp, D. Stavens, A. Aron, J. Diebel, P. Fong, J. Gale, M. Halpenny, G. Hoffmann, K. Lau, C. Oakley, M. Palatucci, V. Pratt, P. Stang, S. Strohband, C. Dupont, L. E. Jendrossek, C. Koelen, C., … P. Mahoney (2006). Stanley: The robot that won the DARPA Grand Challenge. *Journal of Field Robotics, 23*(9), 661–692. doi.org/10.1002/rob.20147.

18   B. Bilger, "Auto Correct," newyorker.com, November 25, 2013. https://www.
        newyorker.com/magazine/2013/11/25/auto-correct.

19   M. Ramsey and D. MacMillan, "Carnegie Mellon reels after Uber lures away
        researchers," *The Wall Street Journal*, May 31, 2015. www.wsj.com/articles/is-uber-a-
        friend-or-foe-of-carnegie-mellon-in-robotics-1433084582.

20   Accounts of the actual purchase price vary, and some put it as low as $220M. In
        February 2017, Waymo launched a lawsuit against Uber claiming misappropriation of
        trade secrets, and in May 2017, Uber fired Levandowski for not cooperating with Uber's
        investigation into the lawsuit. Many of the Otto engineers left for other self-driving
        start-ups. Waymo and Uber settled the lawsuit in February 2018, with Google receiving
        about $245M of Uber stock.

21   https://www.tesla.com/autopilot#:~:text=Eight%20surround%20cameras%20
        provide%20360,distance%20of%20the%20prior%20system.

22   FLIR, "FLIR systems partners with veoneer for first thermal sensor-equipped
        production self-driving car with a leading global automaker," October 30, 2019. www.
        flir.com/news-center/press-releases/flir-systems-partners-with-veoneer-for-first-thermal-
        sensor-equipped-production-self-driving-car-with-a-leading-global-automaker/.

23   Pixels, short for picture elements, are the little dots that make up digital picture images.

24   The stealth bombers use a plastic covering that does not conduct electricity to make then
        invisible to radar.

25   J. Stewart, "Why Tesla's Autopilot Can't See a Stopped Firetruck," wired.com, August
        27, 2018. www.wired.com/story/tesla-autopilot-why-crash-radar/.

26   en.Wikipedia.org/wiki/Dead_reckoning.

27   A. Noureldin, T. B. Karamat, and J. Georgy, "Inertial Navigation System," *Fundamentals
        of Inertial Navigation, Satellite-based Positioning and Their Integration* (Berlin: Springer,
        2013), 125–166.

28   Since it is not unusual to see twenty-year-old cars on the road, even if we get to the
        point where every new car is outfitted with V2V technology, it could still be over twenty
        years before every car on the road has the technology. The good news is that despite the
        unsettled standards issue, many automakers are already starting to build one of the two
        standards into their cars.

29   KPMG International, "2019 Autonomous Vehicles Readiness Index," 2019. assets.
        kpmg/content/dam/kpmg/xx/pdf/2019/02/2019-autonomous-vehicles-readiness-index.
        pdf.

30   An explanation of the Tesla technology can be found in two videos of talks by Director
        of AI Andrej Karpathy. The first video provides an overview of the technology: www.
        youtube.com/watch?time_continue=40&v=hx7BXih7zx8&
        feature=emb_logo. The second video is more technical and explains that the networks
        aren't completely separate and actually share some layers in what is known as a multitask
        supervised learning architecture: www.youtube.com/
        watch?v=IHH47nZ7FZU.

31   Karpathy noted that development of even a basic component such as a stop sign detector
        is difficult. Stop signs can be mounted on a pole, a car, a school bus, a gate, or held by a
        construction worker. Stop signs can also be occluded by the car in front or by foliage.

32   youtu.be/A44hbogdKwI.

33   All Tesla vehicles have an internet connection that is used to connect each car to servers at Tesla headquarters and to both update the car software and transfer data from the car to the Tesla servers. It is not required, however, for safe operation of the vehicle.

34   For a great blog post on how Lyft's 3D maps work, see medium.com/lyftlevel5/https-medium-com-lyftlevel5-rethinking-maps-for-self-driving-a147c24758d6.

35   www.youtube.com/watch?v=y57wwucbXR8&feature=emb_rel_end.

36   lexfridman.com/tesla-autopilot-miles-and-vehicles/.

37   www.youtube.com/watch?time_continue=40&v=hx7BXih7zx8&feature=emb_logo.

38   The simulator, named Carcraft, is located on the Alphabet campus in Mountain View, California. A. C. Madrigal, "Inside Waymo's secret world for training self-driving cars: An exclusive look at how alphabet understands its most ambitious artificial intelligence project," *The Atlantic*, August 23, 2017. www.theatlantic.com/technology/archive/2017/08/inside-waymos-secret-testing-and-simulation-facilities/537648/.

39   Waymo, "Building maps for a self-driving car," *Medium*, December 14, 2016. medium.com/waymo/building-maps-for-a-self-driving-car-723b4d9cd3f4.

40   C. Urmson et al., "High speed navigation of unrehearsed terrain: Red team technology for grand challenge 2004," The Robotics Institute, Carnegie Mellon University, June 1, 2004. www.ri.cmu.edu/pub_files/pub4/urmson_christopher_2004_1/urmson_christopher_2004_1.pdf.

      J. Levinson and S. Thrun, "Robust vehicle localization in urban environments using probabilistic maps," in *Proceedings - IEEE International Conference on Robotics and Automation*, 2010, pp. 4372–4378, doi: 10.1109/ROBOT.2010.5509700.

41   As of July 2018, Waymo had logged 8 million self-driving miles. T. Randall and M. Bergen, "Waymo's self-driving cars are near: Meet the teen who rides one every day," *Bloomberg*, August 1, 2018. www.bloomberg.com/news/features/2018-07-31/inside-the-life-of-waymo-s-driverless-test-family.

42   A group of MIT researchers have detailed a system for using low-dimensional topographical maps on rural roads: T. Ort, L. Paull, and D. Rus, "Autonomous vehicle navigation in rural environments without detailed prior maps," in *Proceedings - IEEE International Conference on Robotics and Automation*, 2018, doi: 10.1109/ICRA.2018.8460519.

43   www.youtube.com/watch?time_continue=40&v=hx7BXih7zx8&feature=emb_logo.

44   B. Hood, "Hackers Tricked Self-Driving Teslas Into Accelerating 50 MPH With a Piece of Tape," robbreport.com, February 19, 2020. www.robbreport.com/motors/cars/hackers-manipulate-teslas-50-mph-2900057/.

45   T. Huddleston, "These Chinese hackers tricked Tesla's Autopilot into suddenly switching lanes," cnbc.com, April 3, 2019. www.cnbc.com/2019/04/03/chinese-hackers-tricked-teslas-autopilot-into-switching-lanes.html.

46   G. Rapier, "Why trees have wreaked havoc on Uber's self-driving program," markets.businessinsider.com, November 27, 2018. https://markets.businessinsider.com/news/stocks/trees-are-wreaking-havoc-on-uber-self-driving-car-software-2018-11-1027759300.

47   J. Kaplan, R. Glon, S. Edelstein, and L. Chang, "Deadly Uber crash was 'entirely avoidable' had the driver not been watching Hulu," digitaltrends.com, June 22, 2018. https://www.digitaltrends.com/cars/self-driving-uber-crash-arizona/.

48   C. Sullengerger, *Sully: My Search for What Really Matters* (New York: HarperCollins, 2016).

49   B. Lewis, "Student intentionally causes a car crash, and it may have saved a woman's life," wtsp.com, January 17, 2019. https://www.wtsp.com/article/news/clearwater-senior-saves-seizing-driver-with-heroic-car-crash/67-aebb4a34-2eea-4fc2-bb69-4254b804c4a2.

50   R. Stumpf, "Autopilot Blamed for Tesla's Crash Into Overturned Truck," thedrive.com, June 1, 2020. https://www.thedrive.com/news/33789/autopilot-blamed-for-teslas-crash-into-overturned-truck.Another Tesla fatality occurred in 2019 when a Tesla crashed into a different truck. The crash sheared off the top of the Tesla.

51   R. Nazarov, "Russian wake-up call from winter autonomous-vehicle (AV) trials," *Urgent Communications*, February 18, 2020. urgentcomm.com/2020/02/18/russian-wake-up-call-from-winter-autonomous-vehicle-av-trials/.

52   Insurance Institute for Highway Safety, "Self-driving vehicles could struggle to eliminate most crashes," iihs.org, June 4, 2020. https://www.iihs.org/news/detail/self-driving-vehicles-could-struggle-to-eliminate-most-crashes.

53   D. Newcomb, "Don't believe the self-driving car crash hype," *PC Mag*, March 31, 2017. www.pcmag.com/opinions/dont-believe-the-self-driving-car-crash-hype.

54   P. Keating, "Florida Mayo Clinic using autonomous vehicles to transport coronavirus tests," foxnews.com, April 14, 2020. https://www.foxnews.com/auto/florida-mayo-clinic-autonomous-vehicles-coronavirus.

55   Sidewalk delivery robots are a special case of delivery vehicles. From a timeline perspective, these vehicles are more like campus shuttles than delivery vehicles that operate on city streets. For example, Starship Technologies robots are the size of a large cooler, operate no faster than six miles per hour, and have been approved for use on university campuses and in some states in the US.

56   A. J. Hawkins, "Waymo's driverless car: Ghost-riding in the back seat of a robot taxi," *The Verge*, December 9, 2019. www.theverge.com/2019/12/9/21000085/waymo-fully-driverless-car-self-driving-ride-hail-service-phoenix-arizona.

57   waymo.com/journey/.

58   Zoox is testing its autonomous taxis in San Francisco. In early 2020, the company posted an impressive video (venturebeat.com/2020/04/17/watch-zooxs-autonomous-car-drive-around-san-francisco-for-an-hour/) of an autonomous vehicle driving the streets of San Francisco for an hour without the human safety driver taking over at all. The video shows the Zoox car doing the following:

•   Driving on Market Street when it was very busy with pedestrians

•   Stopping for pedestrians in crosswalks and when making turns

•   Avoiding pedestrians who walk out from behind parked cars

•   Navigating around double-parked cars and delivery trucks

•   Going through a tunnel that blocked the GPS signal

- Waiting for a car to back into a spot

- Driving on hilly Lombard Street

59   There is always the possibility that vehicle makers simply relabel Level 2 vehicles as Level 3 vehicles and still require drivers to pay attention to the road. This would not be a true Level 3 capability.

60   I am far from the first person to articulate this position. For example, self-driving car pioneer Chris Urmson predicted in 2017 that it would be thirty years or more before we eliminate the need for drivers: www.vox.com/2017/9/8/16278566/transcript-self-driving-car-engineer-chris-urmson-recode-decode.

Chapter 9

1   Reinforcement learning has also been used in many other types of applications. For example, two MIT researchers used reinforcement learning to determine how to dose glastoblioma patients with the least amount of toxic anticancer drugs that would still be effective: G. Yauney and P. Shah, "Reinforcement learning with action-derived rewards for chemotherapy and clinical trial dosing regimen selection," *Proc. Mach. Learn. Res,* vol. 85, 2018.

Another example is financial trading strategies; e.g., C.-Y. Huang, "Financial trading as a game: A deep reinforcement learning approach," arXiv preprint arXiv:1807.02787, 2018.

2   Applying reinforcement learning to elevator control was first discussed at the 1996 NIPS conference by Robert Crites and Andrew Barto: R. H. Crites and A. G. Barto, "Improving elevator performance using reinforcement learning," in *Neural Information Processing Systems 8,* S. Touretzky, M. C. Mozer, and M. E. Hasselmo, Eds. (Cambridge, MA: MIT Press, 1996), pp. 1017–1023.

3   A trillion-trillion is a one plus twenty-four zeroes. The number of combinations of 118 buttons is 2^{118}, which is three plus thirty-five zeroes.

4   In this case the state would be the location of each elevator, whether each of the thirty-eight hall call buttons is pressed, and whether each of the twenty buttons inside each of the four elevator cars is pressed.

5   This is a bit of an oversimplification. There are two primary types of learned functions in reinforcement learning termed policies and Q-functions. For an overview of how each of these are learned, see www.AIPerspectives.com/rl.

6   Crites and Bartow found that the function learned by their reinforcement learning system was superior to most industry algorithms at the time, including SECTOR, a sector-based algorithm similar to what was being used in many actual elevator systems: Dynamic Load Balancing, which attempts to equalize the load of all cars; Highest Unanswered Floor First, which gives priority to the highest floor with people waiting; Longest Queue First, which gives priority to the queue with the person who has been waiting for the longest amount of time; ESA, Empty the System Algorithm, which searches for the fastest way to "empty the system" assuming no new passenger arrivals.

7   Making a poor choice of reward function can result in unintended behaviors. For example, OpenAI researchers built a reinforcement learning system to learn a game

named *CoastRunners* where the goal of the game is to navigate a boat race faster than the other players and extra points are won by hitting targets along the route. As it turned out, the reward function put too much emphasis on hitting the targets, and the reinforcement learning system learned to drive around in a circle, hitting the same three targets over and over and never finishing the race.

J. Clark, "Faulty reward functions in the wild," *OpenAI,* December 21, 2016. openai. com/blog/faulty-reward-functions/.

8   Simulators are not a panacea. One big problem with simulators is that the real world is almost always different from the simulator assumptions. People will arrive at elevators in unexpected clumps. Robots that pick up objects and move them can encounter unexpected environmental conditions such as winds, uneven floors, and dogs and people. Self-driving cars can encounter unexpected conditions such as blizzards, fog, construction blockages, and deer crossing the road.

9   The mathematics behind learning policy weights for a given reward function is beyond the scope of this book. For an overview of how reinforcement learning policies are learned, see www.AIPerspectives.com/po. For the most prominent textbook on reinforcement learning, see R. S. Sutton, and A. G. Barto, *Reinforcement Learning: An Introduction,* 2nd ed. (Cambridge, Mass.: MIT Press, 2018).

10   *Pong, Breakout, Enduro, Beam Rider, Q*bert, Sequest,* and *Space Invaders.*

11   V. Mnih et al., "Playing Atari with deep reinforcement learning," 2013. arxiv.org/ pdf/1312.5602.pdf.

V. Mnih et al., "Human-level control through deep reinforcement learning," *Nature,* vol. 518, pp. 529–541, 2015, doi: 10.1038/nature14236.

12   *Pong, Breakout,* and *Enduro.*

13   D. Silver et al., "Mastering the game of Go with deep neural networks and tree search," *Nature,* vol. 529, pp. 484–489, 2016, doi: 10.1038/nature16961.

14   D. Silver et al., "Mastering chess and shogi by self-play with a general reinforcement learning algorithm," *Science,* 2017, doi: 10.1126/science.aar6404.

15   A. Gleave, M. Dennis, C. Wild, N. Kant, S. Levine, and S. Russell (2020). "Adversarial Policies: Attacking Deep Reinforcement Learning." *Eighth International Conference on Learning Representations.* adversarialpolicies.github.io/.

16   For example, the Sophia (www.hansonrobotics.com/sophia/), Erica (robots.ieee.org/ robots/erica/), and the Geminoid line of robots (www.geminoid.jp/en/robots.html).

17   www.YouTube.com/watch?v=xb93Z0QItVI.

18   See this video of Boston Dynamics robots: www.YouTube.com/ watch?v=rVlhMGQgDkY.

19   M. Hayes, "The creepy robot dog botched a test run with a bomb squad," *OneZero,* February 19, 2020. onezero.medium.com/boston-dynamics-robot-dog-got-stuck-in-sit-mode-during-police-test-emails-reveal-4c8592c7fc2.

20   P. Abbeel and A. Y. Ng, "Apprenticeship learning via inverse reinforcement learning,"

in *Proceedings, Twenty-First International Conference on Machine Learning, ICML 2004*, 2004, doi: 10.1145/1015330.1015430.

21   As researchers Pieter Abbeel and Andrew Ng (Abbeel and Ng, 2004) point out, it would be very hard to define a reward function for driving because of the number of constraints (e.g., do not hit a pedestrian, stay in your lane, do not speed, obey traffic signals, and on and on).

22   There are also other difficult pick-and-place problems. For example, if a robot is trained to pick up a box, ideally that training would generalize to boxes of different sizes and surfaces with different friction coefficients. Otherwise, separate training for each box and surface will be required. More generally, the goal is to train on the strategy observed in the demonstrations and to generalize that strategy so that it can be applied to states that were not observed during training.

23   youtu.be/YBVR-TRXEc4.

24   P. Pastor, H. Hoffmann, T. Asfour, and S. Schaal, "Learning and generalization of motor skills by learning from demonstration," in *2009 IEEE International Conference on Robotics and Automation*, pp. 763–768, 2009, doi: 10.1109/robot.2009.5152385.

25   K. Muelling, J. Kober, O. Kroemer, and J. Peters, "Learning to select and generalize striking movements in robot table tennis," in *AAAI Fall Symposium - Technical Report*, 2012, pp. 38–45.

26   M. A. Rana, M. Mukadam, S. R. Ahmadzadeh, S. Chernova, and B. Boots, "Towards robust skill generalization: Unifying learning from demonstration and motion planning," in *Conference on Robot Learning*, 2017.

27   www.YouTube.com/watch?v=52QTL7v_-vo.

Chapter 10

1   G. Orwell, *1984* (New York: Berkley, 2003).

2   English translation is "Sharp Eyes."

3   R. Dixon, "China's new surveillance program aims to cut crime. Some fear it'll do much more," *Los Angeles Times*, October 27, 2018. www.latimes.com/world/asia/la-fg-china-sharp-eyes-20181027-story.htmll. Also, according to *Time* magazine (Dec 2–9, 2019), the city of Chongqing has 2.58 million surveillance cameras for its 15.35 million people.

4   Phys.org, "China shames jaywalkers through facial recognition," *Phys.org*, June 20, 2017. phys.org/news/2017-06-china-shames-jaywalkers-facial-recognition.html.

5   J. C. Hernandez (n.d.), "China's High-Tech Tool to Fight Toilet Paper Bandits," *New York Times*, March 17, 2017. Retrieved March 23, 2020, from www.nytimes.com/2017/03/20/world/asia/china-toilet-paper-theft.html.

6   L. Ong, "In Beijing, 'Big Brother' now sees all," *The Epoch Times*, October 5, 2015.

7   C. Campbell, "What the Chinese Surveillance State Means for the Rest of the World," time.com, November 21, 2019. https://time.com/5735411/china-surveillance-privacy-issues/.

8   D. Alba, "The US government will be scanning your face at 20 top airports, documents show," *Buzzfeed News*, March 11, 2019. www.buzzfeednews.com/article/daveyalba/

these-documents-reveal-the-governments-detailed-plan-for.

9   www.airportfacescans.com/.

10   K. Rector and A. Knezevich, "Maryland's use of facial recognition software questioned by researchers, civil liberties advocates," *Baltimore Sun*, October 18, 2016. www.baltimoresun.com/news/crime/bs-md-facial-recognition-20161017-story.html.

11   R. Brandom, "How facial recognition helped police identify the Capital Gazette shooter," *The Verge*, June 29, 2018. www.theverge.com/2018/6/29/17518364/facial-recognition-police-identify-capital-gazette-shooter.

12   G. L. Goodwin, "Face recognition technology: DOJ and FBI have taken some actions in response to GAO recommendations to ensure privacy and accuracy, but additional work remains," June 4, 2019. www.gao.gov/assets/700/699489.pdf.

13   www.banfacialrecognition.com/.

14   D. Harwell, "Both Democrats and Republicans blast facial-recognition technology in a rare bipartisan moment," *Washington Post*, May 23, 2019. www.washingtonpost.com/technology/2019/05/22/blasting-facial-recognition-technology-lawmakers-urge-regulation-before-it-gets-out-control/.

15   D. Harwell, "Parkland school turns to experimental surveillance software that can flag students as threats," *Washington Post*, February 18, 2019. www.washingtonpost.com/technology/2019/02/13/parkland-school-turns-experimental-surveillance-software-that-can-flag-students-threats/.

16   S. Bushwick, "How NIST tested facial recognition algorithms for racial bias," *Scientific American*, December 27, 2019. www.scientificamerican.com/article/how-nist-tested-facial-recognition-algorithms-for-racial-bias/.

17   G. Goswami, N. Ratha, A. Agarwal, R. Singh, and M. Vatsa, "Unravelling robustness of deep learning based face recognition against adversarial attacks," in *32nd AAAI Conference on Artificial Intelligence, AAAI 2018*, 2018.

18   Many other companies offer similar software, including Google, Microsoft, and IBM.

19   www.banfacialrecognition.com/map.

20   www.banfacialrecognition.com.

21   J. Snow, "Amazon's face recognition falsely matched 28 members of Congress with mugshots," *American Civil Liberties Union*, 2018.

22   California Legislative Information. (2019, Oct. 8). AB-1215 Law Enforcement: Facial Recognition and Other Biometric Surveillance. [Online]. Available: leginfo.legislature.ca.gov/faces/billTextClient.xhtml?bill_id=201920200AB1215.

23   A. Pressley, "Reps. Pressley, Clarke & Tlaib Announce Bill Banning Facial Recognition in Public Housing," *Representative Ayanna Pressley*, July 25, 2019. pressley.house.gov/media/press-releases/reps-pressley-clarke-tlaib-announce-bill-banning-facial-recognition-public.

24   J. Delcker and B. Smith-Meyer, "EU considers temporary ban on facial recognition in public spaces," *Politico*, January 16, 2020. www.politico.eu/pro/eu-considers-temporary-ban-on-facial-recognition-in-public-spaces/.

25   For an example of how badly facial recognition errors can completely ruin someone's life, see this article: A. Kofman, "Losing face: How a facial recognition mismatch can ruin your life," *The Intercept*, October 13, 2016. theintercept.com/2016/10/13/how-a-facial-recognition-mismatch-can-ruin-your-life/.

26   A. M. McDonald and L. F. Cranor, "The cost of reading privacy policies," *I/S A J. Law Policy Inf. Soc.*, vol. 4, no. 3, pp. 543–568, 2008.

27   R. Copeland, D. Mattioli, and M. Evans, "Inside Google's quest for millions of medical records," *Wall Street Journal*, January 11, 2020. www.wsj.com/articles/paging-dr-google-how-the-tech-giant-is-laying-claim-to-health-data-11578719700?mod=searchresults&page=1&pos=1.

28   H. Fry, *Hello World: Being Human in the Age of Algorithms*, 1st ed. (New York: W. W. Norton & Company, 2018).

29   K. Hill, "How Target figured out a teen girl was pregnant before her father did," *Forbes*, February 16, 2012. www.forbes.com/sites/kashmirhill/2012/02/16/how-target-figured-out-a-teen-girl-was-pregnant-before-her-father-did/#4a304a7c6668.

30   J. Mikians, L. Gyarmati, V. Erramilli, and N. Laoutaris, "Detecting price and search discrimination on the Internet," in *Proceedings of the 11th ACM Workshop on Hot Topics in Networks, HotNets-11*, pp. 79–84, 2012, doi: 10.1145/2390231.2390245.

      A. Hannak, G. Soeller, D. Lazer, A. Mislove, and C. Wilson, "Measuring price discrimination and steering on E-commerce web sites," in *Proceedings of the ACM SIGCOMM Internet Measurement Conference, IMC*, 2014, doi: 10.1145/2663716.2663744.

31   Federal Trade Commission v. Compucredit Corporation and Jefferson Capital Systems, LLC, US Dist. Court Atlanta, 1:08-CV-1976, 2008. [Online]. Available: www.ftc.gov/sites/default/files/documents/cases/2008/06/080610 compucreditcmptsigned.pdf.

32   "Facebook Says Cambridge Analytica Harvested Data of Up to 87 Million Users," *New York Times* (n.d.). Retrieved February 17, 2020, from https://www.nytimes.com/2018/04/04/technology/mark-zuckerberg-testify-congress.html.

33   Norwegian Consumer Council, "Deceived by design: How tech companies use dark patterns to discourage us from exercising our rights to privacy," July 6, 2018. fil.forbrukerradet.no/wp-content/uploads/2018/06/2018-06-27-deceived-by-design-final.pdf.

34   https://marketing.acxiom.com/rs/982-LRE-196/images/Acxiom%20Global%20Data.pdf.

35   S. Zuboff, *The Age of Surveillance Capitalism: The Fight for a Human Future at the New Frontier of Power*, 1st ed. (New York: PublicAffairs, 2019).

Chapter 11

1   See www.AIPerspectives.com/fe for more information on image feature extraction methods.

2   O. Russakovsky, J. Deng, H. Su, J. Krause, S. Satheesh, S. Ma, Z. Huang, A. Karpathy, A. Khosla, M. Bernstein, A. C. Berg, and L. Fei-Fei (2015). "ImageNet Large Scale Visual Recognition Challenge." *International Journal of Computer Vision*,

115(3), 211–252. https://doi.org/10.1007/s11263-015-0816-y.

3   A. Krizhevsky, I. Sutskever, and G. E. Hinton, "ImageNet classification with deep convolutional neural networks," *Commun. ACM*, 2012, doi: 10.1145/3065386.

4   It should be noted that the AlexNet top-1 error rate was still around 37 percent.

5   There are two types of neural networks. The human brain is a type of **biological neural network**. The type of neural network that will be discussed in this book is an **artificial neural network**. I will use the term "neural networks" to refer to "artificial neural networks" in this book.

6   T. B. Brown, B. Mann, N. Ryder, M. Subbiah, J. Kaplan, P. Dhariwal, A. Neelakantan, P. Shyam, G. Sastry, A. Askell, S. Agarwal, A. Herbert-Voss, G. Krueger, T. Henighan, R. Child, A. Ramesh, D. M. Ziegler, J. Wu, C. Winter, … D. A. Openai (2020). *Language Models are Few-Shot Learners. arXiv preprint arXiv*: 2005.14165, 2020.

7   Mathematical methods, the most popular of which is termed backpropagation using gradient descent (and which is explained at www.AIPerspectives.com/ba), determine how the weights are learned.

8   The details of how ConvNets work can be found on www.AIPerspectives.com/cn.

9   The discussion in this section will focus on image classification. However, facial recognition uses similar algorithms. For more information on facial recognition see www.AIPerspectives.com/fr.

10   Y. Le Cun, L. Bottou, and Y. Bengio, "Reading checks with multilayer graph transformer networks," in *ICASSP, IEEE International Conference on Acoustics, Speech and Signal Processing - Proceedings*, 1997, doi: 10.1109/icassp.1997.599580.

11   C. Szegedy, W. Liu, P. Sermanet, S. Reed, D. Anguelov, D. Erhan, V. Vanhoucke, and A. Rabinovich. *Going deeper with convolutions. arXiv preprint arXiv*: 1409.4842, 2014.

12   K. He, X. Zhang, S. Ren, and J. Sun (n.d.). *Deep Residual Learning for Image Recognition. arXiv preprint arXiv*: 1512.03385, 2015.

13   C. A. G. Grajales, "The statistics behind Google Translate," *Statistics Views*, June 23, 2015. www.statisticsviews.com/details/feature/8065581/The-statistics-behind-Google-Translate.html.

14   F. Och, "Statistical machine translation live," *Google AI Blog*, April 28, 2006. ai.googleblog.com/2006/04/statistical-machine-translation-live.html.

15   Actually, many phrases have more than one possible translation, so it would store all possible phrasal translations.

16   The process was more complex because the system needed to handle multiple translations for phrases and account for word order differences between languages. See www.AIPerspectives.com/pb for more details.

17   In English, French, and Italian, the word order for a sentence is SVO (SUBJECT VERB OBJECT). Subjects are typically noun phrases that appear before the verb, and objects appear after the verb. In contrast, in German and Japanese the typical word order is SOV (SUBJECT OBJECT VERB). For example, in English, one would say "John hit the ball." In German, one would say the equivalent of "John has the ball hit" (*"John hat*

den Ball getroffen"). Other languages are OVS, VOS, and VSO, and many languages tolerate multiple word orders.

18   B. Turovsky, "Ten years of Google Translate," *Google Blog*, April 28, 2016. blog.google/products/translate/ten-years-of-google-translate/.

19   B. Turovsky, "Found in translation: More Accurate, Fluent Sentences in Google Translate," *Translate* (blog), November 15, 2016, https://blog.google/products/translate/found-translation-more-accurate-fluent-sentences-google-translate/.

20   "The Great A.I. Awakening," *New York Times.* Retrieved February 17, 2020, from https://www.nytimes.com/2016/12/14/magazine/the-great-ai-awakening.html.

21   Unfortunately, as good as Google Translate has become, as of February 2020 it supported only 104 of the world's more than seven thousand languages (see cloud.google.com/translate/docs/languages for an updated list). Further, this situation might not improve rapidly, as the technology requires large bilingual texts for each language pair.

22   The encoder and decoder deep neural networks are termed *recurrent neural networks* (RNNs), and many use a specialized form of RNN termed a *long short-term memory* (LSTM) network. See www.AIPerspectives.com/rn for details on RNNs, LSTMs, and the evolution of sequence-to-sequence models.

23   How NMT systems works is explained on www.AIPerspectives.com/nm.

24   K. H. Davis, R. Biddulph, and S. Balashek, "Automatic recognition of spoken digits," *J. Acoust. Soc. Am.,* vol. 24, no. 6, pp. 637–642, 1952, doi: 10.1121/1.1906946.

25   See chapter 7 and also www.AIPerspectives.com/lm for more information on language models.

26   See www.AIPerspectives.com/sr for more information on how earlier speech recognition systems work.

27   A. Mohamed, A. Mohamed, G. Dahl, and G. Hinton (2009). "Deep belief networks for phone recognition." In *Proceedings of the NIPS Workshop on Deep Learning for Speech Recognition and Related Applications.* citeseerx.ist.psu.edu/viewdoc/summary?doi=10.1.1.587.3829.

28   G. E. Dahl, D. Yu, S. Member, L. Deng, and A. Acero (2012). "Context-Dependent Pre-Trained Deep Neural Networks for Large-Vocabulary Speech Recognition." *IEEE Transactions on Audio, Speech, and Language Processing,* 20(1). doi.org/10.1109/TASL.2011.2134090.

29   A more in-depth explanation of current speech recognition technologies can be found at www.AIPerspectives.com/s2.

30   Ibid.

31   The deepfake network illustrated here is based on the technology behind the Faceswap app. See forum.faceswap.dev/viewtopic.php?f=6&t=146.

32   www.YouTube.com/watch?v=r1jng79a5xc.

33   Research has shown it is possible to create a deepfake image using only eight training images of the target person plus one image of another person wearing the desired

facial expression. E. Zakharov, A. Shysheya, E. Burkov, and V. Lempitsky, "Few-shot adversarial learning of realistic neural talking head models," in *Proceedings of the IEEE International Conference on Computer Vision,* 2019.

34   https://www.descript.com/lyrebird.

35   J. Wang et al., "Visual concepts and compositional voting," *Ann. Math. Sci. Appl.,* vol. 3, no. 1, pp. 151–188, 2018, doi: 10.4310/amsa.2018.v3.n1.a5.

36   J. Su, D. V. Vargas, and K. Sakurai, "One pixel attack for fooling deep neural networks," in *Proceedings of the IEEE Computer Society Conference on Computer Vision and Pattern Recognition,* 2019, doi: 10.1109/TEVC.2019.2890858.

37   A. Nguyen, J. Yosinski, and J. Clune, "Deep neural networks are easily fooled: High confidence predictions for unrecognizable images," in *Proceedings of the IEEE Computer Society Conference on Computer Vision and Pattern Recognition,* 2015, doi: 10.1109/CVPR.2015.7298640.

38   J. R. Zech, M. A. Badgeley, M. Liu, A. B. Costa, J. J. Titano, and E. K. Oermann (n.d.). *Confounding variables can degrade generalization performance of radiological deep learning models. Author summary. arXiv preprint arXiv:* 1807.00431, 2019

39   N. Carlini and D. Wagner, "Audio adversarial examples: Targeted attacks on speech-to-text," in *Proceedings - 2018 IEEE Symposium on Security and Privacy Workshops, SPW 2018,* 2018, doi: 10.1109/SPW.2018.00009.

Chapter 12

1   M. Minksy, "Why People Think Computers Can't," *AI Magazine,* Fall 1982, p. 5.

2   In spoken language, it also implies the ability to interpret vocal tone, body language, and facial expression—all of which can alter the literal meaning of the words, sometimes making the meaning the opposite of what was said, such as with the use of sarcasm.

3   A. M. Collins and M. R. Quillian (1972). "How to make a language user," PsycNET. In E. Tulving and W. Donaldson (Eds.), *Organization of Memory.* Academic Press. psycnet. apa.org/record/1973-08477-002.

4   R. C. Schank and R. Abelson, *Scripts, Plans, Goals, and Understanding: An Inquiry into Human Knowledge Structures (Artificial Intelligence Series),* 1st ed. (East Sussex, England: Psychology Press, 1977).

5   R. C. Schank, "Conceptual dependency: A theory of natural language understanding," *Cogn. Psychol.,* vol. 3, no. 4, pp. 552–631, 1972, doi: 10.1016/0010-0285(72)90022-9.

6   J. Weizenbaum, "ELIZA-A computer program for the study of natural language communication between man and machine," *Commun. ACM,* vol. 9, no. 1, pp. 36–45, 1966, doi: 10.1145/365153.365168.

7   The natural language processing portion of a personal assistant is just one small part. Developers use conventional programming techniques to create many of the other aspects of a successful personal assistant such as the following:

   • Sending and receiving text messages from Slack, Facebook Messenger, Twilio, and other text messaging tools

- Adding images, videos, and other media to messages
- Creating dialogues to collect data from users
- Adding click buttons that give the user choices in a text dialogue
- Storing data input by the user
- Querying knowledge sources (e.g., knowledge bases, FAQs) for data requested by the user or data needed by the bot (e.g., is an appointment available at the time requested by the user?)
- Linking commands to smartphone app actions
- Security and authentication
- Performance monitoring
- Adding speech capabilities
- Management of the dialogue state
- Synchronization across devices such as smartphones and smart speakers (e.g., Google Home and Amazon Alexa)
- Notifications
- Localization
- Chatbot personas
- Payment service interactions
- Vehicle integrations (e.g., Android Auto and Apple CarPlay)

8   Third-party developers are programmers who do not work for the company.

9   "Amazon Announces 80,000 Alexa Skills Worldwide and Jeff Bezos Earnings Release Quote Focuses Solely on Alexa Momentum," *Voicebot.ai.* (n.d.). Retrieved September 17, 2020, from https://voicebot.ai/2019/01/31/amazon-announces-80000-alexa-skills-worldwide-and-jeff-bezos-earnings-release-quote-focuses-solely-on-alexa-momentum/.

10   These are proprietary systems, and the vendors do not reveal much in the way of details.

11   For example, Apple used deep learning to identify intents in Siri conversations. X. C. Chen, A. Sagar, J. T. Kao, T. Y. Li, T. Klein, S. Pulman, A. Garg, and J. D. Williams (n.d.). *Active Learning for Domain Classification in a Commercial Spoken Personal Assistant, Interspeech,* September 15-19, 2019.

Similarly, developers of automated online customer support systems can use their question/answer history to train deep networks to map natural language questions to a set of pre-defined questions that have canned answers or suggest support articles based on user questions.

12   developer.amazon.com/alexaprize.

13   H. Fang, H. Cheng, E. Clark, A. Holtzman, M. Sap, M. Ostendorf, Y. Choi, and N. A. Smith (n.d.). *Sounding Board-University of Washington's Alexa Prize Submission, 1st Proceedings of Alexa Prize,* 2017.

14   C. Y. Chen, D. Yu, W. Wen, Y. M. Yang, J. Zhang, M. Zhou, K. Jesse, A. Chau, A. Bhowmick, S. Iyer, G. Sreenivasulu, R. Cheng, A. Bhandare, and Z. Yu (n.d.). *Gunrock:*

Building A Human-Like Social Bot By Leveraging Large Scale Real User Data. Retrieved May 12, 2020, from aws.amazon.com/lambda.

15   I. V. Serban, C. Sankar, M. Germain, S. Zhang, Z. Lin, S. Subramanian, T. Kim, M. Pieper, S. Chandar, N. R. Ke, S. Rajeswar, A. De Brebisson, J. M. R. Sotelo, D. Suhubdy, V. Michalski, A. Nguyen, J. Pineau, and Y. Bengio (n.d.). *A Deep Reinforcement Learning Chatbot (Short Version) 31st Conference on Neural Information Processing Systems,* 2017, Long Beach, CA, USA.

16   D. Adiwardana, M. T. Luong, D. R. So, J. Hall, N. Fiedel, R. Thoppilan, Z. Yang, A. Kulshreshtha, G. Nemade, Y. Lu Quoc, and V. Le (n.d.). *Towards a Human-like Open-Domain Chatbot.* arXiv preprint arXiv: 2001.09977.

17   S. Roller, E. Dinan, N. Goyal, D. Ju, M. Williamson, Y. Liu, J. Xu, M. Ott, K. Shuster, E. M. Smith, Y. L. Boureau, and J. Weston (n.d.). *Recipes for building an open-domain chatbot.*arXiv preprint arXiv: 2004.13637.

18   S. Baker (2011). *Final Jeopardy: man vs. machine and the quest to know everything.* Houghton Mifflin Harcourt.

19   J. Chu-Carroll, J. Fan, N. Schlaefer, and W. Zadrozny, "Textual resource acquisition and engineering," *IBM Journal of Research and Development,* vol. 56, no. 3/4, pp. 1–11, 2012, doi: 10.1147/JRD.2012.2185901.

20   Here, "BornIn" is an arbitrary label that represents the relationship connoted by sentences like "Obama was born in Hawaii."

21   See www.AIPerspectives.com/el for a detailed description of entity linking.

22   The term "entity" in an NLP context means a word or phrase that refers to a person, place, or thing.

23   C. Wang, J. Fan, A. Kalyanpur, and D. Gondek, "Relation extraction with relation topics," in *Proceedings of the EMNLP 2011 - Conference on Empirical Methods in Natural Language Processing,* 2011.

24   Open source means freely available and collaboratively developed by people all over the world.

25   YAGO also contains hierarchical information about concepts. For example, YAGO lists an animal hierarchy (animal->mammal->dog). When the entity and LAT were both available in YAGO, DeepQA used conventionally coded hierarchical rules to determine if the entity matched the LAT concept exactly or matched a subtype or supertype in the YAGO concept hierarchy.

26   D. C. Gondek et al., "A framework for merging and ranking of answers in DeepQA," *IBM Journal of Research and Development,* vol. 56, no. 3/4, pp. 1–12, 2012, doi: 10.1147/JRD.2012.2188760.

27   We could consider the conventionally coded rules used to match the time frame and location to be a trivial form of human-like reasoning if one stretches the definition. The same is true for the conventionally coded rules that match the entities and relations in the question to the candidate answers. And the same is also true for the hierarchical concept reasoning. However, a more apt description of the entire system is clever conventional programming.

28   P. Rajpurkar, J. Zhang, K. Lopyrev, and P. Liang, "SQuad: 100,000+ questions for machine comprehension of text," in *EMNLP 2016 - Conference on Empirical Methods in Natural Language Processing, Proceedings*, 2016, doi: 10.18653/v1/d16-1264.

29   D. Chen, J. Bolton, and C. D. Manning, "A thorough examination of the CNN/ Daily Mail reading comprehension task," in *54th Annual Meeting of the Association for Computational Linguistics, ACL 2016 - Long Papers*, 2016, doi: 10.18653/v1/p16-1223.

      R. Kadlec, M. Schmid, O. Bajgar, and J. Kleindienst, "Text understanding with the attention sum reader network," in *54th Annual Meeting of the Association for Computational Linguistics, ACL 2016 - Long Papers*, 2016, doi: 10.18653/v1/p16-1086.

      C. Xiong, V. Zhong, and R. Socher, "Dynamic coattention networks for question answering," in *5th International Conference on Learning Representations, ICLR 2017 - Conference Track Proceedings*, 2017.

      M. Seo, A. Kembhavi, A. Farhadi, and H. Hajishirzi, "Bi-directional attention flow for machine comprehension," in *5th International Conference on Learning Representations, ICLR 2017 - Conference Track Proceedings*, 2017.

      For descriptions of many of these RC systems, see www.AIPerspectives.com/rc.

30   A. Linn, "Microsoft creates AI that can read a document and answer questions about it as well as a person," *Microsoft AI Blog*, January 15, 2018. blogs.microsoft.com/ai/ microsoft-creates-ai-can-read-document-answer-questions-well-person/.

      A. Najberg, "Alibaba AI model tops humans in reading comprehension," *Alibaba*, January 24, 2018. www.alibabacloud.com/blog/alibaba-ai-model-tops-humans-in-reading-comprehension_396923.

31   Numerous word and sentence alignment techniques were developed in machine translation research. See www.AIPerspectives.com/wa for more information.

32   K. M. Hermann et al., "Teaching machines to read and comprehend," in *Advances in Neural Information Processing Systems*, 2015.

33   D. Chen, J. Bolton, and C. D. Manning, "A thorough examination of the CNN/ Daily Mail reading comprehension task," in *54th Annual Meeting of the Association for Computational Linguistics, ACL 2016 - Long Papers*, 2016, doi: 10.18653/v1/p16-1223.

34   R. Jia and P. Liang, "Adversarial examples for evaluating reading comprehension systems," in *EMNLP 2017 - Conference on Empirical Methods in Natural Language Processing, Proceedings*, 2017, doi: 10.18653/v1/d17-1215.

35   See www.AIPerspectives.com/sp for additional research showing that superficial patterns are also used on other RC tests.

Chapter 13

1   S. M. Kosslyn, S. Pinker, G. E. Smith, and S. P. Shwartz, "On the demystification of mental imagery," *Behav. Brain Sci.*, vol. 2, pp. 535–581, 1979, doi: 10.1017/ S0140525X00064268.

2   A. M. Turing, COMPUTING MACHINERY AND INTELLIGENCE, *Mind*, Volume LIX, Issue 236, October 1950, Pages 433–460, doi.org/10.1093/mind/LIX.236.433.

3   M. Roemmele, C. A. Bejan, and A. S. Gordon, "Choice of plausible alternatives: An evaluation of commonsense causal reasoning," in *AAAI Spring Symposium - Technical Report*, 2011.

     H. J. Levesque, E. Davis, and L. Morgenstern, "The Winograd schema challenge," in *Proceedings of the International Workshop on Temporal Representation and Reasoning*, 2012.

4   See www.AIPerspectives.com/tr for more details.

5   R. C. Schank and R. Abelson, *Scripts, Plans, Goals, and Understanding: An Inquiry into Human Knowledge Structures (Artificial Intelligence Series)*, 1st ed. (East Sussex, England: Psychology Press, 1977).

6   J. Walker, A. Gupta, and M. Hebert, "Patch to the future: Unsupervised visual prediction," in *Proceedings of the IEEE Computer Society Conference on Computer Vision and Pattern Recognition*, 2014, doi: 10.1109/CVPR.2014.416.

7   S. Singh, A. Gupta, and A. A. Efros, "Unsupervised discovery of mid-level discriminative patches," in Lecture Notes in Computer Science (including subseries Lecture Notes in Artificial Intelligence and Lecture Notes in Bioinformatics), pp. 1–15, 2012, doi: 10.1007/978-3-642-33709-3_6.

8   A. Perfors and J. B. Tenenbaum, "Learning to learn categories," in *Proceedings of the 31st Annual Conference of the Cognitive Science Society (CogSci 2009)*, 2009, pp. 136–141.

9   D. G. T. Barrett, F. Hill, A. Santoro, A. S. Morcos, and T. Lillicrap, "Measuring abstract reasoning in neural networks," in *35th International Conference on Machine Learning, ICML 2018*, 2018.

10   J. Piaget, *The Construction of Reality in the Child* (New York: Basic Books, 1954).

11   See, for example, B. M. Lake, T. D. Ullman, J. B. Tenenbaum, and S. J. Gershman, "Building machines that learn and think like people," *Behav. Brain Sci.*, pp. 1–72, 2017, doi: 10.1017/S0140525X16001837.

12   A. Lerer, S. Gross, and R. Fergus, "Learning physical intuition of block towers by example," in *33rd International Conference on Machine Learning, ICML 2016*, 2016.

Chapter 14

1   M. Lewis, *Moneyball: The Art of Winning an Unfair Game* (New York: W.W. Norton & Company, 2004).

2   K. T. May, "The moneyball effect: How smart data is transforming criminal justice, healthcare, music, and even government spending," *TED Blog*, January 28, 2014. blog.ted.com/the-moneyball-effect-how-smart-data-is-transforming-criminal-justice-healthcare-music-and-even-government-spending/.

3   B. Marr, "How Experian is using big data and machine learning to cut mortgage application times to a few days," *Forbes*, May 25, 2017. www.forbes.com/sites/bernardmarr/2017/05/25/how-experian-is-using-big-data-and-machine-learning-to-cut-mortgage-application-times-to-a-few-days/#28742440203f.

4   Electronic Privacy Information Center, "Algorithms in the Criminal Justice System: Pre-Trial Risk Assessment Tools." epic.org/algorithmic-transparency/crim-justice/ (accessed March 19, 2020).

5   J. Selingo, "How colleges use big data to target the students they want," *The Atlantic*, April 11, 2017. www.theatlantic.com/education/archive/2017/04/how-colleges-find-their-students/522516/.

6   R. Feloni, "I tried the software that uses AI to scan job applicants for companies like Goldman Sachs and Unilever before meeting them—and it's not as creepy as it sounds," *Business Insider*, August 24, 2017. www.businessinsider.com/hirevue-ai-powered-job-interview-platform-2017-8.

7   W. M. Grove and P. E. Meehl, "Comparative efficiency of informal (subjective, impressionistic) and formal (mechanical, algorithmic) prediction procedures: The clinical-statistical controversy," *Psychol. Public Policy, Law*, vol. 2, pp. 293–323, 1996, doi: 10.1037/1076-8971.2.2.293.

8   P. W. Greenwood and A. Abrahamse, *Selective Incapacitation*. (Santa Monica, CA: Rand, 1982). www.rand.org/pubs/reports/R2815.html.

9   "Opinion: Sentencing, by the Numbers," *New York Times* (n.d.). Retrieved February 17, 2020, from https://www.nytimes.com/2014/08/11/opinion/sentencing-by-the-numbers.html.

10   M. Bertrand and S. Mullainathan, "Are Emily and Greg more employable than Lakisha and Jamal? A field experiment on labor market discrimination," *American Economic Review*, 2003.

11   R. Bartlett, A. Morse, R. Stanton, N. Wallace, M. Adelino, S. Das, A. DeFusco, A. Fuster, A. Liberman, M. Puri, R. Rau, A. Seru, A. Walther, J. Wolfers, and participants at Berkeley, seminar U. (2019). *Consumer-Lending Discrimination in the FinTech Era*. faculty.haas.berkeley.edu/morse/research/papers/discrim.pdf.

12   A great overview of this issue can be found in the book *Weapons of Math Destruction* by mathematician Cathy O'Neil (New York: Crown Random House, 2016). The nonprofit group Future of Privacy Forum put out a nice overview of the different ways that automated decision-making can harm both individuals and society as a whole: L. Smith, "Unfairness by algorithm: Distilling the harms of automated decision-making," *Future Privacy Forum*, 2017. fpf.org/wp-content/uploads/2017/12/FPF-Automated-Decision-Making-Harms-and-Mitigation-Charts.pdf.

13   J. Angwin, J. Larson, S. Mattu, and L. Kirchner, "Machine bias," *ProPublica*, May 23, 2016. www.propublica.org/article/machine-bias-risk-assessments-in-criminal-sentencing.

14   R. Richardson, J. M. Schultz, and K. Crawford, "Dirty data, bad predictions: How civil rights violations impact police data, predictive policing systems, and justice," *New York Univ. Law Rev.*, 2019.

15   AdAge, "Apple co-founder Steve Wozniak says Goldman's Apple Card algorithm discriminates," November 10, 2019. adage.com/article/digital/apple-co-founder-steve-wozniak-says-goldmans-apple-card-algorithm-discriminates/2214331.

16   J. Dastin, "Amazon scraps secret AI recruiting tool that showed bias against women," *Reuters*, October 10, 2018. www.reuters.com/article/us-amazon-com-jobs-automation-insight/amazon-scraps-secret-ai-recruiting-tool-that-showed-bias-against-women-idUSKCN1MK08G.

17   M. Evans and A. W. Mathews, "Researchers find racial bias in hospital algorithm," *Wall Street Journal*, October 25, 2019. www.wsj.com/articles/researchers-find-racial-bias-in-hospital-algorithm-11571941096.

18   R. Speer, "ConceptNet Numberbatch 17.04: Better, less-stereotyped word vectors,"
      ConceptNet Blog, April 24, 2017. blog.conceptnet.io/posts/2017/conceptnet-
      numberbatch-17-04-better-less-stereotyped-word-vectors/.

19   J. Larson, J. Angwin, L. Kirchner, and S. Mattu, "How we examined racial
      discrimination in auto insurance prices," *ProPublica,* April 5, 2017. www.propublica.
      org/article/minority-neighborhoods-higher-car-insurance-premiums-methodology.

20   J. Guynn, "Google Photos labeled Black people 'gorillas'," *USA Today,* July 1, 2015.
      www.usatoday.com/story/tech/2015/07/01/google-apologizes-after-photos-identify-
      black-people-as-gorillas/29567465/.

21   J. Buolamwini and T. Gebru, "Gender shades: intersectional accuracy disparities in
      commercial gender classification," in *Proceeding of Machine Learning Research, Conference
      on Fairness, Accountability, and Transparency,* vol. 81, pp. 77–91, 2018.

22   G. McMillan, "It's not you, it's it: Voice recognition doesn't recognize women," *Time,*
      June 1, 2011. techland.time.com/2011/06/01/its-not-you-its-it-voice-recognition-
      doesnt-recognize-women/.

23   A. Koenecke, A. Nam, E. Lake, J. Nudell, M. Quartey, Z. Mengesha,
      C. Toups, J. R. Rickford, D. Jurafsky, and S. Goel (2020). Racial disparities in
      automated speech recognition. *Proceedings of the National Academy of Sciences of the
      United States of America, 117*(14), 7684–7689. doi.org/10.1073/pnas.1915768117.
      www.pnas.org/content/117/14/7684.

24   Research Next: Research, Scholarship and Creative Activity for a Brighter Future, "Our
      changing language," *University of Massachusetts Amherst.* www.umass.edu/researchnext/
      feature/our-changing-language.

25   See, for example, R. Chowdhury, "Tackling the challenge of ethics in AI," *Accenture,*
      June 6, 2018. www.accenture.com/gb-en/blogs/blogs-cogx-tackling-challenge-ethics-ai.

      F. D. P. Calmon, D. Wei, B. Vinzamuri, K. N. Ramamurthy, and K. R. Varshney, "Data
      pre-processing for discrimination prevention: Information-theoretic optimization and
      analysis," *IEEE J. Sel. Top. Signal Process.,* vol. 12, no.5, pp. 1106–1119, 2018, doi:
      10.1109/JSTSP.2018.2865887.

26   See, for example, J. Zhao, Y. Zhou, Z. Li, W. Wang, and K.W. Chang, "Learning
      gender-neutral word embeddings," in *Proceedings of the 2018 Conference on Empirical
      Methods in Natural Language Processing,* pp. 4847–4853, 2018, doi: 10.18653/v1/d18-
      1521.

      T. Bolukbasi, K. W. Chang, J. Zou, V. Saligrama, and A. Kalai, "Man is to computer
      programmer as woman is to homemaker? Debiasing word embeddings," in *Advances in
      Neural Information Processing Systems,* 2016.

      A. Caliskan, J. J. Bryson, and A. Narayanan, "Semantics derived automatically from
      language corpora contain human-like biases," *Science,* vol. 356, no. 6334, pp. 183–186,
      2017, doi: 10.1126/science.aal4230.

      H. Gonen and Y. Goldberg, "Lipstick on a pig: Debiasing methods cover up
      systematic gender biases in word embeddings but do not remove them," *arXiv preprint
      arXiv:1903.03862,* 2019.

      K. Ethayarajh, D. Duvenaud, and G. Hirst, "Understanding undesirable word embedding associations," in *Proceedings of the 57th Annual Meeting of the Association for Computational Linguistics*, pp. 1696–1705, 2019, doi: 10.18653/v1/p19-1166.

27   R. Jiang, A. Pacchiano, T. Stepleton, H. Jiang, and S. Chiappa, "Wasserstein fair classification," in *35th Conference on Uncertainty in Artificial Intelligence, UAI 2019*, arXiv preprint arXiv:1907.12059, 2019.

28   fairlearn.github.io/.

29   R. Perrault et al., "The AI index 2019 annual report," AI Index Steering Committee, Human-Centered AI Institute, Stanford University, Stanford, CA, December 2019. [Online]. Available: hai.stanford.edu/sites/g/files/sbiybj10986/f/ ai_index_2019_report.pdf.

30   One could argue that many bias issues are caused by facial recognition technology. I would argue that the problem is in the data used to train the facial recognition systems. Deep learning systems also tend to be less interpretable, but we should not focus on the underlying technology; we should focus on agreeing on and regulating the degree of interpretability we need in automated decision systems.

31   AI techniques like deep learning sometimes result in improved decision-making; however, it is often not significantly better. An MIT study examined the degree to which deep learning techniques improved marketing analytics predictions versus a fifty-year-old linear regression technique. They found that linear regression had a 70 percent accuracy and deep learning had a 74 percent accuracy (G. Urban, A. Timoshenko, P. Dhillon, and J. R. Hauser, "Is Deep learning a game changer for marketing analytics?" *MIT Sloan Management Review*, November 25, 2019. sloanreview.mit.edu/article/ is-deep-learning-a-game-changer-for-marketing-analytics/). If deep learning had never been invented, the older technique could still have been used. Both techniques are subject to concerns about bias, discrimination, and fairness.

32   For example, researchers at the University of Texas at Austin have developed CERTIFAI, which tests tools for explainability, nondiscrimination, and robustness to adversarial attacks and can be used by third parties to certify ADS systems. R. Bartlett, A. Morse, R. Stanton, N. Wallace, M. Adelino, S. Das, A. DeFusco, A. Fuster, A. Liberman, M. Puri, R. Rau, A. Seru, A. Walther, J. Wolfers, and participants at Berkeley, seminar U. (2019). *Consumer-Lending Discrimination in the FinTech Era*.

33   See www.AIPerspectives.com/in for more information on the technical aspects of interpretability.

34   P. Crosman, "Is AI making credit scores better, or more confusing?" *American Banker*, February 14, 2017. www.americanbanker.com/news/is-ai-making-credit-scores-better-or-more-confusing.

35   For a framework for assessing the interpretability of machine learning algorithms, see Z. C. Lipton, "The mythos of model interpretability," *Commun. ACM*, 2018, doi: 10.1145/3233231. There is also ongoing research on how to make deep learning systems more interpretable, e.g., L. Hardesty, "Making computers explain themselves," *MIT News*, October 27, 2016. news.mit.edu/2016/ making-computers-explain-themselves-machine-learning-1028.

36   K. Crawford, "The hidden biases in big data," *Harvard Business Review*, April 1, 2013.

hbr.org/2013/04/the-hidden-biases-in-big-data.

37   There have been some interesting court cases on this topic. A Pennsylvania death penalty defendant was denied access to the source code of a forensic software program that produced the key evidence against him due to trade secret laws, and the Wisconsin State Supreme Court ruled that a defendant had no right to know the details of an algorithmic risk assessment used to sentence him: R. Wexler, "Life, liberty, and trade secrets: Intellectual property in the criminal justice system," *Stanford Law Review*, vol. 70, pp. 1343–1429, 2018, doi: 10.2139/ssrn.2920883.

38   L. Hardesty, "Making computers explain themselves," *MIT News*, October 27, 2016. news.mit.edu/2016/making-computers-explain-themselves-machine-learning-1028.

   M. T. Ribeiro, S. Singh, and C. Guestrin, "Local Interpretable Model-Agnostic Explanations (LIME): An introduction," *O'Reilly*, August 12, 2016. www.oreilly.com/content/introduction-to-local-interpretable-model-agnostic-explanations-lime/.

39   T. Frey, "Increasing transparency with Google Cloud Explainable AI," *Google Cloud*, November 21, 2019. cloud.google.com/blog/products/ai-machine-learning/google-cloud-ai-explanations-to-increase-fairness-responsibility-and-trust.

40   "Model interpretability in Azure Machine Learning," *Microsoft Azure*, October 25, 2019. docs.microsoft.com/en-us/azure/machine-learning/how-to-machine-learning-interpretability. See also fairlearn.github.io/.

41   R. Perrault et al., "The AI index 2019 annual report," AI Index Steering Committee, Human-Centered AI Institute, Stanford University, Stanford, CA, December 2019. [Online]. Available: hai.stanford.edu/sites/g/files/sbiybj10986/f/ai_index_2019_report.pdf.

42   A. Amrein-Beardsley, "Breaking news: A big victory in court in Houston," *VAMboozled!*, May 5, 2017. vamboozled.com/breaking-news-victory-in-court-in-houston/. See also R. Richardson, J. M. Schultz, and V. M. Southerland, "Litigating algorithms 2019 US report: New challenges to government use of algorithmic decision systems," September 2019. ainowinstitute.org/litigatingalgorithms-2019-us.pdf for a discussion of other court cases.

43   L. Hardesty, "Making computers explain themselves," *MIT News*, October 27, 2016. news.mit.edu/2016/making-computers-explain-themselves-machine-learning-1028.

   M. T. Ribeiro, S. Singh, and C. Guestrin, "Local Interpretable Model-Agnostic Explanations (LIME): An introduction," *O'Reilly*, August 12, 2016. www.oreilly.com/content/introduction-to-local-interpretable-model-agnostic-explanations-lime/.

Chapter 15

1   B. Zhang and A. Dafoe, "High-Level Machine Intelligence," in *Artificial Intelligence: American Attitudes and Trends*. (Oxford, UK: Center for the Governance of AI, Future of Humanity Institute, University of Oxford, 2019).

2   There have been many critiques of AI systems over the years like the ones in this chapter. The goal of this chapter is to tie the commentary back to the explanations in the rest of

this book concerning how the various AI systems work. Previous critiques include J. A. Fodor and Z. W. Pylyshyn (1988). "Connectionism and cognitive architecture: A critical analysis." *Cognition, 28*(1–2), 3–71. doi.org/10.1016/0010-0277(88)90031-5;

S. Pinker and A. Prince, "On language and connectionism: Analysis of a parallel distributed processing model of language acquisition," *Cognition*, 28(1–2), 73–193, 1988;

G. Marcus, "Deep learning: A critical appraisal," *arXiv preprint arXiv:1801.00631*, 2018;

A. Darwiche, "Human-level intelligence or animal-like abilities?" *Commun. ACM*, vol. 61, no. 10, pp. 56–57, 2018, doi: 10.1145/3271625;

A. L. Yuille and C. Liu, "Deep nets: What have they ever done for vision?" *arXiv preprint arXiv:1805.04025*, 2019.

M. Mitchell, *Artificial intelligence: A Guide for Thinking Humans* (New York: Macmillan, 2019).

3   There has been some success in transferring low-level representations such as word embeddings and the initial layers of image classification systems to other tasks. However, the systems still require some training on the new task. Also, word embeddings do not help image classification, and image classification layers do not help natural language processing tasks. Lastly, there has been some progress on multitask learning where systems are trained simultaneously on multiple similar tasks (e.g., multiple natural language processing tasks). This is equivalent to learning a single task with multiple similar subtasks. See www.AIPerspectives.com/ml for more information.

4   AI researchers have developed systems that have some ability to transfer from one domain (e.g., recognizing cats) to another (e.g., recognizing dogs), but only for very similar domains. This is known as **transfer learning**. See www.AIPerspectives.com/tl for more information on this topic.

5   S. LeVine, "Artificial intelligence pioneer says we need to start over," *Axios*, September 15, 2017. www.axios.com/artificial-intelligence-pioneer-says-we-need-to-start-over-1513305524-f619efbd-9db0-4947-a9b2-7a4c310a28fe.html.

6   Y. LeCun, "Learning World Models: The next step towards AI," in *International Joint Conference on Artificial Intelligence*, 2018, minute 37.04.

7   www.youtube.com/watch?v=OpSmCKe27WE.

8   For example, B. M. Lake, T. D. Ullman, J. B. Tenenbaum, and S. J. Gershman, "Building machines that learn and think like people," *Behav. Brain Sci.*, pp. 1–72, 2017, doi: 10.1017/S0140525X16001837.

9   Interview with MIT Professor Joshua Tenenbaum in M. Ford (2018). *Architects of Intelligence: The truth about AI from the people building it.* Packt Publishing.

10   This article in *Brain and Behavioral Sciences* contains both a proposal for this approach by NYU researcher Brenden Lake, as well as commentary from many other prominent researchers: B. M. Lake, T. D. Ullman, J. B. Tenenbaum, and S. J. Gershman, "Building machines that learn and think like people," *Brain and Behavioral Sciences*, pp. 1–72, 2017, doi: 10.1017/S0140525X16001837.

11   For example, M. Sap et al., "ATOMIC: An atlas of machine commonsense for if-then reasoning," in *Proceedings of the AAAI Conference on Artificial Intelligence,* 2019;

A. Bosselut, H. Rashkin, M. Sap, C. Malaviya, A. Celikyilmaz, and Y. Choi, "COMET: Commonsense transformers for automatic knowledge graph construction," 2019, doi: 10.18653/v1/p19-1470.

12   G. Marcus (2018). "Deep learning: A critical appraisal," *arXiv preprint arXiv:1801.00631.*

G. Marcus (2020). "The Next Decade in AI: Four Steps Towards Robust Artificial Intelligence." *arXiv preprint arXiv:2002.06177.*

13   G. Marcus and E. Davis, *Rebooting AI: Building Artificial Intelligence We Can Trust.* (New York: Pantheon, 2019).

14   See this April 2019 video interview with Greg Brockman for more information on the OpenAI approach: www.youtube.com/watch?v=bIrEM2FbOLU.

15   https://www.aiperspectives.com/gpt-3-does-not-understand-what-it-is-saying/.

16   Y. LeCun (2020). "Self-Supervised Learning." *Presentation at the 34th AAAI Conference on Artificial Intelligence.* drive.google.com/file/d/1r-mDL4IX_hz ZLDBKp8_e8VZqD7fOzBkF/view;

Y. Bengio (2019). "Yoshua Bengio: From System 1 Deep Learning to System 2 Deep Learning." *Presentation at the NeurIPS 2019 Conference.* journalismai.com/2019/12/12/yoshua-bengio-from-system-1-deep-learning-to-system-2-deep-learning-neurips-2019/.

17   Y. Bengio, T. Deleu, N. Rahaman, N. R. Ke, S. Lachapelle, O. Bilaniuk, A. Goyal, and C. Pal (2019). "A Meta-Transfer Objective for Learning to Disentangle Causal Mechanisms." *ArXiv Preprint ArXiv1901.10912v2;*

A. Goyal, A. Lamb, J. Hoffmann, S. Sodhani, S. Levine, Y. Bengio, and B. Schölkopf (2019). "Recurrent Independent Mechanisms." *ArXiv Preprint ArXiv:1909.10893.* arxiv.org/pdf/1909.10893.pdf;

Y. Bengio (2019). "The Consciousness Prior." *ArXiv Preprint ArXiv:1709.08568.* arxiv. org/pdf/1709.08568.pdf.

18   They have also generated an interesting debate between NYU professor Gary Marcus and Yoshua Bengio: montrealartificialintelligence.com/aidebate/ and this article by Gary Marcus: G. Marcus, "The next decade in AI: Four steps towards robust artificial intelligence," arXiv preprint arXiv:2002.06177, 2020.

19   For example, venturebeat.com/2020/05/02/yann-lecun-and-yoshua-bengio-self-supervised-learning-is-the-key-to-human-level-intelligence/.

20   www.humanbrainproject.com.

21   S. Makin (2019). The four biggest challenges in brain simulation. In *Nature* (Vol. 571, Issue 7766, p. S9). Nature Publishing Group. doi.org/10.1038/d41586-019-02209-z. www.nature.com/articles/d41586-019-02209-z.

22   S. Levy, "The Brief History of the ENIAC Computer," *Smithsonian Magazine,* November 2013, https://www.smithsonianmag.com/history/the-brief-history-of-the-eniac-computer-3889120/.

23   T. Everitt, G. Lea, and M. Hutter (2018). "AGI Safety Literature Review," *International Joint Conference on Artificial Intelligence (IJCAI). ArXiv: 1805.01109.*

V. Vinge (1993). "The Coming Technological Singularity: How to Survive in the Post-Human Era." In *Vision-21: Interdisciplinary Science and Engineering in the Era of Cyberspace.* National Aeronautics and Space Administration. ntrs.nasa.gov/archive/nasa/casi.ntrs.nasa.gov/19940022855.pdf.

24   S. Pinker, "Tech Luminaries Address the Singularity," in IEEE Spectrum, *Special Report: The Singularity,* June 2008. spectrum.ieee.org/static/singularity.

25   J. McCarthy, M. L. Minsky, N. Rochester, and C. E. Shannon, "A proposal for the Dartmouth summer research project on artificial intelligence," August 31, 1955.

26   M. Minsky, *Computation: Finite and Infinite Machines* (New Jersey: Prentice-Hall, 1967) 2.

27   D. Michie, "Machines and the theory of intelligence," *Nature,* vol. 241, pp. 507–512, 1973, doi: 10.1038/241507a0.

28   S. Armstrong and K. Sotala, "How We're Predicting AI—or Failing to," in *Beyond AI: Artificial Dreams,* J. Romportl, P. Ircing, E. Zackova, M. Polak, and R. Schuster, Eds. (New York: Springer, 2015, pp. 52–75).

29   K. Grace, J. Salvatier, A. Dafoe, B. Zhang, and O. Evans, "Viewpoint: When will AI exceed human performance? Evidence from AI experts," *Journal of Artificial Intelligence Research,* 2018, doi: 10.1613/jair.1.11222.

30   M. Ford, *Architects Of Intelligence: The Truth about AI from the People Building It.* (Birmingham, UK: Packt Publishing, 2018).

Chapter 16

1   I am focusing on regulatory activity here. A positive impact on society can also be accomplished by creating standards for the ethical use of AI technology that people follow on a voluntary basis. For example, the Institute of Electrical and Electronics Engineers has published a set of guidelines for its large membership. There are also corporate consortiums, such as The Partnership on AI to Benefit People and Society that was founded by Apple, Amazon, Facebook, Google, IBM, and Microsoft and now has over one hundred members, guidelines from several other nonprofit consortiums, guidelines from centers for AI ethics research created by universities, and from governmental bodies. The comments in this section apply to both regulatory efforts and efforts to create ethical frameworks and best practices.

2   Isaac Asimov, in his novel *I, Robot*, proposed three simple laws to regulate AGI-based robots:

The First Law was "A robot may not injure a human being or, through inaction, allow a human being to come to harm." The Second Law was "A robot must obey orders given to it by human beings, except where such orders would conflict with the first law." The Third Law was "A robot must protect its own existence as long as such protection does not conflict with the first or second law." AI futurists have since identified many flaws in these laws (e.g., R. R. Murphy and D. D. Woods, "Beyond Asimov: The three laws of responsible robotics," *IEEE Intell. Syst.*, vol. 24, no. 4, pp. 14–20, 2009, doi: 10.1109/ MIS.2009.69. www.researchgate.net/publication/224567023_Beyond_Asimov_The_ Three_Laws_of_Responsible_Robotics). See also S. Russell, *Human Compatible: Artificial Intelligence and the Problem of Control* (New York: Viking Press, 2019).

M. Tegmark, *Life 3.0: Being Human in the Age of Artificial Intelligence* (New York: Knopf, 2017).

M. Ford, *Architects of Intelligence: The Truth about AI from the People Building It* (Birmingham, UK: Packt Publishing, 2018).

J. Brockman, *Possible Minds: Twenty-Five Ways of Looking at AI* (London: Penguin Books, 2019).

For a great summary of the history of humanity's fear of robots see U. Barthelmess and U. Furbach, "Do we need Asimov's Laws?"; *arXiv preprint arXiv:1405.0961*, 2014.

INDEX

ABOUT THE AUTHOR

Steve Shwartz began his AI career working with Roger Schank as a postdoctoral researcher in the Yale University Artificial Intelligence Lab. Starting in the 1980s, Steve was a founder or cofounder of several AI companies, one of which created the award-winning Esperant business intelligence product. As the AI Winter of the 1990s set in, Steve transitioned into a career as a successful serial software entrepreneur and investor and created several companies that were either acquired or had public offerings.

Steve uses his unique perspective as an early AI researcher and statistician to explain how AI works in simple terms, why people shouldn't worry about intelligent robots taking over the world, and the steps we need to take as a society to minimize the negative impacts of AI and maximize the positive impacts.

Made in the USA
Coppell, TX
04 March 2021